Management Information Systems

Management Information Systems

BRIEFING 1

Consultant editor: RV FRANKS

published by Kogan Page Ltd
in association with
the Chartered Institute of Management Accountants
|C|I|M|A|
Incorporated by Royal Charter
63 Portland Place London W1N 4AB

First published in 1988 by
Kogan Page Ltd,
120 Pentonville Rd, London N1 9JN
by arrangement with the
Chartered Institute of Management Accountants,
63 Portland Place, London W1N 4AB.

Printed and bound in Great Britain by
MacKays Ltd, Chatham, Kent

British Library Cataloguing in Publication Data

Management information systems: briefing I.
1. Information systems. Technological development – for management
I. Franks, R.V. (Ray V.) II. Chartered Institute of Management Accountants
001.5

ISBN 1-85091-469-9

CONTENTS

Foreword

Developments in Information Technology (IT) have transformed the business environment in recent years and there is every sign that the pace of technological advancement will continue to accelerate in the future. While there are obvious advantages to be gained from the more sophisticated and efficient treatment of information, these developments have also brought many problems, particularly in the way in which traditional organisational structures and disciplines have had to be adapted to accommodate the various changes. The finance function is frequently at the centre of such developments and management accountants, in particular, have been quick to realise the need to keep abreast of evolving technology and to review its suitability for their own information systems.

The material contained in this briefing, contributed by a number of subject specialists, has been produced to assist with the task of keeping the management accountant informed as to the current developments in the area of IT and their implications in practical terms. Diverse subject matters are covered, linked by the IT theme, and they include the 'latest' issues as well as consolidating on more established areas. Intended to provide an easy-to-read introduction to the various topics, the material, although not pretending to be exhaustive in content, is sufficient to provide a sound basis for proceeding to more detailed study or practical application.

The scene for the briefing is set in the first contribution, a discussion of the impact of IT upon accountants. Four recent research studies in this area are reviewed and their findings analysed to provide pointers as to the ways in which accountants are meeting the challenges provided by the changes to their working environments. While the rate of acceptance and utilisation of IT by accountants differs markedly, it is clear that those who do not react will suffer in both personal and corporate terms as time progresses.

The next three contributions concentrate on areas close to the accountant's specialist environment. In 'Choosing Accounting Software' the principal criteria for the selection of accounting ledger systems are discussed and guidelines set out for the potential purchaser. Obviously, as there can be no 'right' answer for every company, there is no intention to deal with specific products but the advice given should help to minimise the occurrence of expensive (in terms both of time and cost) mistakes. In 'Financial Modelling Systems' an overall picture is set out of the history and use of financial models. Following the design of a simple conceptual model, the role of the model is set into context so that its proper place in the manager's decision-making armoury can be understood. 'Control in the Computing Environment' deals with a subject which should never be far from the accountant's mind. The recent spread of critical business systems based on microcomputers outside of a controlled DP environment has accentuated the need for accountants to be fully aware of control techniques and concepts as they frequently will have sole responsibility for their definition and implementation.

The following three contributions deal with more general computing matters but which will still be of interest to accountants. In 'Database Systems' the theory of such systems is discussed and particular attention paid to the oepration of relational database systems. In looking outward from the pure finance function, many accountants are realising the importance of such systems and the opportunities for corporate information management and control which are presented by them. The normal development cycle of computer systems is described in 'Systems Analysis' and, although this was once a subject which the accountant saw only from the 'end user' viewpoint, it is now a discipline with which he or she is becoming increasingly involved at all stages. 'The Strategic Control of IT' is aimed directly at those responsible for the development of the IT strategy in organisations. If the response to this statement is: 'what IT strategy?', then there is a particularly pressing need to read further as, such is its importance, it is suggested that it should rank alongside other major corporate ventures.

The final contributions in this briefing deal with two rather more specialist areas. In 'Micro Multi-User Systems and Networks' a summary is provided of the principles behind multiple access systems on microcomputers. This is an area in which many accountants are becoming directly involved and it is imperative that they should have at least a basic understanding of the concepts and limitations of such systems. A look towards the future is provided by 'Expert Systems in Context' although an excellent summary of the current state of the art is also included. The use of expert systems and, indeed, the whole sphere of artificial intelligence, from which such systems are derived, have exciting implications for all those working in the business environment.

While the topics covered by this briefing are varied, to say the least, this only serves as an indication of the wide spread of knowledge that accountants, or anyone involved in management, are increasingly expected to possess. As with most functions of business operation there is little substitute for practical experience but it is hoped that these briefings can at least shorten the learning process and stimulate thinking on the various aspects.

Ray Franks
January 1988

1
The impact of IT on accountants

G R Kaye BA, MSc, FCMA, MBIM, MIDPM

Introduction

The working environment of practising accountants has been transformed by information technology (IT). The purpose of this contribution, written by a qualified accountant who is also an academic working in the area of computerised accounting, is to inform both the practising manager and the accountant of these changes.

Several research projects, recently completed by various accountancy bodies, form this briefing paper which may be used by organisations as a discussion guide in any consideration of their strategy towards IT in the areas of accounting.

The publication of the individual research reports, particularly those by the accounting bodies, took place in a fanfare of publicity implying that the accountant had '*moved into the twentieth-century*' and was both a user and innovator of IT. These views were, however, inconsistent with the image being projected by much of the IT industry, which indicated lack of innovation and a rigidity of accounting practice standing in the way of progress. Perhaps, therefore, the fanfares were those of the image builders trying to change the generally accepted image of accountants whilst also placating the sponsoring bodies. What, then, is the truth?

The issues covered raise more questions than they answer but it is essential that accountants and related managers consider these aspects if they are to control their own future and not become further '*casualties*' in the development of IT. This viewpoint has been put forward by those outside the profession and will be increasingly heard if the accountant fails to adapt.

Some coverage of what is meant by IT is included here, but this is approached from the user viewpoint and it is in no way comprehensive or repetitious of texts on IT. Perhaps a significant feature here is the relationship between accountants in the professional practice and their industrial colleagues who are surrounded by technology in a variety of guises.

The intended stance taken is one of constuctive criticism of the profession and allows a wider view than that available to practicsing accountants, who may not be able to stand back and look at the changes occurring in their working environment.

Research studies

Four recent studies undertaken on behalf of the accounting bodies will be considered, but reference will also be made to other studies. In addition the author has undertaken a survey (Kaye & Dixon 1986), to which references are also made.

The four studies forming the core material are:

Collier	*The Impact of Information Technology on the Management Accountant* (ICMA – 1984)
Carr	*Information Technology and the Accountant* (ACCA – 1985)
Bhaskar & Williams	*The Impact of Microprocessors on the Small Accounting Practice* (ICAEW – 1984)
Coopers & Lybrand	*The Chartered Accountant in the Information Technology Age* (ICAEW – 1985)

Several other studies and reports also address the accounting environment and provide evidence of change and some relevant publications are listed in the bibliography at the end of this contribution.

In addition to publications, several conferences have been held at which both academics and practitioners have made statements about the change taking place in the profession. These assertions tend to lead to confusion rather than clarity of view, and hide an underlying feeling of uncertainty and lack of clear direction. This is a reflection of the failure of any single research study to provide a comprehensive and masterly overview. This is not surprising since each study had its own objectives, reflecting the particular interests of the researcher and the sponsoring organisation. It has been left to individual accountants to interpret this evidence and abstract the meaning and relevance to their own unique situations. It is hoped that this briefing will give some guidance as to interpretation of the various views expressed.

Before reviewing the findings of these studies the traditional view of accountants is considered together with their roles and tasks within and outside the organisation. This is followed by a general synopsis of what is understood by IT. In this way a picture of the current situation can be formed and the forces of change understood.

Traditional views of accountants

Categorisation of accountants

The traditional view of accounting is usually simplified into the following categories:

- accountants in practice
- accountants in industry.

This can be viewed as an alarming simplification as accountants in prsactice provide a variety of services ranging from book-keeping and taxation to consultancy and brokerage, whilst their industrial counterparts are working for a spectrum of organisations – small and large, public and private, manufacturing and service. In addition, the industrial accountant may be undertaking work which the professional counterpart in practice can recognise as accounting or alternatively be undertaking activities of a managerial nature which seem to have little relationship to the normal definitions of accounting. These conflicting views represent a starting point from which an explanation will be attempted as to how the activities of accountants will change as a result of adaptation to IT.
The American Association of Accountants defined the accounting objectives as:

'to provide information for the following purposes:
1 To make decisions concerning the use of limited resources, including identification of crucial decision areas, and determination of objectives and goals;
2 To effectively direct and control an organisation's human and material resources;
3 To maintain and report on the custodianship of resources;
4 To facilitate social functions and control.'
(Source: *A statement of basic accounting theory 1966*)

The American Institue of Certified Public Accountants, in *APB statement 4*, provides a contrast with the above view in that it states that '*Accounting is a service function*'. This view of accounting as a service function is reflected in the definitions of accounting given by the UK institutes and strongly reflects the auditing and stewardship functions associated with the accountant in professional practice. These definitions fail to reflect the role of the accountant, the expectations of the users of accounting information and the associated management perceptions.

Perception of the accountants role

Perhaps one consequence of the IT revolution has been to highlight the various roles of accountants:

Service function	known services drawn upon as and when required – auditing, stewardship, taxation, trusteeship etc.
Marketing	marketing of services and extensions into brokerage, advisory, consulting etc.
Consultant	expert in specific financial and related services.
Expert	providing specific expertise.
'G.P.'	like the doctor a general practitioner providing a range of roles and a point of initial advice.
Manager	managing accounting information services, financial resources or other functions, as per production and sales managers in their respective functions.
Participant in power game	whether within the organisation or on a wider stage.

If the principle of focusing on an Accounting Information System (A-I-S) is adopted then this wider framework might provide an all embracing category. Otley (1978) suggested that A-I-S could be identified in four categories:

- answering machines
- learning machines
- rationalisation machines
- ammunition machines.

This provides another instance of an apparent variety of categories without an obvious means of reconciliation.

Summary

The above examples represent just a few of the interpretations of what an accountant actually does. They also reflect the conflicting expectations of those who define the roles. The assumptions upon which all of the studies have been based is that the subject of study is one and the same. This view is misleading and results in conflicting statements as to how the accountant is going to change. In reality, however, there is not just one accountant, but many, and generalisations, which may be reasonable in collective terms, when considered on an individual basis, may be as unrealistic as the

statement that the number of children in a family is 2.5! The use in this discussion of Industry and Practice represents a polarisation of the variety of accountants which may be encountered.
The traditional views of the accountant are often distorted, which makes for an unclear starting position. The one certainty is that readers will have their own disparate views as to what an accountant is, and that these will form the basis for individual judgements of the impact of IT. Even those readers who are accountants may have a biased perception of the role of accountants and some benefit may be gained by asking non-accountant colleagues or clients for their views!

Information technology

There is an ample supply of literature describing the various aspects of information technology and there is little point, therefore, in detailing these aspects further in this booklet. The following paragraphs, together with the accompanying diagram, serve to summarise the relevant areas.

Overview of Information Technology

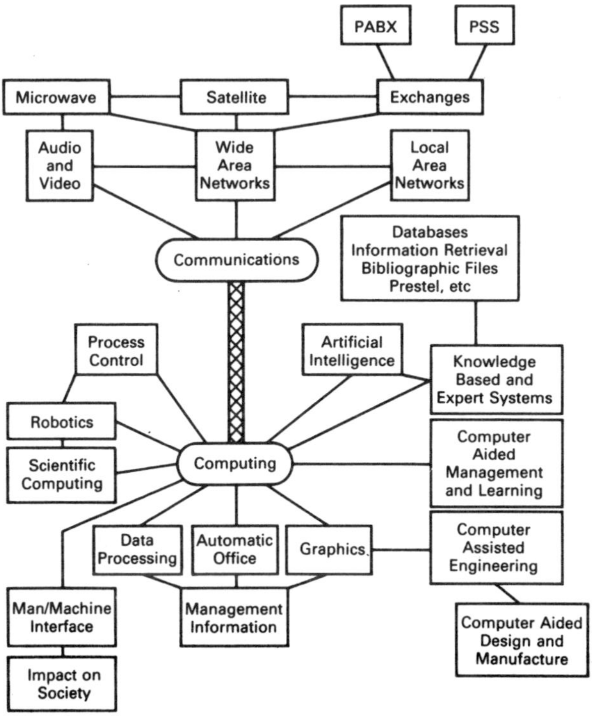

Views of information technology

Zorkoczy (1982) suggested that IT was synonymous with '*new technology*' for many people, but that the technology being referred to went back a long way. IT is both topical and controversial as its consequences are unclear. Some consider that people feel threatened by IT or its effects and hence adopt a Luddite mentality towards it. Alternatively, IT is viewed as a liberator from drudgery and the creator of new opportunities. With such a divergence of views a starting place must be established, and a suitable common basis can be taken to be the definition of terms as found in the Oxford English Dictionary. Technology is defined as 'the practice of applied science' and information is defined as 'items of knowledge'. The first definition raises the question of which science? – information science, a science of knowledge? Whilst this definition is highly acceptable, many would feel this is too wide. This breadth, however, reflects the variety of disciplines currently operating in this field, ranging from computer scientists to behavioural analysts.

Collier (1985) used the definition of the British Advisory Council for Applied Research and Development:

> 'The scientific, technological and engineering disciplines and the management techniques used in information handling and processing; their applications; computers and their interaction with men and machines; and associated social, economic and cultural matters.'

Coopers & Lybrand (1985) suggest that a 'middle course' would lead to 'the use of technology to process, store and transmit information in various forms (text, data, image and voice)'. Carr (1985) views IT as a term 'coined to describe the phenomena created by the convergence of the technologies associated with computing, communications and office systems'.

The diagram illustrates the variety inherent in the study of IT, but the dominant domains are those of computing and communications. These domains are showing increasing integration, stemming both from the technologies and their application to social and organisational problems. Currently, the weighting seems to be in favour of computing but, increasingly, the accountant will detect a shift towards communications as analogue and digital systems become integrated within the same networks. The implications for accountants can already be felt in the area of finance as banks and financial services move over to integrated systems and electronic funds transfer (EFT) systems are used for their normal business services.

The findings

Rather predictably, the results of reviewing the studies with regard to the adoption of IT display varying degrees of adaptation and various attitudes towards the impact of IT. These results are not, however, necessarily inconsistent.

In order to provide an external comparison with the accounting profession, the recently published report by Kearney (1985) provides a study of management's adaptation to IT. In this study, parallels were drawn between adaptation attitudes and business succes, with its classification into *leaders and laggards* in industrial performance. This approach was not followed in any of the four studies reviewed, although Coopers & Lybrand found that the awareness of accountants with regard to IT varied, and that generally they were reactive to IT rather than proactive. Kearney's division into leaders and laggards, whilst clearly a simplification, emphasises the strategic potential of IT, with the innovators exploiting the opportunities to snatch an advantage over their competitors.

One may expect to find similar positions existing in the accountancy profession, with early adaptors to the technology (leaders) and late maturers (laggards). Possibly these studies implied this hypothesis but did not attempt to evaluate it. In the case of Carr the organisational studies precluded such an evaluation whilst Collier did not attempt to measure it and Bhaskar & Williams tended to assume it. Perhaps these static studies missed the possibility of different rates of adaptation and the consequence that individuals and organisations will be at different positions on the IT life cycle. This may result from the over-concentration of the studies on accountants themselves rather than the relationship between accountants and their environment.

As the studies were based around the respective professional institutes, they have perhaps predictably produced different classifications of accountants, as follows:

Collier (ICMA)

The accountant as a manager-employee working within organisations to provide information and advice for planning, control and decision making.

Carr (CACA)

The accountant as a professional general practitioner working in a mixture of locations providing accounting services.

Bhaskar & Williams (ICAEW)

The accountant engaged in auditing, taxation and provision of accounting and consultancy skills to business.

Coopers & Lybrand (ICAEW)

The accountant as a professional employed in practice or industry.

These differing classifications, which the marketeer may describe as product differentiation, may be expected to generate the same conclusions if they are, in fact, classifying the same 'product'. If, however, they are classifications of different 'products' and their markets, then it is reasonable to expect different conclusions. As discussed previously, the classifications may be polarised into *Industry* and *Practice*, which portray significantly different structures and relationships with their environment as shown in the accompanying diagram.

(a) Practice Based Accountants (b) Industrial Based Accountants

The four studies should not be treated *en bloc* but should be reviewed both individually and comparatively. The latter comparison may be treated collectively as a comparison of overall professional change or individually, comparing findings about the Practice based accountant or the Industrial accountant. The findings for Industry and Practice accountants should not be compared directly as their role is significantly different in each situation.

Collier

Collier's study covered a wide spectrum of accountants, although a possible model of a *'typical'* management accountant would be one aged in his or her thirties who tended to be reporting directly to a director and working for a subsidiary of a UK parent company with a turnover in excess of ten million pounds. This person will generally have already adapted to IT and will be actively using relevant technology and techniques.

Collier found that, for members working in the accounting function, access was almost certainly available to a variety of computers which, in particular, supported the financial and management accounting applications. In addition it is probable that they would have access to financial modelling and spreadsheet software, perhaps to utilise in their work. This picture is consistent with the theory that computerisation is closely and essentially linked with the large scale data handling activities of growing companies. Indeed, Weizenbaum (1984) suggested that the history of development of data processing, and the subsequent IT revolution, is closely linked to the large scale data handling problems experienced by the big corporations in the 1950s and 1960s, who initially solved their problems by employing increasing number of clerks, typists and comptometer operators. This solution was, however, found to be punitive in both time and monetary terms. The former was particularly important as it led to delays, slower administration and, potentially, to a 'final seizure' of the system. These problems were eventually overcome by the development of mechanical and electronic data processing methods which are now assumed in such situations.

The specific use of decision support systems may be seen to reflect the cost benefits of information economics, where reduction of costs of information and benefits of increased sensitivity can be compared directly with the employment of additional staff or the risks associated with decision making in the absence of this information.

In addition to the use of computer facilities, Collier found that management accountants were involved throughout the selection, development and implementation stages of computerised systems. This involvement ranged from merely participating in the selection of accounting software to writing systems specifications, programming and adapting and tailoring systems. The involvement was clearly varied, with some individuals being active 'information processing managers', whilst others were merely problem-solving in the accounting function. This varied experience was not found to be linked to the age, size or type of company. Subsequent studies of management accounting students showed that, whilst they were higher users of IT in terms of both hardware and software, their involvement in selection and implementation reflected their junior position, although their youth increased their adaptability (Kaye & Dixon).

This picture of adaptation by management accountants was reflected in the recognition of the implied changes and the desire to adapt, and survive, perhaps as a new type of management accountant, termed 'information accountant' or 'management analyst' by Fawthrop (1984). The expectation of employment prospects displayed clear confusion as to whether a contraction or expansion could be expected. There was doubt cast, however, about the relevance of existing training and education and this message should ring warning bells for those responsible; these warnings were echoed by Bhaskar & Williams who found that those students who had already received IT related training were the greatest advocates of increased training in IT areas.

Carr

Whilst Collier's study was predominantly descriptive of the state of IT in management accounting, the studies of both Carr and Bhaskar & Williams emphasised the normative approach, providing indications of development routes for the professions. For this reason, their studies read differently from Collier's, emphasising throughout the direction in which the profession should be going rather than what has happened to date, even though all three are based firmly in empirical studies. In particular, Carr's study, in describing the environment, office automation and its links with the accountancy profession through data processing, could well have been written some years ago and reflects heavily the studies by Booz Allen and IBM on the future of office systems. Essentially, Carr emphasises the direction in which accountants should be proceeding and how they should use office automation and IT to expand their capabilities and improve their professional practice. To this end, the report is divided into eight sections:

- environment
- office automation
- the accountant and office automation
- the account as a user of data processing
- auditing
- professional practice (including time-keeping, fees, ledger work, the practice accounts, payroll and taxation)
- employment and attitudes
- changes in knowledge and skills.

Throughout the Carr study, the professional practice is emphasised, with the industrial counterpart being seen essentially as an in-house professional accountant having the same IT resources available as to any other manager. This picture fails to recognise that industrial based accountants have been involved with data processing since the pioneering days of LEO in the 1950s. They are, therefore, likely to possess greater experience in the use of data processing and will have helped with the evolution of general office automation systems as well as those relating specifically to the accounting function.

The overall message on professional practice and auditing is a 'prescription' for the increased use of IT. Essentially, the report postulates that there will be no change in employment of accountants, but that they will increase their productivity, a view which appears to be current among accountants. This raises an interesting point that, if accountants are going to be more productive then somebody, somewhere, must be contracting accordingly (assuming minimal growth as currently experienced in the western economies). Who will this be? Clearly this generalisation is countered by individual situations as organisations expand and contract, but the professions are concerned with overall employment prospects.

Carr's study along with the others indicates that there should be more of the same studies in the future. The argument for this is principally that the use of case studies and static data points will cumulatively provide a dynamic picture of what is happening to the profession. This seems to bear a close relationship to a series of autopsies being undertaken on patients dying at various stages, thereby discovering the ageing process! To lighten the picture, however, Carr also indicates that the views of non-accountants should be included, e.g. the clients of professional practices, the customers of management accountants' companies, other employees, and the technology providers (i.e. suppliers and manufacturers of hardware and software).

Bhaskar & Williams

The study by Bhaskar & Williams provides a suggested route for development into the IT era by professional practices. This development path takes an application base and suggests that, since practices spend substantial time typing various reports for presentation, then a starting point would be word processing. From this base accountants would then gain some experience of IT, which they could then apply in two directions. Firstly, towards data processing in the use of retrieval of data and numerical computation; and secondly in the use of productivity tools such as databases, word processing, spreadsheets, communications and graphics, i.e. the same elements that can be found in office automation and integrated systems.

Having identified the direction of development, consideration is given as to how this development may be funded and recognition is placed on the fact that any small practice would require fee income in order to develop such resources. On this basis it is recommended that new services are offered in the area of:

- assistance and advice on small business systems
- data processing bureau work
- financial director consulting roles
- decision support systems

- cash flow forecasting
- bank monitoring
- financial modelling services (including taxation and portfolio) and sub-contract work
- communication and office facilities.

Not only would these new services generate additional fee income but they would also provide a competitive edge for those who choose to practice them. Whilst these new roles for small practitioners are being developed they must additionally come to terms with IT and learn about new systems at the same time as using them and advising on them! Bhaskar & Williams believe that the small practice may disappear since it is vulnerable due to a lack of expertise, lack of services offered to the market and a lack of credibility and, given the current debate on small business audits, the small practitioner, whose work is predominantly in this area, may in any case be considered to be under serious threat.

The recently expressed view that: 'It is evident that the profession has been deficient in reacting to technology development' is one which is threatening to the profession and shows a lack of awareness as to the potential of IT. However, since the study in 1983/84, the ICAEW has begun to react to this threat. Recently, this failing was illustrated at a discussion of examiners within one of the bodies on the place of taxation in the syllabus, and it was apparent that the examiners had failed to recognise the availability of taxation packages on, for example, Prestel (the British Telecom viewdata service) which assist private individuals with the preparation of their income tax returns. Such services have been provided by exploiters of IT who are leading the way in the marketplace. The view of Bhaskar & Williams that 'Survival of the "big eight" UK accountancy firms is not in question' is supportable in that these organisations have a high degree of market awareness in their provision of services, in response to demands by users.

In reviewing the specialist work of auditing in the small practice, Bhaskar & Williams considered that a particularly serious problem existed when auditing microcomputer based systems, in which a lack of standards and controls has led to a proliferation of accounting packages which do not have the auditing aids traditionally available for larger systems. In such cases, greater control of standards through the profession and the development of audit guides and packages is recommended.

In summary, the Bhaskar & Williams study identifies problems for the profession in the areas of:

- auditing
- expertise
- operation
- range of services.

Their solutions are for further research to be undertaken, training and development initiatives and greater control by the profession of its own destiny.

Coopers & Lybrand

Coopers and Lybrand's study is similar to that of Carr in the respect of its emphasis on attitudes, awareness and usage. It confirms some of the beliefs engendered by the other reports, particularly with regard to the split between industry and practice and, within practice, between large and small. Generally the industrial based accountants are considered to be more aware and involved and consequently are greater users of IT and will tend to use more innovative systems. The larger practices do not lack awareness of IT and are using the technology strategically witht heir consultancy wings involved with the development of systems for clients, systems evaluation and the provision of computerised auditing techniques. Smaller practices, however, are considered to be followers rather than leaders with limited awareness and usage of IT and an attitude which was highly reactive to client and competitor threats, but only in respect of following established routes.

In general, accountants in professional practice who have access to IT have a more even usage over the available software, although the variety in use was constrained. The usage by their industrial based colleagues was more concentrated, being in specific areas associated with their work (e.g. decision support systems), but the variety of software available was greater. The expectations of future developments and anticipated benefits reflected the different nature of their work, with industrial based accountants concerned with better information services to management and cost effectiveness, whilst their practice based counterparts concentrated on market oriented issues such as new services and improved performance of existing services.

Summary

Collectively, the reports generate a varied picture of current attitudes, usage and awareness with all of them indicating a trend towards the increased utilisation of IT. Given that there is such a variation in the level of usage, the overall picture must indicate either varying rates of adaptation, with the associated consequences identified by Kearney, or a need for some rapid training and education of those who are currently behind. All of the reports tend towards this view, preferring to leave the individual to determine the consequences of failing to adapt. This maintains uncertainty and perhaps leads to the older member hoping to retire before the threat becomes real whilst the younger colleague may become more withdrawn, retiring into specific services or changing career. This view, which implies age-attributable differences, is not, however, supported by the studies, which indicate that adaptation is not age related. More realistically, the view recognises the alternative choices available to individuals under threat and these reflect their careers and working life cycles.

Survey methods

Whilst researchers have a variety of methods available to them, the dominant traditions in social sciences have tended towards literature surveys, questionnaires, analysis of published data, and more recently, case studies. This latter approach has been criticised by those who favour the 'so called' scientific methods because of the lack of generalisation which may be propounded from representative sampling techniques. The studies under review have clearly followed different approaches.

Collier

Collier's approach was strictly to use the postal questionnaire method, with 400 questionnaires being sent to a potential population of some 12,000 ICMA members working in the private sector. Excluded from the population were those working overseas and those in public service, utilities, consultancy and education. The 2 per cent sample was randomly generated and the 273 usable responses provided 225 replies from members fulfilling accounting roles. Past experience of postal questionnaires indicated a likely response rate of about ten per cent. The high overall response rate, 73 per cent, presumably reflects the interest of accountants in the IT issue. Comparison of these replies with existing data on members and subsequent telephoning of non-respondents indicated the representativeness of the sample. The survey was further verified by follow-up interviews with 31 interested parties.

Carr

The studies by both Bhaskar & Williams and Carr have followed a more mixed approach, with Carr having the most explicitly defined and intr-related methodology. Carr identified three themes:

- technology review
- organisation studies
- individual accountants.

These themes were tackled separately through three different approaches. Firstly, through the use of literature searches and discussions with users and providers of technology. Secondly, organisational studies were undertaken by case reports on selected organisations representative of the UK economy who either had, or had planned, innovatory work in IT and were willing to provide access to researchers. Twenty-four organisations were approached and twenty co-operated in the study. Thirdly, a questionnaire survey was undertaken of members of the CACA in two selected branch societies, comprising 1,192 members. Despite the encouragement of the president of the Association in an accompanying letter, a response rate of only 30 per cent was achieved. The sample was compared with the Institute distribution of occupations and was deemed to be representative. Carr's questionnaire included some 60 questions whilst Collier's comprised 40 questions. Both used multiple choice questions and sectionalised the questionnaire.

Bhaskar & Williams

Bhaskar & Williams' study commenced with an initial literature search which was maintained throughout the study period and was supported by in-depth case studies of small practices. In addition a technology review was undertaken using discussions with users and providers of technology whilst a watching brief was maintained and laboratory type research undertaken in the manner of natural sciences. This study was the least empirical of those reviewed in terms of hard data gathering, this position being defensible since the study attacks the issue of attitudes towards microprocessors within the accountancy profession. In order to gather such data a 'softer' methodology was used in which discussions with practioners were less formal and sought to gain insight into their attitudes and ambitions.

Coopers & Lybrand

Coopers & Lybrand's study was undertaken by full-time researchers employed by the firm and was sponsored by the department of Trade and Industry and two computer manufacturers (Data General Ltd and IBM UK Ltd). The methodology was a combination of case studies and questionnaires. The case studies were developed from interviews with the heads of the finance function and other accounting personnel and, in the case of industrial organisations, additional interviews were carried out with two clients of the finance function and the information service manager. Twenty case studies were compiled covering ten practices (three small, four medium-sized and three large) and the following industries:

- water authority
- chemical conglomerate
- mechanical engineering
- distributive trades
- electronics
- building society
- merchant bank
- insurance broker
- hotel catering and leisure
- construction and civil engineering.

In addition 1,000 questionnaires were sent to accountants, divided equally between industry and practice. A 70 per cent response rate generated 669 usable responses in the ratio 51:49 between industry and practice. All of the questionnaires were sent to ICAEW members in a targetted distribution similar to that of the membership.

Summary

The research methods employed tended to use questionnaires to collect the overall hard data whilst limited case studies were employed to establish detailed situations and to collect the softer data. Unfortunately, all the methods were aimed to collect static data (i.e. the state now) rather than to establish a dynamic picture of change, although Coopers & Lybrand did ask specific questions on future usage and Carr made some predictions based on forecasts of computer manufacturers.

It is interesting to note that the estimated costs of conducting the studies by Collier, Carr and Bhaskar & Williams varied considerably, ranging from £1,500 to £50,000. Costs for Coopers & Lybrand's study are not available and would in any case be difficult to compare as the study was carried out by full-time researchers as opposed to being undertaken by academics alongside their other duties.

Forecast of future trends

Forecasting the future of IT is an activity which embodies science fiction and crystal-gazing together with a true insight into the technologya nd its social and economic consequences! Some general thoughts and principles are, however, set out in the following paragraphs.

Knowledge

As knowledge progresses, so more sophisticated products become available, although cost may become a constraint to their development. Whilst the costs of manufacture seem continually to decrease, various limitations exist, for example:

(a) mechanical devices such as printers and disk drives only have a limited range of improvements that can possibly be made, without them moving from mechanical to electronic mechanisms.
(b) the costs of developing electronics with larger scales of integration can only decrease with increased volumes of production.
(c) competition drives prices down but with an increasing dominance of one operating system or manufacturer. This trend may reverse with fewer alternative suppliers.

The increased number of installations and short life cycles before technical obsolescence must in any case be set against cost reductions.

Communications

With the integration of digital and analogue communications, savings must result from investment in new communications systems. These will provide opportunities for public and private databases, electronic funds transfer, procurement etc.

Programming

Programmer productivity will increase with program generation facilities and more 'English-like' languages permitting user-written systems. Sources of cheap software could create forces to reduce costs but these will be countered with cost increases as copyrights become effective.

Software

The general trend will be towards an increasing level of software products which will be cheaper, better, more user-friendly and, in particular, user/application oriented.

Man-machine interface

Such advanced devices as the mouse and the touchscreen, as well as voice activated systems, already exist but the real limitation relates to users' needs for access to more than one screen at a time, reflecting the problems of display and human interaction. The development of WIMPS (Windows, Icons, Mice and pull-down Screens) addresses this area, and brings together many disciplines. Applications too are varied, ranging from the design of control systems in military aircraft to the desk top work station.

Artificial intelligence (AI)

AI has a charisma which attracts much research and currently the subset of Expert Systems is the focus of attention in many areas, including accounting. Opportunities exist for expert supports to managers and decision-makers such that the variety of decisions can be filtered, thus permitting concentration on issues of judgement. Many projects are already exploiting the potential in this area and are generating results in, for example, fields such as taxation.

Distributed processing

With more compact and portable microcomputers the trend is towards local processing with mainframes continuing to undertake major DP activities, hence the developing concept of a hierarchy of processing from local to department to central with an associated mixture of mainframes, minicomputers and microcomputers. This concept demands policies on upward compatibility, transportability and systems architecture.

Security and safety

Issues of security, at both the accounting and DP level, will become more significant, as will general considerations of safety.

Multiprocessing

There will increasingly be moves towards multiprocessing activities which will lead to improvements in operating software and hardware configurations. These will be demanded by users who, with higher levels of expectation, will not wish to wait for processing on a sequential basis.

Standards

Whilst the concept of standards in hardware, software, data and communications will be sought, strong forces against them will exist in the market-place, as owners of systems defend their territory and continue to charge committed users who are unable to afford the choice of change.

Training

The costs of training will rise and thus justify the application of technology to training, with such techniques as computer assisted learning, interactive video etc.

Privacy and protection

Data and information have a value and their possession has always been a source of power. The opening of communications will dramatically affect current attitudes and policies towards the management of these resources.

Environmental

The wider impact of IT will be found in all parts of the environment, ranging from that directly impacting the user and the micro-environment of the organisation to the wider social, economic, legal, political, national and international areas.

Conclusion

This contribution has reviewed four major studies of the accountancy profession and has recommended that accountants should become aware of the impact of IT on their future. To this end, it is recommended that accountants should read these studies so that they can deliberate on their own positions and, to assist with these considerations, an Action Plan, including a Checklist, is given on the following pages.

It is apparent from the studies that accountants are reacting in various ways to the changing work environment. This is not surprising and one may always expect to find people who are either 'early innovators' or 'latterly laggards' in adapting to change. What is of interest, however, is the apparent position of the three major professional bodies.

Four classifications of accountants have been identified, one from each of the studies. That attributed to the Coopers & Lybrand study can be subsumed into the others, leaving three clearly defined categories of accountant which, for ease of reference, can be termed:

- professional practitioner
- industrial
- general practitioner.

The latter two categories can be considered to be 'employee accountants', in contrast to the professional practitioner.

It would seem reasonable to suggest that accountants in each of these classifications will have differences in their associated behaviour patterns. Firstly, accountants in professional practice have as their reference group services provided by fellow professional practitioners, i.e. they are not under pressure from their 'users' in the same way that applies to the employee accountant. Their failure to satisfy users will be discovered only if users make their demands elsewhere. On this basis, it can be concluded that the professional practice has generally been much slower than the other categories in adapting to changes in IT. The exceptions to this are, of course, the larger professional practices who have been IT users for some time. This is partly as a result of demands from their large clients for services commensurate with their advancing systems.

The employee accountant is in a similar position, being at the 'beck and call' of the employer or user manager. User managers expect accountants to be effective and efficient in satisfying their needs and this has long involved keeping abreast of latest developments in the area of IT. It is not unusual, therefore, to encounter management accountants who actively participate in data processing activities and, indeed, the accountant and the DP manager within an organisation are occasionally one and the same person. The suggestion is that, if accounting is seen as a service function, then like all services it must adapt to suit the needs of the users. In the case of employee accountants the users' needs are paramount and clearly linked to their own employment position. This contrasts clearly with the position outlined above for the professional practitioner. This would support the view of Bhaskar & Williams that, whilst the small practice is under threat, the 'big eight' firms are not.

A further problem existing for those who are late in adapting to IT is the learning curve upon which they will need to embark. Early innovators will already be well advanced on the learning curve and, additionally, will adapt more rapidly to new developments as they will have acquired confidence, experience and basic knowledge. Latecomers may have to work hard to catch up but at the same time they should benefit from the mistakes made by the 'pioneers' thus avoiding the need to 'reinvent the wheel'.

The remaining conflict is the view presented by Carr that employment of accountants will not change and yet their productivity will increase. This view does not seem feasible unless other management disciplines are going to contract, or at least expand less rapidly. Given the delay mechanism for change in professional bodies referred to previously, it is highly unlikely to suppose that other management disciplines will not adapt to IT whereas accountants will. If this is accepted, then it is likely that a section of the accounting community will suffer and this could reasonably be expected to be at the lower level of staff, including clerical functions. Perhaps, therefore, the same compression of the accounting function can be anticipated as that which will apply to the organisation as a whole. If this is the case then trainee accountants and the lower tier accounting bodies will be under threat; alternatively, the view must be put forward that accountants themselves may not expect to enjoy the same employment opportunities when productivity increases.

The view of the author is that accountants are adapting to IT at varying degrees and, as per the Kearney report, there are 'leaders and laggards'. The leaders will exploit IT and move forward, whilst the laggards must chase to stay in business.

Action plan and checklist

Action plan

It is hoped that readers will now be aware of some of the changes being felt in the accountancy profession and will feel encouraged to be proactive in shaping the future course of the profession and their own careers. To assist with this, a series of questions in the form of a Checklist have been compiled which can be reviewed individually or in discussion with colleagues.

Having worked through the Checklist it is suggested that clear objectives are identified, both pesonally and organisationally, and that these are translated in terms of tasks and deadlines. In this way it should be possible to move from the current state to the desired state in a controlled manner rather than reactively, i.e. being subject to the latest threat and uncertainty.

Managing IT is no different from managing other aspects of business and the tried and tested techniques of management accounting such as Corporate Planning and Budgetary Control still apply. Management accountants are equipped to manage change and to evaluate effectiveness and efficiency and these skills are now required for dealing with **Inforamtion Technology**!

Checklist for Information Technology adaptation

1 Do you or your organisation operate any of the following:

mainframe computer
minicomputer
microcomputer
intelligent terminal
dumb terminal
wordprocessing facilities
viewdata/videotext
facsimile equipment
electronic mail
networks
PABX
PSS

2 Do you or your organisation use any of the following software packages:

wordprocessing
spreadsheets
databases
graphics
statistics
production planning
communications
general ledger
sales ledger
purchase ledger
stock control
payroll
fixed asset register
product cost
budgets

standard costs
financial packages
audit packages
taxation
CAD/CAM

3 Do you collect data electronically through:

shop-floor terminals
terminals at remote locations
portable terminals
optical character reading equipment
point of sale devices

4 Are you or your organisation involved with:

electronic funds transfer (CHAPS/CHIPS)
automated teller machines
SWIFT (Society for worldwide interchange of financial transactions)
BACS (Bankers automated clearing services)

5 Do you or your organisation transfer data from system to system:

manually, by rekeying
electronically
magnetically

6 Do any of your suppliers or customers have electronic communication systems with you?

7 Do you and the staff around you have their own computing facilities including personal productivity tools?

8 Do you or your organisation use IT equipment for:

planning purposes
investment appraisal and other special reports
risk analysis
routine reporting (budgets, monthly accounts, correspondence, accounting formats, report writing)

9 Are you or any of your staff involved in:

hardware selection and installation
software selection, conversion, implementation
system specification
programming

10 Does your organisation have a policy towards the acquisition of IT equipment, hardware and software (including micros), training, security and the management of its life cycle?

11 Does your organisation have a strategy incorporating IT as a strategic element alongside other elements such as marketing?

12 Do you have a personal strategy for adapting to IT?

Analyse your responses between self and organisation. Then apply the following interpretation firstly to yourself and secondly to the organisation.

If you answered YES to any of the above questions, consider whether you have an adequate policy for:

- the control of the hardware and software
- determining its effectiveness and efficiency

If you answered NO to any of the above questions then you should investigate fully the potential of **Information Technology**, together with the actions you should take to make yourself more aware.

Bibliography

The four principal studies reviewed are:
Collier – *The Impact of Information Technology on the Management Accountant* (ICMA — 1984)
Carr – *Information Technology and the Accountant* (CACA — 1985). Pubished by Gower
Bhaskar & Williams – *The Impact of Microprocessors on the Small Accounting Practice* (ICAEW — 1984). (Published by Prentice Hall International 1985)
Coopers & Lybrand – *The Chartered Accountant in the Information Technology Age* (ICAEW — 1985)

Other references and works of interest in this field are:
Kearney – *The Barriers and the Opportunities of Information Technology, a Management Perspective* (The Institute of Administrative Management and Department of Trade and Industry — 1985)
Weizenbaum – *Computer Power and Human Reason* (Pelican — 1984)
Fawthrop – *Management Accountants and Infromation Technology* (1984). Submission to the Institute of Cost and Management Accountants, Information Technology working party.
Barras & Swan – *The Adoption and Impact of Information Tecnology in the UK Accountancy Profession* (The Technical Change Centre — 1984)

Manpower – *The Personal Computer Survey* (Manpower Ltd — 1985)
Arthur Andersen – *Trends in Information Technology: 1985* (Arthur Anders & Co — 1984)
Touche Ross – *The Impact of Technology on Banking: World Summary* (Touche Ross — 1985)
ASA National IT Task-force – *The Impact of Developments in Information Technology on Australian Accountants* (Australian Society of Accountants — 1984)
Bessant, Guy, Miles & Rush – *IT Future* (National Economic Development Office — 1985)
Kaye G.R. and Dixon R., – *The Impact of Information Technology on the Students of the ICMA* (ICMA — 1986)

2

Choosing Accounting Software

R V Franks BSc, MBCS, FCMA, MIDPM

Introduction

Any contribution entitled 'Choosing Accounting Software' is likely to be worth while setting out some points before proceeding. The most important is that it is *not* a guide as to which product to buy. Apart from the fact that new accounting software packages appear (and sometimes disappear!) with amazing rapidity and existing products are frequently updated, it will become increasingly clear that there cannot possibly be a universal answer to the question: 'which is the best accounting system for me?' Every organisation has its own individual characteristics of operation and a system which is perfect in one situation may not even be capable of implementation or operation in another. There are, however, a number of basic guidelines which, if borne in mind during the selection process, can greatly increase the chances of a successful installation of an accounting system and it is these which I have attempted to address here. The selection of an accounting system can often be a complex task with perhaps many conflicting requirements, both operational and technical, to be satisfied. While there are more options today, both in terms of the range of products and the facilities which they provide, this serves merely to increase the pressure on the prospective user to be sure that the correct approach is being adopted and emphasis correctly placed on the myriad of factors which comprise the selection decision.

Having said this, there are many very successful computerised accounting systems in operation, although one suspects that there is at least an equal number which have never worked properly or efficiently for one reason or another. Like most things, there is no magic solution and, even if the right selection decision is made today, the nature of an organisation (not to mention management information requirements) may soon change so fundamentally that the system which started so well quickly becomes wholly inappropriate.

This contribution deals mainly with the three principal ledger systems, ie the sales, purchase and nominal ledgers, and assumes that readers will have at least a passing acquaintance with their functions and basic methods of operation. It is, however, recognised that such systems are often acquired in the context of integration with other systems, such as sales invoicing or stock control and these related systems are briefly considered later.

It is hoped that by reading this contribution the prospective (or even existing) user of accounting software will gain some insight into the principal criteria to be applied in selection. It is important to remember, however, that the two most fundamental questions are:

- does the software work?
- does the software enable proper accounting records to be maintained?

With all the complexities of accounting software selection it is often easy to forget these most basic of selection criteria.

A brief history

The computerisation of accounting functions was one of the first commercial applications tackled by computer systems, a fact which largely explains why DP departments and computing are often strongly linked to the finance function. Indeed many of the early proponents of business computing emanated from the finance discipline. While systems on mainframe and minicomputers are well established, the advent of business microcomputers in the late 1970s has revolutionised the accounting software market-place and has brought computerised accounting within the reach of many organisations for which it was previously prohibitive in terms of cost and technical expertise.

It must be said that some of the early ledger systems which became available for microcomputers left a lot to be desired in both accounting and computing terms. There were various tales of systems which, for example, allowed single-sided entries to be made to the ledgers (one in my experience even permitted triple-sided entries to be effected!), payroll systems in which the payees and their details needed to be keyed in as data statements in a program (effectively necessitating a program amendment each time the payroll was run!) or ledgers which mysteriously 'lost' transactions during end-of-period operations. Unfortunately, instances such as these were largely responsible for the failure of many to take microcomputers seriously as effective business tools, an attitude which changed only with the subsequent widespread acceptance of spreadsheet and word processing systems.

In the early days, many microcomputers offered only two floppy diskette drives as storage devices, providing for as little as 250K of total on-line storage. Software designers were, therefore, faced with designing accounting systems with an acute shortage of disk space and this gave rise to 'balance-forward' ledger systems in which merely the balance on each customer or supplier account was brought forward from one period to the next. This approach contrasts with the 'open-item' method in which individual transactions which are outstanding can be carried forward to the ledgers; this method, of course, has a greater storage requirement. Another problem tended to revolve around the update of the nominal ledger from the sales or purchase ledgers; this often involved juggling diskettes between the various available drives with amazing frequency. The general concern for space also meant that additional information fields, such as customer telephone numbers or remarks for transactions were kept to a bare minimum, thereby in turn reducing the overall usefulness of such systems. Nevertheless, there were some good systems and the better of these have lasted (although in improved versions) to the present day.

The advent of hard disk systems reduced concern about disk space and, as all elements of the system were always on-line, the mechanics of ledger updates became less involved. Open-item systems with more emphasis on the provision of management information became available and there has been a steady progress as technology and users' expectations and sophistication have developed over the years. Accounting systems for microcomputers are now well established and whilst aspects such as multiple-access requirements, large data-volumes and speed of processing may have occasionally dictated against their use in the past the differences in capabilities that contributed to these decisions are continually being eroded.

General considerations

While it may seem like stating the obvious, the starting-point for selection of a system involves the definition of the elements of the accounting and related tasks which are to be computerised. Naturally, while this can often be a trivial task, for example if the requirement is merely to computerise the three ledgers, this is by no means always the case, particularly in large organisations where the accounting functions may be split with, for example, a number of purchase ledgers in operation on microcomputers at local sites but with the nominal ledger centralised on a mainframe computer. If anything other than a complete accounting suite is to be acquired it will be necessary to check that any proposed software will operate piecemeal, for example will the sales or purchase ledgers operate without a nominal ledger also being installed, or will sales invoicing function as a stand-alone module without the stock control or sales ledger systems? Although some software packages provide a high level of modularity, others are much more integrated in concept and design and may not lend themselves to partial implementations. Having arrived at the requirement, there are a number of considerations which apply to the operation of any accounting software and these are considered in this chapter before going on to look at the specific elements of the systems in later chapters. The emphasis of the various criteria may vary according to circumstances, but the following are likely to apply in many situations:

- coding structures
- control of transaction input and method of ledger update
- preservation of ledger integrity
- user interface
- flexibility and means of modification
- envisaged and potential volumes
- suitability and reliability of the proposed hardware and operating system environments
- security of access
- interface with other software
- documentation and training/support
- 'auditability' and approval of systems

Coding structures

Although this subject is returned to later, the size, nature and structure of the various account codes are among the most important factors to be considered when initially determining whether or not a system is likely to be suitable for use in a particular organisation. In terms of sales and purchase ledgers, the structure of the customer/supplier code may not be too problematic. Most systems will permit at least six alphanumeric characters as the account code and, unless there is some fundamental reason for not conforming to this, it is not normally an area for great concern.

The structure of the nominal code, however, may be crucial to the suitability of a particular accounting system and this is an area which will need to be looked at critically before firmly deciding upon a course of action, particularly as the nature of the code will largely determine the reporting and analysis capabilities of the system. Most nominal ledger systems will have some form of hierarchical coding structure but the number of levels, and the number and nature of the characters permitted within each level, vary considerably. The capability of systems to produce an autonomous analysis by cost centre or department may also be critical. It is worth noting that some systems allow for specification of the structure of the nominal code by the user, although obviously within certain parameters.

For many potential users of accounting systems this subject will play a major part in their selection decision, as the structure of the nominal code may be well established from previous systems or may be dictated by a corporate policy set, for example, by a parent company. The problem of coding conventions is not confined to ledger systems, as similar considerations exist in the selection of a stock control system.

Control of transaction input and method of ledger update

A few years ago, I asked a salesman from a well-known microcomputer accounting software company whether his product incorporated batch control facilities. His answer was that 'batch control is an old concept which only applied on mainframe computers'. What he probably meant was that he saw his market as being small businesses where all transaction input would be effected by one person (probably the proprietor of the business) who would not want to be bothered either with first totalling the transactions or with a report of the input made. While I could see what he meant, I must admit that the answer did not inspire me with any great confidence in the product.

The concept of using batch controls for the identification and confirmation of user input should be fundamental to any computerised accounting system and any such system should at least provide it as an option even if its use is not made compulsory. Apart from any other consideration, batch listings provide remarkably effective documents if there is ever a need to re-store from an archive copy of data files, as these listings may only require re-keying to return to the current position.

Ledger updates may be performed in one of two ways:

- interactively as transactions are entered or immediately after their entry; or
- in batch mode as a separately selected process.

The latter method is normally to be preferred and this will usually be found in systems which enable batch control of input to be exercised. The batch update simplifies the running of a well-controlled accounting system, enabling proper levels of access, documentation and timing to be brought to the update function. Additionally, it enables input batches which are found to be in error after initial input to be amended or even cancelled prior to being posted to the ledger, thus removing the need for various adjustment transactions to be entered.

Preservation of ledger integrity

There can be no more fundamental test of an accounting system than that it should maintain proper books of account, in accordance with normal double-entry book keeping principles. A ledger integrity test should involve a pass of the complete ledger file to determine that the calculated balance is in agreement with a control figure; for example, an integrity check on a nominal ledger in which debits are held as positive figures and credits as negative should return an overall file total of zero. There are two simple points to consider here:

- is it possible legitimately to enter a single-sided entry (or, indeed, anything other than a double-sided entry) into any of the ledgers? (If the answer is yes, then walk away quickly!)
- how often are each of the ledgers checked for integrity?

Apart from systems which positively allow single-sided entries to the ledger, there are a number of other reasons why a computerised ledger may become out of balance, for example physical corruption of part of the file or loss of power during transaction entry or the ledger-posting routines. The system should never be allowed to continue in such a condition and hence the checking of the integrity of the whole ledger (remember, a file corruption can affect any part of the file and not necessarily just the most recently-added transactions) should be a frequent and routine occurrence, for instance whenever the ledger is updated, although one should be aware of the time overhead that such an operation may carry. Some systems check integrity only at the end of a period and others never at all(!), so it is important to know the level of the risk, as an integrity failure will normally require the data files to be re-stored from a backup copy taken before the corruption occurred.

The importance of the above points cannot be stressed too highly. A good idea of the competence of your supplier and the quality of your proposed software can be gained from the answers to two simple questions in this area:

- can I make single-sided entries to the ledger if I am 'not sure' of the full accounting entry?
- if a transaction goes 'missing' from the ledger (eg through file corruption or even program error), how long will the system continue before I am informed?

Remember that these points apply just as much to sales and purchase ledgers, in which internal control accounts should be maintained to preserve integrity, as to nominal ledgers. Memorandum balances, such as those which may be held on master files, should also be subject to integrity checking if they are used in any significant way.

User interface

The phrase 'user friendly' is probably one of the most overworked in computer marketing, a discipline not known for underworking anything! Even so, it is important for accounting systems to be easy to use as, unlike many other types of software, the users are often non-technical clerical workers or equivalent to whom the concepts of computer processing may be foreign. Additionally, such users are often not even familiar with many accounting terms and conventions so that the need for clarity is even more pressing. In general, most accounting systems now rate quite highly in this aspect and the days of watching a blank screen while a ledger is being purged are largely a thing of the past.

As a general guideline, a screen should at any moment show the name of the function being run, the actual process being effected and, when required, clear instructions and options which are available to the user. Whilst documentation, normally in the form of user manuals, provides an important backup in this respect, the principal functions of ledger operation should be ascertainable, at least to the more experienced user, by virtue of screen prompts and displays.

One area which tends to be the subject of particular criticism is that of error messages which are frequently considered to be too technical or even unintelligible to the user. In fairness, only certain error messages are within the control of the software creators (at any rate those of accounting systems). Certainly error messages relating to the normal operation of the system such as the user selecting an invalid option, or a particular field not being entered correctly, should be clear and unambiguous. Other error messages, however, may originate from the program language, the operating system (including, where relevant, network software) or even the hardware and, given the nature of the errors which cause such messages, it may not be possible for the applications software to intercept these and 'translate' them for the user. Anyone who has stared blankly at a message of the type:

BDOS ERROR ON B: BAD SECTOR

will understand the problem!

Flexibility and modification

Packaged software is designed for general applicability and software companies are able to market these systems at what may appear to be relatively low prices because of the amortisation of the cost over a high volume of sales. Accounting systems are no different in this respect but it is rather more unusual to encounter a user who is able to take a packaged set of ledger systems and be entirely happy with them without modification, particularly if systems such as sales invoicing or order processing are also involved. There is, however, a growing trend for accounting systems to provide some inherent flexibility of configuration, particularly in terms of the definition and generation of specific reports. Such customisation facilities may even extend to the specification of nominal code structures, the types of transactions processed by the system and to the definition of selection menus.

It is important to determine extent of flexibility of a particular software package, as it may save the necessity of commissioning a bespoke (ie purpose-written) system to be written, with its attendant implications of lead time, bugs (ie faults) and cost. Even if a required feature cannot be provided by the user customising the system, it may be possible (with some, but by no means all, accounting packages) for the software to be modified specifically for a given set of requirements, be they additional reports, extra data fields, expanded field sizes etc. This is a perfectly valid route to take, but the user should bear in mind:

- the cost of such an exercise is likely to be large in relation to the initial cost of the software package. This is not surprising, as you will be paying a direct labour cost rather than buying an 'off-the-shelf' system with an amortised cost.
- a modified system may be less robust than one which has not been modified; this will largely depend upon the extent and nature of the modifications.
- the user of a modified system may well be cut off from any upgraded path or improved facilities which may be offered by the software supplier in the future. In the worst cases this may result in a system which the software house becomes unable or unwilling to maintain in the medium term (which, in the computer industry, is anyone else's short term!). This in turn has obvious implications in terms of ongoing support and any future modifications.

Having said all this, many users have standard systems which have been successfully modified in some way to provide a better fit for their businesses and this can represent a good way of deriving a 'bespoke' system without exposure to the more fundamental dangers and costs. Some users are keen to acquire source code (ie program code which they can amend themselves) for their accounting applications; while this also may sound an attractive option this route should only be taken by experts as any rights to ongoing support and program maintenance will normally be forefeited.

Potential volumes

With the general use today of hard-disk systems, the volume of accounts and transactions is not quite so problematic as in the days when all three ledgers were required to run on floppy diskettes. Even so, there are still two aspects to consider:

- whether there will be sufficient disk storage available to run the proposed system. Accounting systems can take up a surprising amount of disk space, particularly if ledgers are rarely purged or some form of ledger archiving is not effected periodically. It is important to take the most pessimistic viewpoint (eg a nominal ledger held open at year end for three months into the following year may cause larger-than-normal files to be held) and to allow for operating system, program and internal work and index files in any calculation of space required. Some accounting packages will provide an algorithm to enable the storage requirements to be calculated for a particular level of accounts and transaction activity.

- it is important to watch for any maxima which are inherently attributable to the software, for example in terms of maximum numbers of customer accounts, transactions or even transactions per account. Particular constraints of this nature will, of course, still be found on the systems which are designed to run on limited storage devices and these should always be checked against projected requirements.

When assessing volumes it is easy to forget that a business may grow significantly during the lifetime of the system. Additionally, it can be very easy to underestimate even current volumes; for example, only a hundred customers may be active at any one time but a high level of activity may result in a thousand records being held on the customer file by the end of the year. Needless to say, volume calculations should be based on the latter figure in such instances but are all too often based on the former. Many systems have become unusable because the increase in volumes over the lifetime of the system has been severely underestimated and the pressure that this places on the system, not to mention on the people who are running it, can be catastrophic.
As a working rule, never install a system that will 'just fit' in terms of space – because it will not! Apart from any other consideration, larger disk systems often bring significant improvements in access times, which may well make the often small extra expenditure involved in having a 'cushion' of storage well worth while.

Hardware environment

Discussion of volumes leads on naturally to a more general discussion of the hardware environment in which the accounting software is to run and perhaps this section should be entitled 'Choosing Accounting Hardware'. Consideration of volumes will lead to some conclusion about the disk storage capacity required although this is, of course, only part of the hardware selection decision. The proposed software may also impose conditions as to the computers on which it will operate and the operating systems to which it can be applied. There are further considerations, such as the minimum amount of memory required and whether any special screen or printer characteristics are necessary. It must be recognised that developments in the microcomputer industry, in particular, are extremely rapid and the environment which is recognised today as being standard may not even be supported in three years time. For this reason some users view the portability of the software between different machines as being important, as this is seen as being most likely to provide an upgrade path in the future when the existing equipment becomes obsolete, even though the software is still perfectly serviceable. One should also remember to allow for any other applications which are to be run on the same computer; these applications will also have requirements in terms of hardware and operating software.

The one place I would suggest that the user of an accounting system does not want to be is at the 'leading edge' of technology. There is always a better computer and a better operating system coming out 'tomorrow'; it is more important, however, that the operating environment for an accounting system passes one simple test above all others, ie DOES IT WORK NOW? There is no greater inconvenience than that which is caused by an accounts system which becomes inoperative, particularly where payroll or sales invoicing are involved. It is much better, therefore, to take a well-proven route, however unexciting this may seem, when acquiring hardware for accounting systems.

The speed of operation of the system is another factor to consider when looking at possible hardware environments. The most frequently voiced and sometimes justified criticism of accounting systems is that they are 'so slow'. In many cases, however, accounting systems have to perform global operations on potentially large files (eg a ledger integrity check or a review of purchase ledger invoices) and, software considerations aside, the level of performance is likely to be heavily dependent on the hardware. Ideally, try to see someone with similar volumes running the same software on the same hardware, but this is often not possible and you may find out too late that the end of period on the nominal ledger means that the system will be unavailable for use for that day!

Multi-user and networked systems bring another dimension into this area of deliberation and these are discussed in more detail later.

Security of access

Security of access to the various facilities in an accounting system is traditionally provided by the means of multi-level password protection. While not perfect, this at least prevents casual misuse of a system and enables functions to be separated between various personnel so that, for example, the person responsible for entry of purchase ledger invoices is not also able to set up a new supplier account. Some considerations relating to passwords are:

- where a multi-level password system is in operation, the holders of higher-level passwords are normally able to access facilities available to holders of lower-level passwords through the same (ie higher-level) password.
- for installations where password protection is not required, it is useful to be able to remove any reference to passwords from the users interface.
- passwords should be capable of definition only through a 'system manager' facility, which should itself be protected by the highest-level, or its own special, password.

While passwords do offer a certain level of protection, which will be reinforced with protection facilities provided by multi-user and network systems, their security should be viewed with some caution. In many systems, the access passwords can be ascertained quite easily by anyone possessing some computing expertise who has access to a file dump or similar utility.

Interface with other systems

With the growing use over recent years of database, word processing, spreadsheet and modelling systems, the ability of an accounting system to transfer data to (and, in appropriate circumstances, to receive data from) such systems may form a critical factor in the selection procedure. Transfer of data between systems is becoming increasingly commonplace thanks largely to the prevalence of certain software packages providing, almost as a by-product, industry standards in terms of data structures.

Even where an interface between accounting and other systems may be possible in principle, the inexperienced user may still find difficulty in using such interfaces effectively, as the required process may entail an understanding of file and record structures and the use of intermediary files for the conversion of the data into a different order or format before becoming useful in the target system.

Training and support

For many users, particularly those for whom this is the first venture into the world of business computing, it will be necessary to rely on initial training and ongoing support for the successful implementation of their accounting systems. This applies even more if the user is also unfamiliar with the maintenance of ledgers, even in a manual form.

In such cases the user should take particular care in ascertaining what services will be available and how much these will cost. For example, many software companies have a user 'hot line' which registered users of their products may contact for advice and support in return for an annual fee. On-site training, particularly that required after initial installation of the system, can be fairly expensive but may be necessary in certain situations. In addition to availability, it is also worth finding out something about the likely quality of support before buying the product, particularly where systems are acquired through dealers rather than direct from the software company.

For many users, again particularly those who are inexperienced in this area, it may well be worth single-sourcing the supply of hardware and software; the theory being that if anything goes wrong with the system there is at least just one point of initial contact.

'Auditability' and approval of systems

Many systems are advertised as containing an 'audit trail'; I must admit to finding this rather confusing as the normal reports produced by a proper accounting system should in themselves provide adequate detail of activities for a satisfactory review by auditors. Sometimes the 'audit trail' relates to a log of events which have taken place on the system and this can indeed provide a useful record, not only from the point of view of security but also if a restoration has to be made from a backup copy of data at any time. In general, and particularly if insufficient expertise exists within the organisation, it is worth involving your accountants in the selection process as it is they who will be undertaking the audit of the records. Remember, however, that even the best system will maintain poor accounting records if it is used in a sloppy and uncontrolled manner.

Over the past few years various attempts have been made to provide users and potential users of accounting software with some form of register to denote that certain systems had been 'approved' as being a proper accounting system. In general, the initiatives for such a scheme have originated from the accountancy profession and have met with resistance or, at best, indifference by software suppliers. It is not difficult to see the problems associated with any such plan; apart from the development and administrative costs involved, there would be difficulties in reviewing on an equitable basis the hundreds (if not thousands) of software packages which would need to be encompassed, thus creating a permanent waiting list. Even if this problem were overcome, difficulties would be posed by systems which are upgraded as time goes on and the scheme could hardly embrace the many systems which are modified forms of a standard package or which are entirely bespoke in origin. In any case, it is difficult to see how any success could be achieved without the active cooperation of the main contenders in the accountancy software market.

Nevertheless, some progress has been made and the NCC (National Computer Centre) is currently attempting to establish a scheme whereby software is reviewed on a 'questionnaire' basis. But however laudable the objectives, it is still far from clear whether any effective approval system can be established and, even if it can, whether this will have any marked effect on the software selection decision.

Personal ledger systems

Normal facilities

The term 'personal ledger systems' encompasses the following:

- sales ledger (often marketed as accounts receivable systems)
- purchase ledger (often marketed as accounts payable or as bought ledger systems)

The systems available on the market range widely, from the very simplistic to the complex and powerful and, though there is a tendency to compare competing ledgers by price (on the basis that one software supplier's 'Purchase Ledger' or 'Sales Ledger' is the same as another's), overall you will get what you pay for. The low-priced system which can be run on a twin floppy-drive machine can hardly be expected to provide the same facilities as its more expensive (in terms of cost and machine requirements) counterpart, although that is not to say that such a system would not be the correct purchase in many situations.

Apart from the obvious differences, purchase and sales ledger systems are very similar in design and operation and, in terms of software development, it is common for one of the ledgers to be programmed initially, with the other ledger then being largely derived from it, thus saving considerable development time and costs. In this way it is also easy to maintain consistency between the two ledgers (eg in terms of screen messages and prompts), as only the areas which are specific to each ledger need to be programmed separately. Although many variations exist, all personal ledger systems will be expected to include at least the following facilities:

- maintenance of customer/supplier master files
- transaction entry routines for invoices, credit notes, adjustments and cash receipts/payments
- analysis of transaction input, (eg coding for posting to the nominal ledger)
- some method for allocating (ie matching) cash and credit note transactions with the invoices to which they relate
- screen enquiry facilities
- accounting and management reporting facilities
- period accounting and ledger purging
- interface with a nominal ledger system

The above subjects, which are common to both sales and purchase ledgers, are considered in this chapter, and some of the areas which are specific to one or other ledger are covered in the next.

Maintenance of customer/supplier files

Systems vary considerably in the specific data which is held for customers (sales ledger systems) or suppliers (purchase ledger systems), the bare minimum normally being:

- account number
- name and address
- other contact details (eg contact name, telephone number, telex number)

(Indeed the absolute minimum amount of information comprises merely an account number and name and some smaller systems operate on this basis, although obvious difficulties are presented with the production of external documents such as sales ledger statements and purchase ledger remittance advice notes).
Most systems provide far more information than this, particularly for customer files, which will generally contain fields relating to:

- credit control facilities (eg credit limit and period)
- information for the further analysis of sales, for example sales representative, geographical area, type of customer
- details for statement printing; some systems, for example, hold the ageing analysis as a set of fields on the customer master file.
- facilities for maintenance of further address fields, for example, as required for invoice, delivery or statement addresses, where these are different from the customer's normal contact address
- sales invoicing information, such as trade discount percentages and stock price bands

- VAT-related information, such as the customer's normal status in respect of VAT.

Many of the above fields are relevant only when the sales ledger system is interfaced to a sales invoicing or order-processing system and have no direct effect on the operation of the sales ledger itself. For example, credit control facilities are often seen as desirable features of sales ledgers but, in reality, the 'horse has already bolted' by the time an invoice is posted to the sales ledger and such facilities are in practice most effective at the order entry or despatch stages.
For obvious reasons, supplier master files tend to contain less information, although systems with automated payments procedures will include fields for the various selection processes.
Master file maintenance facilities will include options for the addition of details of new customers/suppliers and their subsequent amendment or deletion. Obviously, the system should not allow any balance details to be amended through these procedures, nor should it be possible to delete accounts which are still active in terms of transactions held on the ledger, even where the sum of these transactions is zero (ie there is a zero balance). Many users will require that a printed record of master file activity is automatically produced and some systems (although by no means all) provide for this.

Transaction entry procedures

Transaction entry procedures encompass the input routines for the entry of the following principal transaction types:

- invoices
- credit notes
- cash payments (and discounts received)
- cash receipts (and discounts allowed)
- ledger adjustments

Transaction entry procedures are normally very similar for both sales and purchase ledgers although the actual method employed can vary between different systems. For example, some systems adopt the normal batch entry method, allowing the user to exercise external control over the input function with the possibility of amending or cancelling a batch of transactions before it is 'approved' for posting to the ledger. At the other extreme, other systems adopt a process whereby transactions are posted directly onto the ledger at the time of entry with no provision of batch control. The latter concept is

generally to be found in low-cost systems operating in a limited-hardware environment and, while many would regard this as far from perfect, it can provide a viable option for the very small business where most accounting functions are performed by one person.
The basic information entered for each transaction will normally include the following:

- customer/supplier account number
- transaction reference (ie 'our' reference); this may, for example, be the cheque number in respect of purchase ledger payments or the invoice number in respect of sales ledger invoices
- an external reference, for example, the supplier invoice number or customer order number
- transaction value, with a separate entry for VAT or settlement discounts received/allowed, as appropriate
- the date of the transaction; this has added significance in systems in which aging is effected by reference to the actual date rather than by period or month number
- some form of remarks field, effectively enabling the ledger to be annotated in respect of the transaction, being used, for example, to provide further identification details
- anlysis information

The method for the entry of VAT can sometimes be over-complicated and there are systems which provide for some form of automatic calculation of the VAT amount to be effected at the input stage. This is, of course, superfluous other than for providing a check of the VAT calculation, as the VAT amount will already be available from the source document (eg the purchase or sales invoice) from which the input is being made and it is this amount which must be used. It must, however, be possible to analyse the invoice in terms of amounts at the various rates of VAT which apply, as noted in the next section.

Analysis of input

In addition to the basic details referred to above for transaction entry, some form of analysis of the transaction will be required, at least in respect of nominal ledger coding for invoices, credit notes and adjustments (many systems will deal automatically with the analysis of cash transactions in terms of the nominal ledger although users with multiple bank accounts will need to note carefully the mechanics of such an operation). The VAT element of the transaction will normally be analysed automatically to a nominated

VAT control account leaving only the analysis of the net amount to be performed by the user. Nominal code analysis (including, where appropriate, analysis by cost centre or department) is most usefully effected by enabling the user to define an unlimited number (at least in theory) of lines of analysis in respect of each transaction; this point should be watched carefully, as many systems enforce a finite limit (sometimes as low as one line of analysis) to the extent of nominal analysis available for each transaction. Whatever method is adopted, the system should ensure that the transaction is fully analysed and that it is not possible to leave the analysis function until this is so; otherwise an imbalance between the nominal and personal ledger concerned will result.

In addition to analysis for nominal ledger purposes, various other forms of analysis may also be provided. Of particular interest will be the method adopted for the analysis of invoice and credit note transactions in respect of the different rates of VAT applying, such that a suitable VAT summary report can be produced later in the period. Analysis of sales and purchases by product may also be required, particularly in systems which encompass a stock control system. For example, entry of a purchase invoice in such a situation should enable each quantity on that invoice to be deducted from the quantity of goods received, but not invoiced, for each relevant stock item.

Allocation of cash and credits

The allocation of cash and credit notes to invoices is often one of the poorer aspects of personal ledger operation. While the concept is easy, there is no simple means of making the allocation procedure right for every situation. For example, in a sales ledger where customers always tend to pay just one invoice it can be tedious to wade through every outstanding transaction on the screen until the required invoice is found and marked in some way. On the other hand, where the payment of multiple invoices is normal, it can be equally tiresome to have to key in the reference of each to enable the allocation to be performed. Although the method adopted may not matter too much on small ledgers, it can make quite a difference in terms of time on larger ledger systems. As allocation is an operation which is generally performed directly on the ledger, this may be even more significant in multi-user systems which incorporate file-locking as the ledger must be locked during this operation.

The facility to allocate a cash item is normally given at the time of entry (although this should not be compulsory, as an allocation cannot always be effected, eg where an advance payment has been made) and a separate function normally exists within the system to allow subsequent allocations as a separate function from the transaction entry, indeed some systems only have this latter facility. Another variance in this area relates to the ability or otherwise to effect partial allocations, these being allocations which enable, for example, an invoice of £1000 to be matched with a payment on account of £750. Following the next purge of the ledger, just one transaction (of £250) is carried forward rather than two (of £1000 and £750) which would otherwise have applied. Even though the concept of partial allocation may look attractive, and in some industries may be essential, it can lead to 'messy' ledgers which become difficult to follow, particularly where a number of partial allocations have been effected over successive periods.

Before leaving this topic, it is worth considering the manner in which allocated transactions are shown on ledger reports and screen enquiries. If transactions are merely marked as being allocated it can be difficult to determine precisely which cash transactions have been allocated against which invoices; such information may be valuable if, for example, there is a dispute with a customer/supplier as to the transactions to which a particular payment related. It is useful, therefore, if some indication of the history of allocations can be provided, for example by the use of a sequence letter to denote allocations made in any one session.

Screen enquiry facilities

All personal ledger systems will incorporate some form of individual account screen enquiry facility enabling the master file details and ledger transactions to be displayed. Access by alphabetical look-up, in addition to an account number look-up, is a desirable feature, as is an option to display just the unallocated (ie outstanding) transactions on a particular account. An option to print the screen display (which is provided anyway as a hardware facility on many machines) is also helpful.

Reporting facilities

The scope of reporting provided by accounting systems varies enormously although it must, to some extent, be dictated by the amount of information held for customers/suppliers and transactions.

As a minimum, however, a personal ledger system will provide:

- master file detail listings
- ledger prints, showing all transactions currently held on the ledger (a version showing only unallocated transactions can be helpful)
- an aging analysis of balances (particularly important for the sales ledger)
- a report of the ledger control account
- a day book report of transactions entered during the period
- a VAT analysis report

The variety and format of reporting is likely to be critical in the selection of an accounting system and many packages now provide report-generation facilities to enable the user to provide (within certain constraints) reports which are not included in the standard system.

Period accounting and purging

Ledger systems are generally designed to operate on a periodic or monthly cycle and some attention needs to be given to the end-of-period operations when selecting a system. Some, but by no means all, systems allow for thirteen (or even more) periods to be operated within the year, thus facilitating '4–5–4–week accounting', and questions such as whether the sales ledger can be in period 4 whilst the nominal is in period 3 and what happens at end of year may be fundamental to individual prospective users. At the end of the period, various reports will be printed, certain transaction files will be cleared down, the ledger may be reorganised and the period number will be incremented. Special procedures will apply at the end of year and the effect on the nominal ledger will be of particular interest, as it is the normal requirement to keep this open in the 'old' year for some time while processing on the personal ledgers continues in the 'new' year.

In 'balance-forward' personal ledger systems, the end-of-period operation involves consolidating the balances into one transaction for every customer/supplier and, while this concept is essential for systems operating in a limited storage environment, the 'open-item' method of operation, in which all unallocated transactions are brought forward into the new period is almost always preferable.

It is worth noting whether a purge of the ledger is forced at the end of period or whether it is available as a separate option, particularly as, for small ledgers, some users prefer to keep a number of months' transactions on the ledger at any one time.

Interface with the nominal ledger

The nature of the interface between the personal and nominal ledgers is an important point to establish before acquiring an accounting system. In terms of timing, this operation generally falls into one of three categories:

- an immediate update following the update of the sales/purchase ledger
- as update only at period end
- an update as and when required, called from within the nominal ledger itself

The nature of the transactions which are passed to the nominal ledger also needs to be investigated; in some systems batch summary totals by nominal code are passed to the nominal ledger, whereas others summarise at transaction, rather than batch, level. The most detailed interface is one in which there is no summarisation at all (ie each line of analysis of each invoice is passed discretely to the nominal ledger); this is good for clarity and establishment of 'trail', but it is generally bad for file sizes and for speed of processing. Whatever method is adopted the system should clearly allow a facility (eg in the form of reports) to enable the balance of the control accounts of the sales and purchase ledgers easily to be reconciled with the corresponding debtors and creditors control accounts on the nominal ledger. This reconciliation is particularly essential in a computerised environment and should be performed monthly (at least) to ensure that the three ledgers are in alignment.

Sales and purchase ledger specifics

While many features of sales and purchase ledgers are similar, if not virtually identical, there are of course some fundamental differences in certain areas of operation. These relate, on the sales ledger side, principally to areas of analysis, either of debtors or of sales made, while the specific features on purchase ledgers are mainly concerned with authorisation for posting to the ledger and with payments to suppliers.
This chapter covers briefly the following areas in sales ledger operation:

- aging of debtor balances
- credit control
- statement printing
- analysis of sales

and the following purchase ledger items:

- purchase invoice logging
- automated payments procedures
- methods of payment

Apart from the above, many other differences between sales and purchase ledger systems produced by individual software companies may be found, particularly in those which relate to specific industries.

Aging of debtor balances

One of the most valuable reports from the sales ledger system is the aged analysis of debtors. In many cases, the availability of this report alone justifies the transition from a manual accounting system, as such an analysis is more or less impossible to produce on a regular basis without a computerised sales ledger. The report provides the user with an analysis of outstanding sales ledger balances by the length of time from the date of the transaction to the current or some other reference date. Ideally, the report should be available in two forms:

- summary, ie one line per customer with just balance figures shown
- detailed, ie the transactions comprising the balances in each aging section.

The aging ranges are frequently fixed at current period, one month, two months to three months and over, although some systems allow for aging by number of days (even one month is too long for some industries!) or for user definition of the aging periods. A percentage analysis of the balances in each aging group can also be a helpful guide for comparative purposes from period to period, as it easily illustrates movement in control over debtors. The presence on the sales ledger of disputed invoices and other uncleared or unallocated 'problem' transactions can hinder the usefulness of the report, as these will tend to be congregated in the 'three months and over' section thus clouding the relevance of the report totals; the moral, of course, is to keep the ledger as 'clean' as possible and not to allow 'odd' transactions to go unattended.

The reference point for aging may also be important. It is useful to allow the user to specify a reference date for aging and for the report to be recompiled, using the actual transaction dates for invoices etc, at the time it is printed. Some systems preclude this, however, and merely operate on a period basis where the transaction is assigned to the period in which it was entered and aged accordingly; this can prove problematic where invoices are entered late or where adjustments are made in later periods.

Although the aging of balances is most useful in sales ledgers, most systems will provide equivalent facilities for creditor balances in the purchase ledger and this too can prove a useful management review and control document, particularly in systems in which no automated payments procedures are provided.

Credit control

In addition to the aging of debtor balances, an operation which is fundamental to the credit control activity, a report of customers who are over their credit limits may also be incorporated within the system. Both these reports provide the credit controller with the information needed to monitor customer performance in respect of agreed payment terms and the reports would usefully incorporate contact details (eg name and telephone number of customer) to make them proper working documents.

Many systems now provide an interface into a word-processing package for the automatic production of letters to be sent to debtors who are in excess of their agreed terms. Such facilities may have a level of sophistication which enables different letters to be sent depending upon the extent and nature of a particular customer's default. Obviously, credit control procedures can be applied even more efficiently in systems incorporating sales invoicing and order processing, as action can then be taken before the despatch of goods.

If the decision to computerise an accounting operation is marginal, the assistance provided in the area of credit control can often tip the balance in favour of computerisation, particularly where a small business is likely to expand (and, therefore, increase its working capital requirements) in the foreseeable future.

Statement printing

In simpler systems the facility for printing customer statements may be served by something closely akin to the ledger print. More sophisticated systems will have a specific function for printing statements and this facility may include:

- definition of scope of accounts to be printed (eg individual accounts, range of accounts or all accounts).

- definition of parameters for printing (eg balances over a certain value, accounts with outstanding items older than a defined period, whether accounts with zero balances are to be printed).
- some facility for customising the layout of the statement print (or this service may be provided by the dealer/software house).

Statement prints will normally include the aging of the balance of the account and some means of facilitating the return of a payment from the customer such as tear-off or undercopy remittance advice. Many businesses view statements partly as a mail-shot to customers and take the opportunity to enclose current product leaflets etc; in this respect a message facility on the statement is useful for advising customers of new products or special offers.

Analysis of sales

The analysis of sales is another area in which the use of a computerised ledger has significant advantages over its manual counterpart. Some sales ledgers provide little more than the nominal analysis capability but others enable analysis by stock code, product type, representative, area, customer type etc. Obviously with more detailed analysis, the user will be required to input more at the transaction entry stage or in customer file maintenance. Systems which interface to stock and sales invoicing systems often produce such analysis information (by volume and/or by amount) as a by-product of input earlier in the transaction cycle.

The imaginative user may also see various other opportunities for information arising from sales ledger data such as reports on 'dormant' accounts (ie customers which have not purchased for a certain length of time), 'best' customers in terms of turnover over a period of time and performance by combinations of parameters, such as product by representative. In many instances specific analysis reports are requested by users as bespoke amendments to sales ledger systems, as different industries tend to have different marketing techniques or barometers of performance. Providing that the base information is already incorporated within the system design, such requirements can often be easily accommodated by software developers.

Some systems provide for analysis of purchases, although this area is generally not so well developed. There is, however, much information which can be usefully gained from a purchase ledger such as purchase price histories, turnover with suppliers (useful knowledge when negotiating trade discounts) and sources of supply.

Purchase invoice logging

One of the most useful 'additional' features to be found in a purchase ledger system is the ability to 'log' purchase invoices on receipt prior to making any accounting entry for them. These invoices can then be sent around the organisation for approval by relevant personnel and, only on return as an approved invoice to the accounts department, is the required input made to post the transaction to the purchase ledger. While the practice may be inappropriate for small organisations (although the concept of not posting 'unapproved' invoices to the ledger is still valid) and may require some redefinition of procedures in larger organisations (particularly where purchase invoices tend to be received initially elsewhere than the accounts department), the use of a purchase invoice logging system has several advantages, including the following:

- the system automatically keeps a sequential register of all purchase invoices received which are not on the purchase ledger, together with the details of the department or person to whom the invoice has been sent for approval.
- as there is no need to post an invoice to the ledger before it is approved, there is a significantly lower chance of an invoice being paid in error.
- the calculation of amounts to be accrued at period ends is facilitated and an automatic posting of these accruals to the nominal ledger may be available.
- invoices which get 'lost' in the organisation can easily be highlighted.
- a record can be maintained of invoices which are not accepted (ie returned to the supplier without a ledger entry being made), such invoices merely being deleted from the logged invoices file at some later stage.

Automated payments procedures

Most larger purchase ledger systems will incorporate some form of automated payments procedure which allows the purchase ledger to be scanned according to predefined parameters, such that payment transactions can be generated in respect of outstanding invoices. These procedures normally work through the following cycle:

- a proposed payments stage, in which the initial parameters are set (eg reference date for payment generation, supplier types to be included etc). This stage produces a list of transactions which, according to the defined parameters, the system 'thinks' should be paid. The treatment of early settlement discounts which may be on offer for individual invoices is an area to be investigated, as this varies between systems.

- having produced a report of proposed payments, there is normally a facility to amend this by:

  - removing or adding a supplier
  - removing or adding transactions
  - 'disallowing' or 'allowing' cash settlement discounts

  A new report of propose payments can then be produced. These operations may be repeated, each time with a revised report being produced, until a 'final' listing is obtained.
- the actual automated payments procedure. This creates ledger entries for the cash payments in respect of the designated transactions and performs the necessary allocations against the relevant invoices. This process will also normally generate remittance advice notes and facilities may also be available for the printing of cheques or credit transfers. Obviously, a report of the ledger postings made must be produced by this operation.

While the facility of automated payments sounds attractive, it can only be used effectively in purchase ledgers which are well organised and have a reasonably stable cycle of payments. The more exceptions to the rule, the more work is created by the need to exclude suppliers or transactions from the automated process, thereby losing some of the advantages and also running the risk that something may be paid erroneously. Another consideration is that, if the automated process is run with incorrect parameters, the effect on the purchase ledger would be devastating; it is, therefore, sensible to take a security copy of data immeditely prior to commencing the automatic process such that the purchase ledger can be easily restored if errors occur.

Some systems may provide special facilities for urgent or one-off payments although many consider that these are better dealt with through the normal cash payment transactions input stream.

Methods of payment

Following the use of an automated payments procedure, the problem of paying large numbers of suppliers may be tackled by the use of cheque printing or by direct transfer using the Bankers Automated Clearing System (BACS) which is available as an on-line transfer or as a floppy diskette transfer for some formats of disk. The use of automatic cheque printing implies stringent control procedures as cheques will invariably be wasted in printer tractor feeds and by alignment routines. Nevertheless, where large numbers of payments are involved on a regular basis the use of cheque printing is almost essential and it is worth checking:

- whether the proposed system provides it and, if so, is it a standard facility or an additional option?
- whether a standard cheque print layout is defined or whether it is possible for specific cheque designs to be accommodated.
- whether cheques can be reprinted, for instance, what happens if there is a printer jam during the cheque printing routine?

When drafting computerised cheque stationery it is advisable to involve your bank and obtain the services of a printing firm used to dealing with this sort of requirement.

Nominal ledger systems

Nominal ledger systems (also marketed as general ledger systems) form the third element of ledger accounting software and their principal features differ markedly from those of the personal ledger systems. Whereas designers of sales and purchase ledgers can make some allowances for the lack of accounting expertise of their potential users (it is, after all, perfectly possible to operate most personal ledger systems without knowing anything about debits and credits) this cannot be so easily achieved with nominal ledger systems and, in the 'wrong hands', such systems can easily fall into disuse, not to mention disrepute!

For some users of accounting software, the nominal ledger element of the system may be the most important part of the whole software, whereas for others, typically those in smaller businesses, it matters least. Differences between software packages are often at their most marked in the area of the nominal ledger and, for accountants, nominal ledgers may be the most difficult to select, partly because of the lack of understanding of accounting principles which is frequently encountered in the developers and sellers of such systems.

It is likely that most serious users will be able to compile a fairly specific set of requirements to be incorporated in a nominal ledger system; the following areas, which are covered in this chapter, will be among those considered in most cases:

- nominal coding structure
- chart of accounts
- periodicity and budgets
- transaction entry
- method of nominal ledger update
- enquiries and reporting facilities
- profit and loss and balance sheet reporting
- end-of-period/year processing

In each of these areas, the selection decision must also take into account the way in which the sales and purchase ledgers impact upon the nominal, where an integrated system is to be undertaken.

Nominal coding structure

One of the most fundamental of the selection criteria for a nominal ledger system will be the coding structure which the user is required to adopt. This assumes such importance because many organisations have predetermined nominal coding schemes which may be dictated by corporate policy to enable uniformity of reporting. Most packages of any sophistication will allow for at least a two-level hierarchical coding structure, eg:
700 = accommodation expenditure
700/001 = rates
700/002 = cleaning
and so on.

The number of levels and the number and nature of the characters permitted within each level varies between different packages and the prospective user should check carefully the facilities provided in this area before committing to a particular system. The type of coding provided will almost certainly dictate the level and sophistication of reporting of which the software will be capable. Much has been written about coding systems and study of these in depth is beyond the scope of this booklet; however, some questions which may be asked include:

- is the coding structure rigidly defined by the software or can it be configured to some extent by the user?
- how many hierarchical levels can be provided and is reporting available at each level?
- how many characters are provided for the nominal code and how are these split between levels?
- is the coding structure purely numeric or are alphanumeric characters also permitted?

In addition to the structure of the principal nominal code, many users will be interested in whether a particular system is capable of providing an 'across the board' coding structure such as may be required for cost centre (or department or project etc) coding and reporting. The availability of reporting on an autonomous basis from the main nominal code can greatly enhance the information capabilities of an accounting system and most organisations will have a use for at least one such facility.

Chart of accounts

Apart from the structure of the nominal code itself, facilities for the maintenance of the chart of accounts should be fairly straightforward in most systems. Apart from the account description, there will normally be fields for:

- the type of account (eg balance sheet or profit and loss); sometimes this is required in a more detailed form for reporting, for example, whether the account is an asset or liability balance sheet account
- budgetary information (discussed in detail later)
- whether the account will normally be used in conjunction with cost centres or equivalent (if present in the system)
- whether the account will 'normally' have a debit or credit balance. Again this information is usually required as part of the profit and loss/balance sheet reporting facilities

In some systems the print position of the account in terms of profit and loss or balance sheet reporting is also defined at the account-entry stage, but separate facilities are more commonly found for the design of the layout of these reports. While amendment facilities should be provided, these should not, of course, extend to balance information and deletion of accounts should be controlled so that 'live' accounts cannot be affected.

Periodicity and budgets

In common with the way that many organisations operate, most systems provide for at least thirteen periods within the accounting year, thus enabling operation of monthly or '4–5–4–weekly' accounting conventions. The number of periods is important not only from the point of view of reporting of actual figures at period end but also because of the requirement to compare with budget information entered. Whatever the number of periods provided, some form of facility for keeping the 'old' nominal ledger open at year end while processing continues in the 'new' year must be provided.

For many, the operation of budget entry and reporting will be of great interest and systems vary considerably in their flexibility and approach in these areas. In general, it should be possible, to define budgets on a period-by-period basis although the entry on an annual basis (with the period budgets being calculated accordingly) should also be permitted. The relationship between the various levels of the nominal code should also enable budgets entered for low-level codes to be aggregated by the system to form the budget for their higher-level counterparts.

The widespread use of modelling systems has also had a significant impact in this area and users now expect either a similar degree of flexibility from their accounting systems or, at least, a simple interface between the accounts and a modelling system. In general, the latter approach can often be best because the design philosophy of accounting systems makes them strong at recording what has happened rather than what might happen, ie the strength of modelling systems. Nevertheless many accounting systems provide 'forecast' facilities for the projection of outturns from year-to-date data and these are often worthy of consideration.

Before leaving the subject of budget definitions, it is worth noting how easily budgets can be revised, an area more important in practical terms than their initial entry. Many systems provide for some form of global update or even for algorithms based upon the previous year's 'actual' figures. Again, this is likely to be an area in which potential users are likely to have fairly specific requirements and these will need to be matched as far as possible against the facilities available.

Transaction entry

Facilities for transaction entry within the nominal ledger will normally provide for at least some of the following transaction types:

- journals
- accruals and prepayments
- cash receipts and payments (ie affecting bank account(s))
- petty cash receipts and payments
- automatic journals

The mode of journal input normally reflects that of the typical journal layout, ie multiple-line entries of assorted debit and credit amounts with each line analysed to a specific nominal code/cost centre as required. Points to note in this type of routine are:

- how much space (if any) for remarks is provided on each line of entry; this is a vital feature for many users and will normally be the only method of annotating ledger entries
- whether it is possible to leave the journal without it balancing. Any system where this is possible should be treated with suspicion, although note that some systems that provide facilities to 'suspend' a journal in such a state require it to be properly completed, or cancelled, before it is posted to the ledger
- the format of the journal reference, for example, whether the journal is automatically numbered by the system, or whether users may enter their own references
- whether journals may be cancelled prior to being posted to the ledger
- reporting facilities in respect of the journal both at the time on input and thereafter
- whether it is possible to enter transactions relating to prior or to subsequent periods (or even years)

Some systems allow for the concept of 'automatic journals' whereby the details of regular and commonly-occurring journals (eg for the depreciation of fixed assets) can be defined in such a way that they can be effected in subsequent periods without the need for rekeying. Obviously, such facilities require a good level of control (eg to ensure that it is not possible accidentally to activate an automatic journal more than once in the same period) and it is also imperative that a mechanism for amending the journal in terms of constituent accounts and amounts in any period is also provided.

The entry of accruals and prepayments often follows more or less the same format as those for journals, although in some systems it is assumed that the contra entry for the accrual will always be a certain nominated account (eg sundry creditors and accruals). The treatment of accruals and prepayments will often require clarification before acquiring a system, particularly as some software developers in the past have had strange ideas about the concept of these items! In general, an automatic reversal of accruals would be expected during the end-of-period operation and, whatever method is adopted, there must be clear documentary evidence of its treatment.

Cash (bank) and petty cash payments and receipts facilities are normally simplified versions of the journal entry with the responsibility of determining the actual accounting entry (ie debit or credit) being removed from the user, this aspect being handled automatically by the system. The contra postings are made to accounts which have normally been predefined as cash/petty cash control accounts. A point of variation here may be the number of bank accounts which the system allows to be defined and this may also have implications in the cash receipt/payment facilities in the personal ledgers. Computerised accounting systems often require the fragmentation of input of cash book transactions between the three ledgers, for example, the majority of a month's cash book payment entries may require posting to the purchase ledger but there will be some which will be entered directly to the nominal ledger and there will even be the occasional sales ledger entry. This can make the production of a 'Cash Book Report' from a system problematic, although the bank account(s) held on the nominal ledger should always be capable of direct reconciliation with the manual cash book. Some systems operate as 'Cash Book' systems and these can be particularly helpful for the very small business. Before leaving the subject of cash and petty cash input, it is always worth noting whether there are any special facilities provided for the entry of the VAT element of payment and receipt transactions. Finally, some systems provide for some assistance in effecting bank reconciliation and this may also be important for certain users.

Method of nominal ledger update

The method and timing of the update of the nominal ledger can vary between systems and some attention needs to be paid to this point, particularly where there is interface with personal ledger systems and different personnel are involved in the maintenance of each of the ledgers. The normal method of posting is on a batch basis where the update is effected from within the nominal ledger itself. Points to consider in this area include:

- at what point do items from the personal ledgers become available for posting to the nominal ledgers? Is there any discretion about the time at which such transactions are taken onto the ledger?
- is the posting of items from the nominal ledger effected in line-by-line detail or are these items summarised to nominal codes by transaction, by batch or even by run of the posting process? In general, the greater the level of detail the better from the point of view of clarity but the large volume of transactions which result may dictate against this, particularly for systems operating in a limited hardware environment
- are there any constraints on timing of the nominal ledger update? For

example, can it only be performed after closing the periods on the sales and purchase ledgers?

- how are transactions relating to prior or subsequent periods treated during the update process?
- what documentary record is produced of the update process?
- are nominal ledger balances maintained separately by period for each account. Alternatively, are merely 'current-period' and 'year-to-date' balances maintained?
- with what frequency is the integrity of the nominal ledger checked and what action is taken if an imbalance is detected, for instance through data corruption?

The nominal ledger update process may be lengthy, depending upon the size of the ledger and the method of update adopted; if integrity checking of the complete ledger is performed at the same time the process is likely to be even more protracted.

Enquiries and reporting facilities

Most systems will provide for a screen enquiry facility of some sort although the degree of comprehensiveness regarding, for example, actual-versus-budget details is likely to vary somewhat. In terms of reporting, however, a system should be expected to provide at least the following:

- chart of accounts (and, if applicable, cost centres)
- trial balance
- nominal ledger listing (available in full or by specified range of nominal codes)
- some form of actuals/budget variance report
- transaction listings for the current period
- profit and loss and balance sheet reporting

Many systems provide considerably more reporting facilities, although these are to some extent dependent upon the degree of sophistication of the ledger in terms of coding structure etc. In particular, the ability for reporting at various levels of the nominal coding structure and by cost centre may be decisive in the selection of a particular software package. Systems which allow users to generate their own reports are also commonly available and, while this is certainly an attractive concept, such 'report generators' are often not easily handled by the inexperienced computer user to whom the concepts of files, records and fields may be entirely foreign and, even with such facilities, there may still be certain reports which cannot be produced. In general, however, the presence of a report generator forms an attractive addition, particularly to a nominal ledger system, and it is likely that such facilities will be increasingly anticipated by prospective users.

Profit and Loss and Balance Sheet reporting

Even where systems do not provide report generators for general use, it is common to find some sort of facility for users to design their own layout and construction for Profit and Loss and Balance Sheet reporting. Such facilities normally take the form of a conceptual blank piece of paper on which one is able to define the order in which Profit and Loss or Balance Sheet lines are to be printed and the constituent elements of these lines. For example such lines may comprise the following types:

Headings – eg SALES
Line text – eg SALE OF GOODS
Accounts – defining the content of the lines in terms of nominal accounts, either by a range of nominal account codes or by specifying a number of individual codes which may appear on that line. These account codes are then added up and printed as a total on that line.
Narrative – for inserting message lines in the completed format.

By using definitions of the above type, together with the nomination of sub-totalling facilities, it is possible to define the Profit and Loss and Balance Sheet reports to meet fairly specific requirements. Whilst the precise techniques used by different systems vary, there are some common points to consider, such as:

- how easy is it to amend the structure, for example if a new line is required in the 'sales' section of the Profit and Loss report?
- how easy is it to accommodate a new nominal code into the line entries?
- how many separate formats for the Profit and Loss and Balance Sheet may be defined in any one system? It is fairly common, for example, for a detailed Profit and Loss print to be required in a different format to that for a summary print or a consolidated form.
- what facilities exist for producing Profit and Loss reports by cost centre (or departments etc)?
- are budget figures produced for comparative purposes?
- are there facilities for the entry of previous year figures?
- is it possible to transfer these reports into a word-processing format so that additional text and documents can be added for presentation purposes?

- can the reports be transferred easily into a modelling package for further manipulation and, where applicable, graphical representation?

It should, of course, be possible to obtain a print of the structure (ie the way in which the reports have been defined) of these reports for reference purposes.

End-of-period/year processing

The end-of-period process in a nominal ledger system will normally comprise the following procedures:

- increment of the period number
- consolidation of transactions into 'balance-forward' figures by nominal code/cost centre. Alternatively, the system may provide for transactions to be carried forward in detail so that a complete record of transactions is maintained throughout the year. Though a good idea for completeness, speed of processing can be markedly affected by such a policy
- automatic reversal of prepayment and accrual transactions
- in some systems, update of the period balance figure for accounts

Many users find that the nominal ledger end of period routine is a useful time for taking an extra security copy of data, partly because it would then be relatively easy subsequently to recreate a particular report should this ever be required. Linked with this, some systems force a print of the principal nominal ledger reports as a part of the period-end procedures although some consider that this somewhat penalises the conscientious user who has already printed these reports!

At the year end, most users will require that the nominal ledger for the 'old' year remains open for some time and the method by which a particular system achieves this will need to be investigated by the potential user, as it is normally at this stage of the year that the most pressure falls on the system in terms of transaction input, file sizes and reporting requirements. Ideally, it should be possible to continue with processing in the 'new' year (in all ledgers) while the 'old' ledger remains open. The same principle applies to nominal period ends, but the need is accentuated at year end because of the additional length of time required.

The additional function required at year end is that balances on accounts designated as profit and loss in type should be cleared by some form of automatic journal to a nominated balance sheet account(s). Again, the methods of approach to this exercise vary considerably and, unless the prospect of a very large journal at the end of the year is not too daunting, it is worth finding out how this operates sooner rather than later. As mentioned previously, the methods for revising budgets for the 'new' year will also require some consideration by the prospective user.

Other considerations

Before leaving the subject of nominal ledger systems it is worth mentioning briefly Incomplete Records systems. These are systems used by firms of accountants to assist with the production of a set of working papers from assorted vouchers, invoices, cheque stubs etc, colloquially known as 'shoebox accounting'. Such systems enable accounting records to be built up through to trial balance and final accounts stages. Most systems of this nature will contain a text editor, or will allow for an easy interface with a word-processing system, so that the final accounts can be produced in a presentable form and other documents (such as notes to the accounts) can be easily compiled. Such systems are in common use by firms of accountants and can be beneficial equally to large or small firms, the latter possibly having a higher proportion of 'shoebox' clients.

The requirements of a nominal ledger system differ enormously between various sizes and classes of business which, apart from any other reason, explains why there can never be a 'best' system for all circumstances. For example, the need to keep an on-line record of *all* transactions in a year may be paramount for some users; this can often be achieved by the use of an archive nominal ledger onto which transactions are passed at the end of each period, thus allowing the 'live' ledger to continue with the minimum number of transactions (and hence fastest processing) while still retaining the ability to enquire or report on historical transactions if required. As another example, the nominal ledger is one of the key areas where compatibility with a modelling system may be a fundamental selection criterion and there is an increasing tendency for such interface to be provided as an integral part of the system, rather than a separate 'add-on'; for other users, however, the existence of such a facility would be entirely superfluous.

Related systems

For some users, the ledgers comprise the only parts of their operation which they wish to computerise. For others, however, the ledgers may form only part, in some instances an incidental part, of the principal computing requirement. There are a large number of systems which interrelate with ledger accounting software and a comprehensive review of all such systems is beyond the scope of this contribution. The more commonly found systems are:

- sales invoicing
- sales order processing
- stock control
- payroll
- fixed assets
- industry specific systems

and these are considered briefly in this chapter.
The first point to note about selection of software in these areas is that, whilst most software suppliers will normally provide sales, purchase and nominal ledger systems, not all may carry the above related systems in their product range. It is, therefore, important to check that the full range of required software can be provided by one software supplier (at least for those elements which are required to be integrated) before commiting to a purchase. The concept of a sales invoicing system from one software company being linked to a sales ledger system from another is likely to prove problematic to say the least! This assumes, of course, that the various modules are required to be integrated, ie data is to be passed directly between them without re-entry by the user; this may not always be a particular requirement and it would, for example, be perfectly acceptable for a stand-alone fixed assets system to be supplied from one software source even though the rest of the accounting suite has been provided by another. Payroll is another system which is often run as a stand-alone application, but the practice is likely to be far more limiting with systems such as sales invoicing and sales order processing which have a fundamental requirement to link with stock control and sales ledger systems.

Sales invoicing

Most accounting systems incorporate a sales invoicing module. The normal mode of operation for the entry of sales invoice data in such systems is:

- identification of the customer by entry of the sales ledger account number (ie that held on the customer master file). In addition to the customer's name and address details, this will also enable other information, such as the discount level applying to that customer and the credit terms, to be retrieved

- entry of other identifying information for the invoice such as delivery note number, customer order number etc
- entry of a succession of charge lines for the invoice. These will take various forms but, where applicable, will include a facility to enable the keying of a stock code to retrieve identifying and other information from a stock master file. For each charge line it should be possible to specify, again where applicable, the quantity, unit price, trade discount amount or percentage and VAT rate applying.

Following the completion of invoice entry, some systems allow for the invoice to be printed immediately (as would be required in a shop for example) whereas others store the invoice details for a subsequent batch print. Following the printing of invoices, some form of automatic entry of the transactions to the sales ledger will be enabled.

The above provides a very general synopsis of an invoicing system and it is reasonable to say that systems vary greatly in their approach, ease of use and flexibility and, in selection, it is important to match requirements very specifically to the facilities provided. The variations which occur between systems is not surprising as most types of business have very specific procedures concerned with their invoicing operations and the software produced over the years has reflected this. Apart from the obvious guidelines in invoice entry and printing, some other points to watch out for include:

- does the system provide full integration with the sales ledger and stock control systems (if applicable) and also with sales order processing?
- how are credit notes dealt with?
- is it possible to annotate invoices with individual message lines?
- does the system facilitate the entry of service type invoices, ie those for which lines of stock items would not be applicable?
- are facilities available for the production of pro-forma invoices?
- is any help provided with the entry of commonly-occurring invoice lines such as, for example, postage and packing?
- can despatch notes be produced from the system?
- how is the invoice print formatted? Is it possible to change the print layout, for example to suit your own pre-printed invoice stationery?
- does the invoice print provide a proper VAT analysis?
- what happens if there is a change to VAT rates or, indeed, to the number of VAT rates?
- what facilities are there in respect of cash-settlement discounts?

- is it possible to reprint invoices? (A good question is: 'what happens if my printer jams whilst the invoice print is in progress?')
- at what point is the sales ledger updated (ie an accounting entry made in respect of the invoice) and what documentary record is produced of the invoices which have been printed and posted to the ledger?

No doubt many other considerations can be raised depending upon the nature of the business. While it is often possible to live with packaged ledger systems which contain a number of imperfections from the viewpoint of a particular organisation (in the end one could take the view that 'a sales ledger is a sales ledger') it is far more difficult to accept shortcomings in invoicing systems.

Sales order processing

Sales order processing systems are used for the entry of orders received from customers to the point at which the goods ordered are despatched or, in some systems which effectively have combined invoicing and order-processing modules, are invoiced. Many of the general considerations outlined above for sales invoicing apply also for order-processing, particularly those relating to the specificity of the business. A good sales order-processing (and stock control) system which is closely aligned to the needs of a particular business can greatly enhance the image of that business in the eyes of its customers and it should be remembered that, however good other systems may be, customers will often judge a business on the basis of the quality of this system. Sales order-processing systems vary enormously in style and content and it is imperative to see a demonstration of such a system before committing to its use in any environment. While the procedures for sales order entry and reporting may be clear from such a demonstration, the following are some points which are often missed during the evaluation exercise:

- is it possible to annotate individual orders with messages such as special-order conditions or delivery instructions?
- how is credit control effected? What happens when an order received places a customer over the credit limit?
- can orders be prioritised on an individual-order basis?
- what procedures are used for allocation of stock to sales orders? What happens when there is insufficient stock to meet all current orders?
- what facilities exist for dealing with urgent or one-off orders?
- can orders be scheduled to operate in a 'call-off' basis?

- can a documentary record of the order be sent to the customer as confirmation of the order?
- what facilities exist for the generation of despatch notes?
- what happens if the quantity *actually* despatched differs from that printed on the despatch note?
- is there a full integration with the stock and sales invoicing (and through this, the sales ledger) systems?

In addition to the above, good reporting facilities are crucial, both on a routine level and on an exception basis. Sales order statistics should also be available on a periodic and year-to- date basis.

Stock control

Stock control, like payroll, is a 'traditional' data processing application, so much so that many people tend to take stock systems for granted. In fact there is considerable variation in the facilities provided by stock control systems and the 'ideal' system will again depend very much upon the environment in which it is to operate. For example, systems for manufacturing companies will generally offer many facilities which are superfluous to those required by a retailer of electrical goods, although the basic requirements will be the same. With this in mind, it is important to identify the needs of *your* organisation and, no matter how sophisticated the system under consideration may appear, some general points to bear in mind when reviewing it include:

- the size, nature and structure of the stock code. As with the account code in ledger systems, the stock code is fundamental to all operations involving stock items (including the operations performed in modules integrated with the stock system). Some industries have adopted standards for stock codes and if, for example, a stock code of sixteen characters in length is required, there would be little point in continuing with the assessment of a system in which the maximum was ten.
- apart from descriptive details, there will normally be many other fields which will be capable of definition for each stock item. Such fields will include selling and cost price information, sources of supply, unit of measure and information relating to the reorder of the item such as minimum, maximum and reorder level quantities. These fields will assume differing levels of importance for potential users of the system
- most stock systems allow for the maintenance of stock quantities at a

number of user-defined locations and such a facility is essential for proper control of physical stock. Reporting should be available by individual location and, in appropriate reports, by aggregated balances. Within locations, many systems allow for the entry of bin numbers or equivalent to assist with locating stock within a particular site

- the method for recording the receipt and issue of goods should allow for a documentary record of such transactions to be produced and a stock 'ledger' to be maintained showing the progress from opening to closing balance within each stock period. Some systems will allow for the printing of goods received notes and despatch notes. Receipts and issues should allow for the recording of exceptional items such as returns to suppliers and returns by customers. On a related theme, the methods for the writing off of stock balances will also be of interest
- there is an almost endless list of reports which could usefully be derived from a stock control system and the potential user should identify those which will be of most value in the intended environment. Apart from the normal listings of stock items and balance information, particular attention should be paid to the level of exception reporting provided as it is here that stock control systems can be the most valuable. For example, information on slow moving stock can often directly influence management decisions. A screen enquiry facility (particularly useful for ad hoc balance queries) is also normally provided
- facilities for assistance with stock counts are a welcome addition to many systems. The better systems recognise that 'life goes on' whilst a stock check is in progress and discrepancies are being investigated and hence it is unreasonable to expect all work to cease on the stock system (and, therefore, on invoicing and order processing systems if they are integrated) until this task is completed; some form of procedure should be provided to enable adjustments resulting from the stock check to be integrated back into the system at a later date
- of particular interest to the accountant will be method(s) employed by the system for stock valuation. The more sophisticated systems provide a choice of methods (eg FIFO, LIFO, average or replacement) but not all systems will provide all methods. In addition, there may be a requirement to value different items of stock on different bases and this also may not be accommodated by all systems
- there are a number of other systems which are commonly associated with stock control systems, each of which could merit contributions in themselves. Two of these, sales invoicing and sales order processing,

have been described earlier; other systems include:

- purchase order processing
- work-in-progress (WIP)
- bill of materials processing (BOMP)
- materials requirements planning (MRP)
- production planning
- job costing.

Payroll

One immediate consideration with payroll is, that, unlike most other systems, the 'rules' change annually, if not even more frequently, and reliance must be placed upon the software supplier to keep producing program modifications as and when statutory or other changes become effective. For this reason it is even more important to choose the product carefully and there must be some confidence that the software supplier will stay in business throughout the intended lifetime of the system. Because of the continual need for amendment, most payroll packages are sold with some form of annual maintenance agreement at an additional cost to the basic cost of the system. In recent years the introduction of such schemes as statutory sick pay (SSP) and statutory maternity pay (SMP), together with fundamental changes to national insurance, have had a marked effect upon computerised payroll systems, some of which have struggled to accommodate the necessary revisions of software.

As with the other systems in this chapter, the requirements of a payroll may be very specific to a particular user. Payroll systems normally operate on an exception basis, ie only changes in pay or circumstances require input each period, with successive attempts at running the payroll being permitted until a final position is reached, at which point that payroll period can be closed. There is little point in trying to list all of the requirements of a payroll system but some of the more general points include:

- can payrolls for more than one company be easily accommodated? (a fundamental question for anyone anticipating running a bureau type of operation)
- can the processing of payrolls of different periodicities (eg weekly and monthly) be accommodated concurrently?
- what form of departmental analysis is provided?
- can the system cope with the various allowances, deductions, pension schemes, methods of payment and overtime rates which

apply in your organisation?

- how comprehensively are schemes such as SSP accommodated?
- what happens if tax or national insurance rates/bandings change? In the better systems, these parameters can be changed by the user without recourse to the software supplier
- what facilities exist for global changes, such as those occasionally required for tax codes or pay rates?
- what facilities are included for part-time or casual labour?
- what is the format of the printed payslip. Can this be reformatted for specific stationery if required?
- are comprehensive end-of-year facilities and documentation provided?
- does the system interface with the personnel records and/or nominal ledger system?
- has the system been reviewed by the Inland Revenue in terms of the tax calculations?
- is there a facility for payment through the Bankers Automated Clearing System (BACS)?

There are many further aspects relating to payroll, not least of which is the ease of use and the production of proper records. The final selection will, therefore, often be a 'best fit' package for the organisation as very few will wish to commission a bespoke payroll system and modifications to standard payroll systems are unpopular with all parties concerned.

Fixed assets

An increasing number of fixed asset recording systems are becoming available for microcomputers, although this is another well-established mainframe application. Such systems allow for the recording of assets by classification and location and for the calculation of depreciation (both historical and current cost) by various methods (eg straight line or percentage) and periodicities. An integration with a nominal ledger system can normally be expected. Within these basic parameters of operation, there exists a wide variety of systems which may differ in such respects as:

- treatment of part disposals
- treatment of costs additional to initial costs
- asset grouping and sub-division of assets
- foreign currency requirements
- text entries for assets

Industry specific systems

In addition to the systems outlined above, a considerable number of accounting and related systems have been specifically designed for particular industries. These have often descended from original bespoke commissions by firms in a particular industry who have experienced problems in finding a packaged solution to their specific requirements. Once a system has been developed it is often marketed jointly by the software and commissioning companies in order to take advantage of what is an obvious gap in the market. It is now difficult to imagine an industry type which does not have at least some packaged products written specifically for it; a glance through a recent directory reveals such diverse accounting systems as those for motor dealers, restaurants and printers. This avenue is certainly worth investigation if the standard systems seem to provide a poor match for your actual requirements and trade associations, publications and exhibitions should prove good starting-points for finding out about any such systems.

Further developments

There was a time not so long ago when users of accounting software were grateful merely for simple ledger systems which worked and which removed the drudgery and inaccuracies from the preparation of accounts. After all, with a computerised system you will at least end up with a trial balance which does balance (I suggest that you change systems if you are able legitimately to have one which does not!) even though it may not be correct. As time has progressed, however, so has the sophistication of computer users and their expectations have increased accordingly. This progress has had to be reflected by software developers who on the one hand are driven by user demands while on the other are limited by current hardware/ operating system/language constraints. Nevertheless, many large steps have been taken over recent years and some of these are reflected in the areas covered by this chapter, as follows:

- multi-company processing
- multi-currency processing
- multi-user systems
- interface with other software

Doubtless further advances will be made in years to come as software suppliers strive to keep pace with users' developing requirements.

Multi-company processing

If you are likely to require your accounting system to operate for more than one company, it is worth while asking in advance how this can be accommodated by the system under consideration. Obviously, the system could be separately installed for each company but this is wasteful in terms of disk resources; more commonly a facility to enable the processing of more than one company's records by using the same program library is provided. This has an additional advantage in that the loading of program revisions is simplified and consistency of processing for each company is guaranteed as they are, by definition, running from the same programs.

While multi-company systems may just provide for a series of different companies for autonomous processing (the maximum number of such companies may be worth establishing if your projected installation is for a large number), many systems provide for some form of interaction between the companies so that 'consolidations' of all or some of selected companies may be compiled. This is, of course, particularly useful in the nominal ledger where corporate reporting at profit and loss/balance sheet stage may be a particularly attractive feature. Where parameters apply to all operational companies, as may be the case for example for nominal codes or currency data, a facility whereby their entry and amendment can be effected once, rather than for each company individually, can save time and minimise inconsistencies. Because of similarities between companies, however, it is particularly important with multi-company systems that all screen displays and reports clearly state the company in current operation; users can also assist themselves by ensuring that specific company data, such as customer account codes, are not duplicated between companies.

A further consideration with regard to multi-company processing is whether there are likely to be any additional software costs involved in operation, such as the payment of further licence fees. Linked with this is the method by which additional companies can be brought on line at a future date; is this within the user's capabilities or is a further release from the software company required? As a final point, the concept of archiving also becomes more complex with multi-company systems, as it may be unwieldy to take security copies for all operational companies at the same time; a utility which enables selective back up by nomination of companies may often be a worthwile acquisition, depending, of course, on the actual form of archiving employed.

Multi-currency processing

Many organisations deal at an international level and hence there is a considerable demand for systems which cater for processing in a number of foreign currencies. Such systems may simply enable purchase and sales invoices to be entered in native currencies, with an immediate conversion to sterling for ledger purposes, whereas more advanced systems allow for a mixture of currencies within the ledgers and various means of effecting conversions to the base currency and for accounting for the exchange differences arising. The automatic handling of bank accounts in various currencies from cash inputs made to the sales, purchase or nominal ledgers would also normally form a part of such systems.

Apart from various differences in input and reporting, the user will also be responsible for the maintenance of a currency file, containing the currencies to be recognised by the system and the exchange rates to be applied at various points. As with so many aspects of accounting software, the requirements of users can vary so widely that there is unlikely to be an ideal system for all applications.

The combination of multi-currency processing with multi-company processing can provide an extremely sophisticated reporting framework for organisations which trade in a number of countries, particularly if it is possible to maintain each company in a different currency with some form of consolidation facility to sterling.

Multi-user system

Multi-user accounting systems were once the preserve of mainframe and minicomputer systems but recent advances in microcomputer technology, together with developments in local area networking (LAN), have resulted in many multi-user systems now being available for microcomputers. The subject of multi-user processing and network operation are beyond the scope of this contribution but there are a number of obvious precautions to be taken before proceeding with the implementation of a multi-user system. Not the least is establishing whether the intended software actually works in multi-user or network environments and, if so, *which* multi-user and network environments. Remember that it is not merely the sharing of files which is required (access to a file in a single user version of a system is often possible by more than one user in some networks), it is the *controlled* sharing of files which is fundamental so that, for example, conflicting requirements from a number of users can be properly processed.

Many people get bound by the concepts of file- and record-locking when selecting multi-user software. While the methods employed by the software are important to some extent, it is the actual performance of the software in a live environment (eg with realistic volumes and levels of access) which is of paramount importance. Although one would expect multi-user software to operate more slowly in some respects than in the single-user version, there may be an unacceptable degradation in some cases. It is also worth checking precisely what functions are allowed concurrently in terms of multi-user access; this varies enormously between systems and the locking applied in a particular system may be restrictive to one company but perfectly acceptable to another which operates in a different manner. For example, at a simplistic level, some systems allow only one user in a particular ledger at any one time; this may, however, be quite sufficient for a small accounts department with a straightforward division of responsibilities between the ledgers. Most users of multi-user software, however, would at least be looking for multiple-transaction entry within the same ledger; this concept applies even more for the entry of sales invoices and sales orders where bottlenecks occur particularly at the input stage. Whatever method is employed, the concept of security of access will also need to be considered.

From a financial viewpoint, it is important to be aware of the additional software costs involved in a multi-user operation. In packaged software there is normally a 40–50% premium to be paid for multi-user operation but this varies somewhat and may also be dependent upon the actual number of users. As with multi-company operation, it is also necessary to establish how additional users may be added at a later stage together with the attendant financial and operational consequences.

As a final thought in this brief look at a complex area, it is useful to determine what happens when there is an abnormal exit from the software as would happen, for example, if a power failure occurred or a machine were accidentally switched off. In this situation, various system locks are likely to be active and there would normally be some sort of procedure for clearing these locks before the system can be restarted. This procedure should also clear the access path for that particular user so that it does not become necessary to set up further users, a problem which has been noted with some packages.

Interface with other software

As information requirements become more refined and more standards (or, at least, more standard software products and conventions) have appeared in the microcomputer market, so the integration of accounting systems with other types of software has grown.

One area which has already been touched on here is that of interfacing (usually of the nominal ledger) with spreadsheet or other modelling systems. This can provide a remarkably effective way of, for example, manipulating budget and actual figures to provide forecasts dependent on various scenarios, something that will be much more difficult to achieve within the more rigid structural confines of the accounting system. The establishment of interfaces with such modelling systems is rapidly becoming an accepted facility which many software companies are building into their accounting products.

The interface of accounting systems with word processing software is, perhaps, a less explored avenue but there are already many instances where profitable use may be made of such a link. The use of word processing to send letters to erring debtors or, on a more optimistic note, mailshots to customers, are examples; the preparation of annotated final accounts with notes is another and there are many more examples.

Interface with database systems is another area worthy of exploration, particularly in an environment where accounting information is seen as just part of the information structure of the organisation rather than something which belongs merely to the accounts department.

A number of more advanced concepts have been mentioned in this chapter and all this is a far cry from the primitive single-user systems described in chapter one. It is worth remembering, however, that the prime selection criterion when choosing accounting software is that the system should enable proper accounts to be maintained; without this all the 'add-ons' and 'features' in the world are worthless and it is essential never to lose sight of this very basic point.

3
Financial Modelling Systems

G R Kaye BA, MSc, FCMA, MBIM, MIDPM

Background to computerised modelling

The proliferation of microcomputers, modelling software, spreadsheets, courses and books on how to develop and utilise computerised financial models has tended to result in confusion rather than knowledge. It is for this reason that this chapter attempts to provide an introductory explanation and a method for modelling independent from any specific software package. It is designed for those who already have some understanding of computers and is aimed primarily at financial managers and associated staff who, whilst working in a variety of organisations, will possess a common understanding of the financial aspects of a business and seek to use computers to assist them in their activities.

Whilst modelling software has existed on mainframe and minicomputers, it is the wide availability of such systems on microcomputers which has made modelling available to a wider audience and it is this aspect which is dealt with in this booklet.

Hardware

The business microcomputer market has, to a large extent, been dominated by the IBM and IBM compatible machines. The IBM machines come in several guises; from the PC junior (discontinued), to the PC, the XT (a hard disc version of the PC), the portable PC and the more powerful AT. The Personal System/2 series of microcomputers, announced by IBM in 1987, are also likely to have a significant impact upon the market. The existing machines have a variety of options in disc drive (hard/soft), colour and communications configuration and there is a multitude of third party add-on cards (including hard disk drives) which can be implemented in the expansion slots provided.

Machines which are truly compatible with those of IBM include those manufactured by Compaq, Columbia, ITT's PC, Olivetti and a host of Japanese, US and European 'look-alikes'. Compatibility is a somewhat subjective term and even IBM have differences between their PC and the PC portable. In the latter case, these differences are small and primarily visible as different character sets but they indicate the problems involved.

The major rivals to IBM and their compatibles include ACT's Apricots, Apple's Macintosh, Hewlett Packard's Series 200 and ICL's new PC, as well as a number of other machines, very often faster and superior in technical specification to the equivalent IBM machine. Even the rivals show some elements of IBM compatibility, with either the software being available in a special version or the operating system providing a level of compatibility which permits the use of IBM software (e.g. DEC, Rainbows and Apricots can run most, but not all, IBM software).

The compatibility/non-compatibility derives from the chip in use in the Central Processing Unit (CPU) and the operating system installed. The current business micro user is likely to be using 16-bit CPU chips such as an Intel 8086/8088/80286 or Motorola 68000 or equivalent. The 8-bit Intel 8080/8085 and Zilog Z80 now belong to a previous generation of micros and we are currently seeing the introduction of machines using 32-bit processors such as Intel's 80386. The most visible distinction to the user is in the operating system being used. Most of the IBM microcomputers use Microsoft's PC-DOS while nearly all the software will run under MS-DOS (the original operating system written by Microsoft). One of the principal alternative operating systems is Digital Research's Concurrent CP/M and latterly Concurrent DOS. The future of the operating systems, like that of hardware, is subject to technical innovation and user acceptance and currently many consider UNIX to be the rising star.

The tradition of modelling and computers

While the variety of hardware may seem substantial the diversity of software systems which claim modelling capabilities is even more enormous. In a report by the Economist Intelligence Unit (No. 162), seventy two packages were reviewed, ranging in price from approximately £40 to £2,000. Indeed this review did not claim to be exhaustive and more recent reports indicate an increase in this number. Such diversity naturally leads to confusion and this section provides some structure for understanding the alternatives.

Originally, modelling used to be carried out using a general- purpose programming language such as BASIC, FORTRAN or PASCAL. There was no alternative in the 1960s and 1970s in terms of the hardware – i.e. a mainframe computer, nor the software – a programming language. A model developed using such a programming language and hardware could, however, take a long time and hence could be costly. This led to the development of modelling systems which were essentially packages to aid building a model; i.e. pieces of software bridging the 'gap' between the model builder and the computer.

The advantages of a modelling system is that it enables a model to be developed in less time (by a factor of between 3 and 5) albeit with some loss of flexibility. On the other hand, it usually uses more computer time in processing (in micro seconds) for a given model than the general purpose language (see the comparison in section 1.4). If the modeller chooses a general purpose language, he or she must then decide: which one? By far the most popular general purpose language is BASIC which is readily available on most micros. The choice of a modelling system is more difficult since there are increasing numbers on offer, with a more even distribution of usage. ICL's PROSPER achieved widespread use on ICL's mainframes whilst EPS-FCS gained acceptance on IBM mainframes. Some modelling packages, such as ORACLE, were available on a time-sharing bureau service.

Since the advent of microcomputers, modelling has increasingly shifted to this form of hardware, particularly as processing power has increased. There still remains, however, a need for mainframe modelling, particularly with networked systems, large scale models, integrated office systems, etc. In addition to this continued activity, developments on mainframes tend eventually to be incorporated on micros. Hence two further developments on mainframes are relevant to microcomputer modellers:

1 General purpose programming languages have continued to be developed to a point where they are very powerful and user- friendly (e.g. DEC's VAX BASIC). Many serious modellers may wish to buy a Micro-VAX 2 and use a language like VAX BASIC for large models.
2 Fourth Generation languages (e.g. FOCUS) have increased programming productivity and allowed users to write their own programs, including faster models.

Both improved general purpose languages and Fourth Generation languages are becoming available on micros and provide modellers with powerful development tools.
The movement of mainframe software to microcomputers is not all one-way; as users become accustomed to user-friendly spreadsheets and other productivity tools, so they become available on the mainframes (e.g. DECALC available on DEC's VAX range of computers).

Comparing languages and modelling systems

General purpose computer programming languages have four principal advantages over modelling systems:

1 Flexibility. General purpose languages tend to be more flexible. Many of the modelling systems cannot perform all the operations necessary for the translation of the mathematical model to a computer.
2 Widespread use. Most computers are able to accommodate, for example, an implementation of BASIC. This means that the modeller can use just about any computer. Modelling systems may be geared to a particular bureau or a particular computer manufacturer.
3 Portability. If the model is developed in a general purpose language, it can be transferred from one computer to another with ease – this is not always true with microcomputers.
4 Cost. General purpose languages tend to use less computer time than modelling systems. Recent developments have tended to reduce, but not eliminate, the advantage.

Modelling systems in turn have a number of advantages. The input and output operations are much easier. Modelling systems usually allow immediate output in a somewhat messy format, whilst with more effort a neat report can usually be generated. The main section of a modelling system deals with the logic of a model; modelling systems are not always as flexible as a general purpose programming language in this instance. There are six principal areas in which they do have an advantage:

1 Multiple products Some (but not all) modelling systems allow the incorporation of multiple products in an easy way and/or facilitate the totalling of rows or columns.

2 Functions or sub-routines. A few modelling systems provide a comprehensive array of functions for calculating tax, depreciation etc which makes it very easy to program the model using these functions as part of the modelling system.

3 Vector approach. Modelling systems automatically adopt a matrix or vector approach to programming. The looping over time is also performed automatically by the modelling system.

4 Consolidation Some modelling systems provide a facility which makes the consolidation of divisional or company models a less complicated task.

5 Sensitivity analysis and 'what if' questions. Modelling systems are usually geared to the modeller performing this task.

6 Totalling over periods. Modelling systems are generally capable of totalling quarterly, half-yearly or cumulative results with a simple instruction.

Spreadsheets

With the explosion of the microcomputer market in the late 1970s and 1980s, a new type of software package was heralded in, i.e. 'the spreadsheet'.

Spreadsheets are based on a large matrix structure in which the cells of the matrix may be thought of as the computer equivalent of a large, multi-column analysis sheet. The accountant has a natural affinity with analysis paper being the normal working document, so many found it easy to adjust to an electronic version. Traditionally, the accountant was restricted to about 20 columns by 30 rows on paper, in which data and relationships were expressed and subsequently subject to calculation in order to arrive at the answer on the bottom line or rightmost column. The electronic version, however, displays on the VDU (screen) only a limited portion of an enormous analysis sheet (e.g. 16,000 cells plus) which can quickly re-calculate as data is modified. The display (the window) may be moved around the spreadsheet for constructing, editing and reading results. It may be used for a variety of purposes, not only by the accountant, but also by other managers and functions.

The essential characteristic of the cell structure is that it imitates the analysis sheet on paper. The imitation runs to the level that each cell may have text, numbers or formulae entered in it. In this way, text may be used to define terms, months, sales, revenue, etc. Numbers may form data associated with the text and formulae may take more than one cell and process them against other cells or process the contents of a particular cell against some defined mathematical base.

In addition, cells in certain software may be used to represent simple graphs by inserting asterisks to represent the number of units in each cell. In using a spreadsheet the technique is to lay out the matrix, showing workings and reports, entering headings, relationships and formulae, subsequently followed by data which may be worked upon to produce results. A major danger with spreadsheets is that the first outcome is assumed to be correct when it may contain errors in logic. Subsequent editing and development of the reporting format is essential, as is a process of verification of logic.

At a conference on *Office Automation and the Professional Worker*, organised by CAET on 1 May 1985, Jim Stone, speaking on the impact of IT on Accounting, referred to a recent survey which had shown that *the highest added value was the simple spreadsheet as a basis for decision support.* It is unlikely therefore that the market for such systems will quickly be replaced.

Software choices

The initial surge of enthusiasm, in which some 250,000 copies of Visicalc, one of the early leaders in spreadsheet packages, were estimated to have been sold led to a general increase in interest in modelling systems for microcomputers. This has resulted in the development of three basic categories of financial modelling packages for this environment:

- relatively cheap and simple spreadsheet packages such as the early versions of Visicalc and Supercalc;
- rather more expensive but sophisticated spreadsheet programs, such as MicroModeller or Plan 80;
- financial modelling packages that have descended, with modifications, from a large computer environment, such as Micro-FCS or Micro Finesse.

The simple spreadsheet programs have two important advantages over their rivals; they are cheap, and, with the acknowledgement in principle of the traditional limitations of models, give a reasonable guideline to possible courses of action. Purely for these reasons many organisations both large and small have invested in microcomputers purely to run simple spreadsheet programs.

There are, however, several limitations built into these programs by their original design. One major shortcoming which has already been referred to is the size limitation. Thus, although several of the simpler spreadsheet programs support approximately 16,000 cells, in practice only a fraction of these can be used before running out of available memory. In many 8 bit microcomputer applications where the RAM (Random Access Memory) is limited, the maximum is usually 1,000 cells, whereas with 16 bit machines it is often about 2,400 cells. Such a limited working area nevertheless generally provides ample space for most applications, although the larger the model the slower the speed of calculation. At maximum capacity this can approach 30 seconds. Given the normal applications and the capacity limitations of these packages, however, such items are likely to cause minor irritation at worst. Other more serious limitations with many of the less sophisticated spreadsheet models are that:

- each model works in isolation, meaning that two models cannot be consolidated;
- facilities which are available for report writing are usually very limited, being confined to printing out the entire model displaying either figures or formulae;
- links with graphics packages are not usually possible and therefore prevent addition of illustrations to reports;
- even if the information required in the model is already stored in the computer, it still has to be input initially to the program through the keyboard unless a database link is available.

The later and more sophisticated spreadsheets and advanced micro modelling packages currently cost in the range of £250 to £800. Many of these packages require users to define their own matrix workspaces and employ so called 'English logic'. As a result, items of information are not merely referenced by the coordinates of a matrix, as in a simple spreadsheet package, but are instead given variable names (such as GROSS PROFIT) which are then used to specify the arithmetic calculations. Whilst many of the packages in this category are driven by commands, however, others are menu-driven and some can be driven by either method. The chief advantage of these packages is that the user is given the opportunity to print reports based on the data held by the program. The operator is thus given much more flexibility in defining the output from the model by being able to create report formats. In addition, with linkages to graphics packages, the presentation of data can be much more meaningful to non-financial personnel in the organisation.

Modelling packages

Packages derived from minicomputer and mainframe models are often in direct competition with the sophisticated spreadsheet programs such as Micromodeller but generally cost considerably more. A typical example would be Micro-FCS, which currently costs between £950 and £2,000, and which was derived from a package called FCS-EPS written by EPS Consultants Limited. The FCS-EPS system is suitable for use on many mini and mainframe computers and typically sells for about £10,000. Unfortunately some of the statistical routines which are available in FCS-EPS are lost in the conversion to the micro version, but this is unavoidable due to the pressure on capacity in microcomputer systems.

To the average user there may not be a great deal of difference between packages like Micromodeller and Micro-FCS. The crucial distinction in this case, however, is that data, logic and reports can be separated and saved as files. Micro-FCS therefore allows the user to run different sets of data through the same logic. This ability greatly facilitates consolidations: for example, where budgets for different departments are added together; a facility only available on the more advanced spreadsheets.

Limitations of systems

Spreadsheets and modelling are increasingly growing closer together as time goes by, but they do essentially have two different basic assumptions. Models are based on mathematical relationships expressed in the logic file which may be utilised in a variety of ways and in a variety of situations. Spreadsheets represent report output systems which will restrict the degree of flexibility of input. The alternative to both of these is the development of specialist programs. An example of this is the use of FORTRAN or other higher level language systems. This route has primarily been replaced by packaged software but it still has some validity as the building of specialist models may exploit a freedom unavailable in the spreadsheet or modelling package which is constrained by the original design specification. For example, spreadsheets are primarily simulation systems and may only achieve an optimising model through iterations in a trial and error manner until the optimum is achieved. Modelling packages have varying degrees of goal seeking abilities but again this tends to be in an iterative manner.

If specific optimising techniques such as linear programming, economic order quantities etc, are sought then this may be achieved in the general purpose modelling and spreadsheet packages through iteration. A genuine optimal solution, however, may best be achieved in a specifically written program using a language such as FORTRAN (mathematically based) or BASIC (general purpose) or their equivalents.

This rather conflicts with the traditional assumptions that decision-makers always seek optimal solutions, e.g. profit maximisation, sale revenue maximisation, cost minimisation, etc. While optimising models may be built, they require a clear understanding of relationships and in a complex world this is not always available. The result is that optimising models tend to be over-simplifications of reality which, whilst elegant, produce results of little use to decision-makers. This view has traditionally been reinforced by the abstract work of OR (Operational Researchers), systems analysts and academics who fail to provide managers with adequate replacements for traditional rules of thumb.

The alternative approach is the building of simulation models in which 'what if' experiments may be undertaken, along with iterations, to achieve an optimal point. It provides not only a tool closer to the manager's own behaviour but also a learning process in which relationships are understood which may permit the development of complex relevant models of the problems being faced. Eventually this may require a shift to more sophisticated optimising, purpose-built models.

This chapter will concentrate on the modelling and spreadsheet packages which are readily available to managers and will permit the development of appropriate models for decision support. In the course of the chapter the various techniques which enable limited goal seeking and iterations associated with attempts at optimisation will be illustrated.

Before describing some of these systems, it must be noted that the rate of technological obsolesence has made some of the distinctions mentioned previously out of date. The market leaders now offer the advantages of a spreadsheet with some of the facilities of micro implementation of a mainframe modelling system.

Trends in software

From the first versions of Visicalc and Supercalc in the early days, two major forces in the shape of Multiplan and Lotus 1-2-3 joined the fray and many others have followed including Symphony (also from Lotus) and Framework (from Ashton-Tate). These latter systems were of the 'integrated' variety although it must be said that it has been the modelling aspects of these systems which have received the most attention. The relatively recent release of Supercalc 4 illustrates that the software developers are continually trying to improve their products in the face of developing competition.

At the same time the continued trend to implement micro versions of mainframe software has provided systems such as MICRO-FCS, IFPS and other proven mainframe systems. The micro implementations offer varying degrees of compatibility with their mainframe parent but for many organisations and modellers, having a growth path at all is a major improvement, particularly when coupled with the flexibility of micro operation.

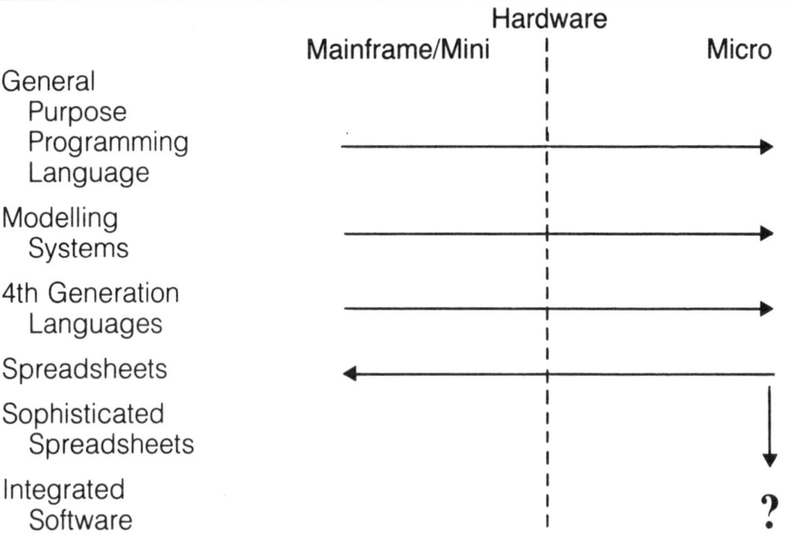

Figure 1 Trends in Software

Finally, the current state of the art is the integrated software combining the productivity tools of spreadsheets, word processing, graphics and data management. This has its origins in the work of software houses who have promoted compatibility in file structures to permit the transfer of files between spreadsheet packages and word processing systems, etc. It also has origins in the mainframe office systems which offer the same compatibility but greater integration. Multi-dimensional worksheets are also now starting to appear which move spreadsheets away from the row by column basis by adding the concept of user-definable pages as a further dimension.

One final point is worth consideration. If you know your system, it may be easier and quicker to stay with your existing system rather than purchasing the 'new improved' one which may have a few more facilities. The cost of moving to a new system is not purely monetary; it is also the time taken to become familiar with the new system. Obviously a modeller must change with the times but these changes should, if possible, be minimised. Only if there is some overriding problem or lack of facility should a modeller rush out and buy a package to overcome a particular problem or limitation. New product launches will continue to be rapid but the growth path and life cycle of a modelling system will be much more gradual, as time is invested in the system resulting in working models which will be costly in transfer time to a new system. Upward compatibility of systems and a general move towards integration between systems will, however, help to facilitate the transfer of files in the future.

Using a modelling system

Spreadsheets and modelling packages

Both spreadsheets and modelling packages share the common start position of identifying the relevant variables and their relationships. They subsequently diverge in their implementation and only become reconcilable at the report stage. The principal differences between the two approaches are shown in Figure 2.

SPREADSHEET	MODELLING PACKAGE
Logic, data and report merged within simple spreadsheet.	Logic, data and report in separated files.
Early consideration of the report format must be undertaken in order to design and separate windows containing working documents and report formats.	The primary consideration is the logical relationship which will subsequently be used to process data and enter it into the desired format.
Both methods require expression of logical relationships.	
Logical relationships will be built into the required cells with the report format resulting in multiple expression.	Logical relationships will be maintained in logic file and may be used repeatedly in report format without requirement of repeated specification.
Data will be entered into the input cells where it will be in the required report format.	Data will be held in a data file which may be used in alternative models.

The formal printed report will be strictly constrained by the windowing, screening and print capabilities which must consequently be considered in the report design and spreadsheet implementation. (Some of these problems may be overcome by incorporating word processing graphics, and specialist print routines.)	The final report format is separately defined and may be customised to the user without affecting the logic or data files.
Spreadsheets, by their very nature are constrained in their flexibility of data input and may require specialist input programs to create appropriate data structures for processing.	The separation of data files from the logical relationships permit greater compatibility with other data systems.

Figure 2 Comparison of Spreadsheets and Modelling Packages

Both systems increasingly permit inferfacing with other systems, such that data may be transferred into the model for automatic processing. At the same time the output may interface with communications systems for onward transmission, graphics packages for pictorial presentation of reports, and word processing for the editing and presentation of reports.

Principles of modelling in financial planning

In everyday life we apply our knowledge, experience and skills to make decisions and solve problems. Most of the time this is undertaken intuitively as a matter of routine, on other occasions there is an explicit process. In all cases there are a series of activities which we know collectively as problem solving and decision making. Both problem solving and decision making have the same route but in the case of the former there may be an absence of choice in the outcome.

In Figure 3 the life cycle of a decision is shown. This life cycle equally applies to problem solving since the only difference may be that of the degree of choice. Initially we must have problem identification. This may be signalled quite clearly (e.g. at what price shall we sell the new product?), or the problem may remain hidden for a period of time before some symptom reveals the existence of the problem (e.g. stocks have risen to the point of creating problems of storage and cash flow due to the poor performance of sales). The problem may exist in the real world or in the conceptual world. The real world problem may be illustrated by the examples above and the conceptual problem may lie in our lack of understanding of the real world. In both cases the problems will be solved only after analysis of the real world. This analysis of the real world should lead to the synthesis of ideas which we term understanding. An alternative definition of this process is modelling.

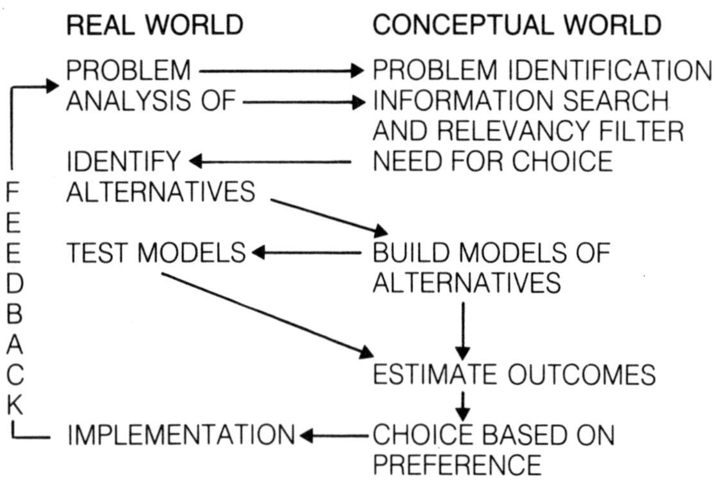

Figure 3 Life-cycle of decision

Representing reality

A model is a representation of reality. It might be a physical model, such as a model of an aircraft undergoing wind tunnel testing, or an abstract model using mathematical formulae to represent size, shape, weight, relationships, etc.

Iconic	– Looks like
Analog	– Behaves like
Symbolic	– Representative of
Mathematical	– Mathematical representative of
Descriptive	– Descriptive of behaviour, relationships, physical characteristics, etc
Deterministic	– Behaves in prescribed patterns
Probalistic	– Behaviour only predicts probabilities
Static	– Static representation
Dynamic	– Changing representation
Algorithmic	– Optimised and structured
Heuristic	– Trial and error

Table 1 Types of Model

A further method of classifying models may be provided, based on the usage of models. For example, simulation models are used to simulate how a real item would behave in a given set of circumstances. The advantage of this approach is one of reduction of risk and cost. An example is the model of the aircraft undergoing wind tunnel testing where the model simulates the real aircraft flying, with which a major cost as well as risk would be associated (i.e. test flying an untried item). Recently Citroen announced the launch of a new car which had been built totally by a computer using simulation techniques to test the characteristics of the car without the need to build a prototype. This resulted in a reduction of cost and time.

Optimising models are associated with the area of operational research in which models are built using mathematical representations, such that the processing of the model will permit the calculation of an optimal solution. This approach has been substantially developed since the last war in the areas of linear programming, queuing theory, economic order quantities etc. The advantages of this approach are that it identifies the best decision, thus eliminating the judgement normally applied by the manager. There is, however, a problem in that the mathematical representation may lead to a simplification of reality. This could eliminate essential characteristics, thus resulting in an optimal solution which may not reflect the variety existing in the environment. Thus it is still up to the individual manager to add the essential judgement basis.

Forecasting models have been available for some considerable time, either based on simple linear regression or multiple regression. The basic principle of forecasting is to project trends, cycles and seasonality into the future. This approach is effectively used in the areas of sales forecasting and budgeting decisions. It has, however, received some bad publicity resulting from the use of historic data simply projected into the future, without consideration of possible changes on the horizon.

In order to understand the elements of the model and their interrelationships, a systems approach is utilised. Figure 4 illustrates the basic assumptions of a business system. The systems view is reflected not only in the accounting system but also in the physical flows of activity through the business. A business model will seek to represent this system. A systems model is an abstract, simulating reality by feeding in data and predicting the likely outcome. Business models are probablistic, i.e. neither true nor false in their predictions. Their usefulness can only be established by comparing their predictions with reality; this probability is independent of how risk and uncertainty have been built into the model. Any abstraction must have an associated degree of probability reflecting the degree of abstraction.

Modelling and decision support systems

A business model offers management one of the most powerful techniques for business planning; it is sometimes referred to as a decision support system. A business model allows management to test out the implications of their plans, strategies and tactics on the business without committing the company either to expensive experiments (toe-testing) or to irreparable steps into the unknown. This is achieved by producing alternative plans and testing out their effect on the business model. The model represents the firm and its behaviour and can be used to generate reports on the outcome of alternatives.

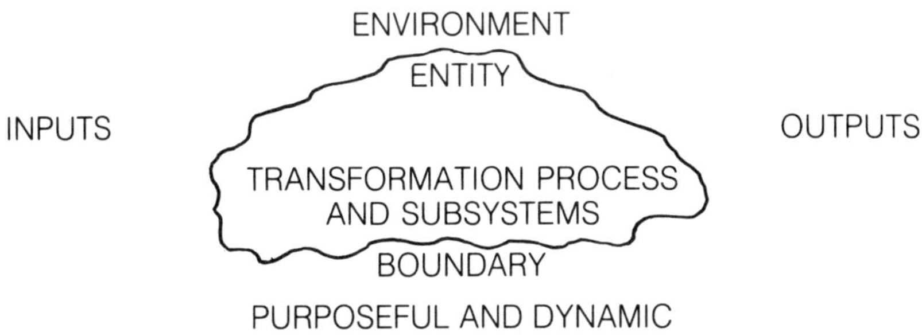

Figure 4 A Business model

The model is, however, only a model and is only as good as the inbuilt assumptions and characteristics. This fundamental rule must not be forgotten otherwise model users are in danger of believing the model is true and that reality is false!

Typical of the type of report mentioned above is the development of a plan which allows the manager to see what happens to such things as profit, assets and liabilities under various circumstances. Once these business variables have been entered into a model a number of different scenarios may be reviewed with changes being made to any input factors; alternatively, sensitivity analyses may be undertaken. Essentially, sensitivity analysis seeks to test the model to identify the model's outcomes and its degree of sensitivity to changes in the inputs. For example, the sensitivity of a cash flow model could be assessed relative to changes in the length of the debtor's period in terms of the cash balance at the end of each month. Of course, the manager can always work backwards from a target profit and thus calculate requirements for sales, debtors, cash, production, inventory or any other business variable as desired. The manager's ability to seek out answers to questions will depend on how the model was built and the model's capabilities. This particularly applies where models are built using standard software which may constrain the model's capabilities.

Business modelling is a tried and trusted management tool which has been available for decades. Computers have been programmed to offer these facilities for quite some years. As recently as a few years ago, however, one needed a large mainframe with highly sophisticated and very expensive software to be able to undertake computerised business modelling. This represented a significant price barrier for businesses seeking to enter the business modelling area, and this was only broken relatively recently with the introduction of microcomputers and low cost software.

A model is built by a process of abstraction from reality, changing attributes and relationships into mathematical symbols. Symbolic models, though the mathematics might seem complex, are often much simpler to construct than physical models. It is the accounting information system which is embodied in this model and hence established accounting routines must be mathematically represented. The process of converting implicit accounting activities into explicit algorithms is perhaps the most difficult step for many accountants to take. But it is one which may be tackled in stages by developing simple models and subsequently amplifying them into more complex, detailed models. Modelling follows the same principles as many activities in data processing, in that data is captured, processed and stored, retrieved and reported. In so doing, data tends to be attenuated, i.e. compressed; this maintains the variety which is particularly pertinent to the model builder's task. In attenuation, however, the process of variety reduction may lead to simplification which limits the potential of the model. The outcome of the model, where 'what if' questions are asked, is essentially data amplification. In other words a limited number of variables interact but produce a larger number of outcomes, thus providing us with the variety with which we need to make our choices. Some of the features of decision making and problem solving may, therefore, be described as data handling, variety handling and judgement. The data handling will be predominantly undertaken by the machine, the variety handling will be defined by decisions in model building and model manipulation and the judgements will remain those of managers. The computer frees the decision maker of the drudgery of 'number crunching' and exploits its speed and accuracy of processing. Modelling, like simulation, is a child of microcomputer technology.

A model consists of a number of attributes, each of which relates to the others in some way which can usually be described mathematically. When data is fed to the model it is manipulated according to these rules and a result is produced. Both data and rules can be changed so that the model reflects the real world as closely as possible.

The best-known business model is the budget. Indeed, few people appreciate that a budget is a model but of course it is, for it seeks to represent the real activities of the business and to predict the likely outcome in the form of a profit. Naturally, its success depends largely upon the model builder's knowledge of the business and the way in which it is abstracted. It also depends upon the data which is entered and the accuracy of the rules portraying the relationship of attributes: e.g. what effect does a price increase have on the volume sold?

Models can be improved with experience but the past is not always the best guide to future events and so it is not possible to rely on experience alone. Some estimate or forecast of relationships has to be added to experience to make the model valuable.

Models are problem-solving tools which are used to try to predict what would happen in the real world if certain events took place. This is why models are often referred to as 'what if' models, the 'if' being the variable data and the 'what' being the outcome.

Advantages of computerised models

The use of models entails a number of significant advantages, as follows:

- they provide a framework for examining problems. Although they may not always lead to solutions, it is possible that they could highlight gaps in information.
- the process of building the model contributes significantly to a better understanding of the problem.
- they allow manipulation of both the rules and the data to test a wide variety of possible outcomes.
- they are easier and less expensive than carrying out a full-scale exercise, saving both time and money.

Other advantages include the ability to aid communication between managers within a business; the ability to consider a longer time horizon, and to act as a check on the consistency of plans. If the sales division is planning to sell X units and the production division to produce Y units the discrepancy will soon show up in a model; that is not to say that the problem should not have been spotted without the aid of a model.

The above list is not, of course, exhaustive. If a computer will be doing the work, the modeller may be prepared to build in additional complexity (both in size and number of calculations), thus providing the business with the ability to explore more complex relationships and inter-relationships between variables. By asking 'what if' type questions, managers can learn more about their business and hence redefine objectives, re-examine problems and search for new options.

Similar such experiments – as well as sensitivity analysis, for example, how sensitive is profit to a change in the pound/dollar exchange rates – permit the manager to make a better assessment of the potential risks. As the arithmetic tedium of calculation is removed, time is released for more strategic and analytical thinking.

Disadvantages of computerised models

Users should, however, be aware that there are some disadvantages associated with computerised modelling, such as the following:

- there is a danger of over-simplification. The model builder may leave out crucial factors for expediency.
- symbolic language, though valuable, has its limitations, and not every relationship can be expressed mathematically.
- model builders can become so enamoured of their models that they begin to believe they are better than reality; and the model may become rigid.
- models produce only predictions of outcome. These might be a simple figure (as in a budget) or a range of results with an indication of the one most likely to occur.
- models are, of course, never (or extremely rarely) absolutely right, leading some people to perceive them as inherently inaccurate.

One of the shortcomings of the modelling process is that it is prone to the 'garbage in, garbage out' syndrome. A salesman making absurdly optimistic assumptions will always produce an excellent profit forecast. Hence quality of the data and assumptions are extremely important. Sometimes models are used to 'prove a point' within an internal conflict whilst what is really at odds is not the model, but the underlying assumptions incorporated within the model. Project Z can be made to look profitable or unviable – depending upon the sales forecasts input. Internal politics may lead to much waving of printouts while the real issue, for example the level of sales that might be reasonably achieved in the future, is missed.

The decision-maker can get into a situation which is extremely difficult to model. For example, in modelling the activities of a timber merchant one might want to break down timber sales into three broad categories: softwood, hardwood and plywood. But across each category there may be many different types of timber, different qualities, differing lengths/widths/depths, from different parts of the world.

Data availability is another problem. Ask for the price of Portuguese pine of certain width and length and you will probably get a straight answer. Ask for the average price of all Portuguese pine last year, and the business's data processing system may be incapable of supplying an answer. Data that is precisely relevant to the particular level at which a model is being built is rarely available. Either the data is too detailed or only readily available in too global a form. Frequently changes to the firm's data processing system have to be undertaken if the relevant data is to be correctly identified. Sometimes, of course, the modeller has to adapt the model to reflect the availability of data. The value of models lie not in their accuracy but in the use that is made of them in the problem-solving activities of managers. A model is a tool to be used with skill and understanding.

Many accountants are now exploring the benefits of using models. They are aware of the advantages of using small computers to manipulate data within a prescribed framework. Modelling software is available which will operate on micros, minis and mainframes. This software provides a means for the accountant to construct a model, without actually writing a program.

The concept of modelling

Problem analysis

Assuming that a problem has been identified, the next stage is the analysis of that problem. To illustrate this, consider the case of the owner of a small business who needs to either build new premises or move to new premises to allow the business to expand. Before a decision can be made on these two alternatives the constraints must be identified together with the relationship between variables. For example, an obvious constraint will be the financial resources available. As part of the problem analysis process the owner must identify and predict future financial resources. This involves forecasting future income and expenditure as well as knowing the extent of existing resources. Information on existing resources can be obtained from the present control systems, particularly the accounting information system. Forecasts of future income and expenditure must be calculated by predicting the behaviour of the elements of the business (the variables). This can best be done by constructing mathematical functions of the relationships of one variable to another and then testing to see if these reflect actual behaviour. This testing may be undertaken by looking at past

records. Once a representative relationship has been found it may be applied to predicting likely future events, such as income and expenditure. In this way the company's financial status becomes known, being one element of the decision portfolio.
From the above, the process of problem analysis can be defined as follows:

1 Problem identification. In this case, the problem was specified as being the need for bigger premises which could be solved by moving or by building an extension to the existing premises. Whilst this problem could be broken down further it was assumed the manager had this understanding of the problem. Problem identification essentially involves setting limits or boundaries to the problem which will enable definition of internal content and external influence.
2 Analysis of the problem. The analysis process identifies the content and influences in two forms: constraints and variables. Constraints are limits which may define feasibility and acceptability. When considering whether to move to bigger premises or build extensions, the availability of financial resources to cover the costs represents a constraint on the decision. Variables, on the other hand, reflect the interaction of elements of the problem. They may be sub-elements of constraints or variables. In the case above we looked at variables which were sub-elements of a constraint. The constraint was financial resource availability, and the variables were current financial resources, future income and expenditure.
3 Analysis of constraints and variables. The process outlined in analysis of the problem continues until two characteristics are established. Firstly, the relationship between variables in a structural form (normally mathematical):

Current		Past		Change in
Financial Resources	=	Financial Resources	+	Financial Resources

These relationships need to be tested and verified to ensure that they are correct otherwise the model will fail. Secondly, variables must be broken down until a known basis, which will allow the entry of data into the relationships to permit calculations, can be established. These known bases may be the existing financial resources (as above) or be forecasts of future elements e.g. sales volume.
4 Testing. Before building any model its conceptual form must be tested rigorously to ensure its validity otherwise the model, when

built, may produce unexpected and unusual results, as per the acronym GIGO (Garbage In, Garbage Out).

The process of problem analysis is one of decomposition into primary elements. This process is somewhat eased in financial modelling, which is built on the basis of financial accounting which is itself a model of the business system. The mathematical relationships are implicit in the accounting model but in order for them to be processed mechanically, they must be made explicit, e.g.:

- *Implicit* – Sales revenue is dependent on the sales volume and the price
- *Explicit* – Sales revenue = sales volume × selling price

This process of making the mathematical relationship explicit is fundamental to the computer's operation. This is because the computer will receive instructions of what to do explicitly from the program and cannot assume the knowledge which the accountant possesses.

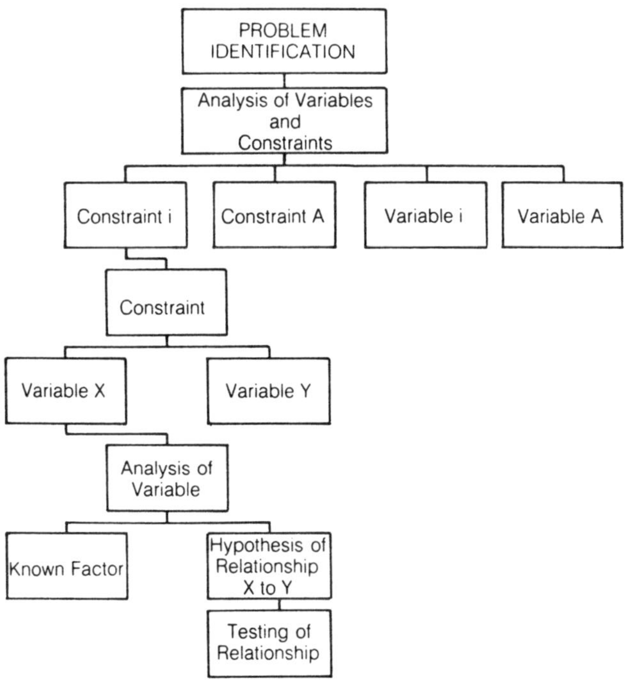

Figure 5 Problem Analysis

Capturing reality

One of the primary influences on attitudes towards financial modelling is the reality of the model. We have all experienced examples of models which fail to capture reality but yet have been applied and have led to incorrect decisions. This failing has led to the rejection of financial modelling and, indeed, of other management sciences. At the same time it has led to excessive criticism of actual performance which has been out of line with some models' predictions. Both of these reactions reflect a failure to understand the objectives and methods of modelling.

The objective of models is to permit the development and testing of ideas and beliefs without the costs and risks associated with building and testing examples in the real world. In the case of financial modelling the alternative is to implement decisions and risk the financial consequences.

In order for models to achieve the objective above, they must be sufficiently realistic to ensure that the results generated from the model are those which may be reasonably expected in reality. At the same time a model captures and affects our understanding and knowledge of the real world. Indeed, if we had a total understanding and knowledge of the real world, we should not need a model as we should be able accurately to predict the outcomes of our decisions. We do not, however, possess this total knowledge and understanding and this results in a risk and uncertainty factor.

It is through model building, with its repeated testing and improvement, that we seek to increase our knowledge and understanding. This process means that modelling is a learning process in which the current model represents our limited understanding and knowledge. Consequently, we should understand that the model will not fully capture reality and must result in a degree of uncertainty in its predictions as opposed to real world events.

A model can only predict and behave within its design constraints and so the output from a financial model must be treated with a degree of caution. This rather negative view should not be interpreted as a rejection of modelling but rather as an encouragement to learn. This is because by learning about modelling we learn not only about the modelling process but also about our business and the world around us.

The logic of modelling

Growing uncertainty and the rapid rate of change combine to increase the need for prediction and the planning of tactics and strategies to survive and prosper. In solving one planning problem another may well have been created, i.e. there may have been insufficient time to evaluate the alternatives before arriving at a decision. Formal management models suggest that we are rational planners. Studies have shown, however, that rational planning is not likely to occur in practice due to the problems of pressure. Pressure often reduces the time available for planning but, conversely, the process of building financial models for planning and decision-making requires an initial investment of time. Subsequently, time will be saved without doubt, but the initial building of a computerised model may take as much as three times as long as for a manual model. It should be noted, however, that whilst in the manual model subsequent changes which require re-calculation may take hours, the computerised version will require only seconds.

The first step in building a model is to compile a complete list of variables which have been identified through the problem analysis process. Once the variables have been identified, their relationship must be analysed and made explicit in the form of mathematical relationships. These variables and their relationships represent rules by which calculations will be performed in order to arrive at the outcomes which are sought from the model. These inter-connections must then be structured in a logical format so that they move in an ascending order from base input through their relationships to the output. This movement will be constrained by the processing capabilities of the software. In the case of financial modelling packages, where reporting and the logic are separate, greater freedom is available than is found in spreadsheets, where the logic and report format are merged.

1	Price 'A'		
2	Quantity 'A'		
3	Revenue 'A'	=	line 1 × line 2
4	Price 'B'		
5	Quantity 'B'		
6	Revenue 'B'	=	line 4 × line 5
7	Total Revenue	=	line 3 + line 6

Figure 6

Figure 6 demonstrates a logical progression with statements including input, e.g. price and quantity, for products A and B, as well as calculations producing results such as:

line 3 : revenue for product A
line 6 : revenue for product B
line 7 : total revenue

These are the basic logical relationships which are used both in financial modelling packages and spreadsheets.

It must be emphasised at this stage that the process of defining logical relationships as algorithms is one which requires accountants, in particular, to make explicit and implicit relationships which they assume daily. Once the process has begun it becomes a simple automatic exercise. With most modelling systems traditional expressions of **x=fy+e** may be more easily understood by using:

LABOUR COST = LABOUR RATE × LABOUR HOURS + DAILY RATE.

Most modelling systems are capable of testing either expression. In the case of the simpler spreadsheets, however, the formula may need to be re-expressed as the representative row/column relationships.

Developing and testing the model

The previous section discussed the problem of capturing reality and it is apparent that there will exist a development process of models. This process is no different to the development of any other product and is reflected in the short run and long run product life cycles.

As each model is developed, understanding of the problem is captured and built into the model. The failure of a model to achieve full representation of reality results in the development of a revised and improved model in which further elements, now understood, have been incorporated. This learning process permits the gradual improvement of validated models, e.g.:

Model 1: *PROFIT* = Sales Revenue − Total Costs
Model 2: *PROFIT* = Sales Revenue − (Fixed Costs + Variable cost)
Model 3: *PROFIT* = Sales Volume × Contribution − Fixed Costs

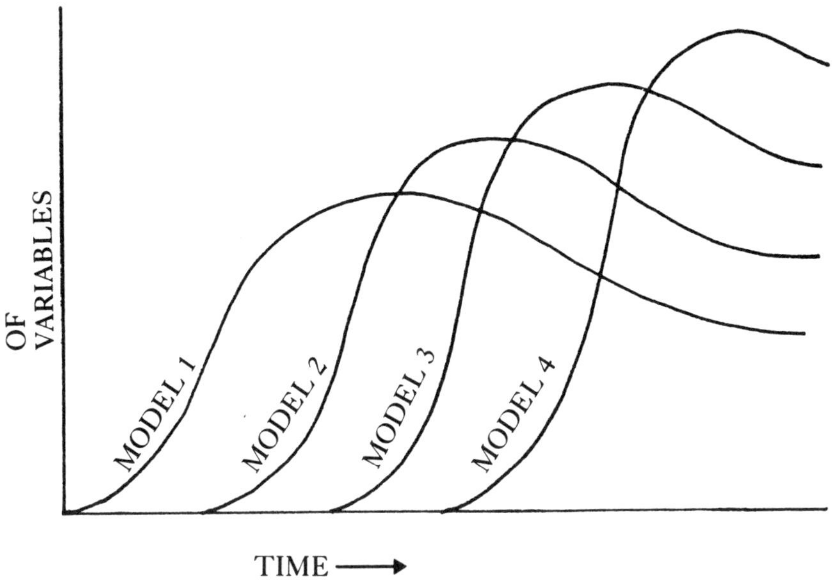

Figure 7 Life Cycle of Models

In the above example, the failure to capture the sensitivity of the model to changes in volume leads to the development of Model 2. Model 3 is the result of understanding the complex relationship of contribution, costs, revenues and profits to volume.

The target of any modeller is not, therefore, the development of the perfect model first time round but rather the gradual development of a more comprehensive and robust model which reflects the current understanding and knowledge, and will permit further improvement as additional experience generates understanding and knowledge.

It seems appropriate to emphasise that, since the modelling process is a long term activity through which learning about a business and its behaviour is undertaken, the modelling task should not be seen as a separate specialist activity but rather the natural activity of management. The separation of the modelling task from management runs counter to the learning process. The learning process permits management to achieve a higher level of control and functional performance. In addition it must be stated that the learning curve promotes support for the view that the investment in learning how to model with a modelling system pays dividends in the long term, rather than the short. Immediate paybacks cannot realistically be expected nor is it likely to be advantageous to keep shifting from one modelling system to another. From experience, however, the rate of learning a new software system is increased with exposure to a variety of systems, but it must first be built on a competence in one system. Lastly, before going further into the mechanics of model building, a few summary points must be made on the process of modelling. Firstly, a structural, rational, top-down analysis approach has been presented owing its origins clearly to systems analysis and design. Whilst this approach ensures a robust, valid model it can be costly in development time and may fundamentally fail to adhere to the user's objectives. An alternative approach, now followed in systems analysis and which may be applied in modelling, is prototyping Prototyping is the approach in which a model is built and tested to gain experience to permit the building of a more robust and relevant second generation model which more closely approximates to the user's needs. A series of generations of the model thus evolve. This approach is feasible with many modelling systems. It may not, however, be used efficiently in systems which demand the definition of all variables at the initial stage and do not permit subsequent editing. The systems which have this characteristic require a more structured approach.

Mechanics of model building

Defining the problem

The problem solving approach is one which can be applied to any financial modelling situation. To summarise, the following points require to be followed:

1 Defining the problem.
2 Identifying the relevant variables, including simplification of reality.
3 Relationships of variables.
4 Specifying the model.
5 Encoding the model.
6 Testing the model.
7 Applying the model.

The information sought from the model by the decision-maker must be specified. The aspects of a system's behaviour of interest to the decision-maker should be stated and the types of questions for which answers are required should be summarised.

We may define a simple problem of identifying the cash flow by month and the resultant financial status of the business. This process of defining the problem also gives the objective of the model against which we can check as we build the model. In the case of cash flow forecasting the objective is to ascertain the changing financial status over time. This is summarised in the form of changing cash balances at the end of each period of trade, i.e. in one dimension months: January, February, March etc and in the other dimension the closing balances for each of the respective months.

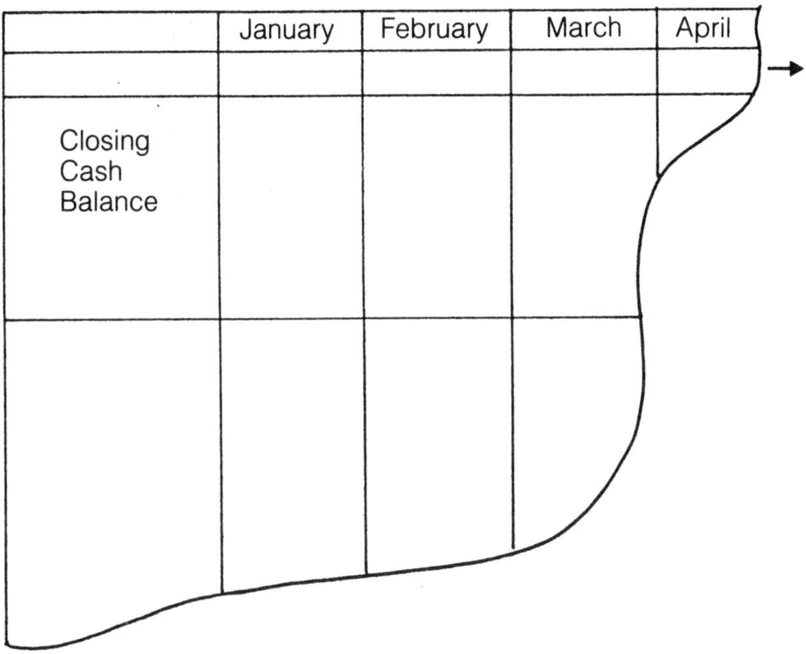

Figure 8 Defining the problem

Identifying the relevant variables

Having defined the problem, the next stage is to break it down into its constituent parts. Whilst this is initially achieved by a global view, the major process involves the decomposition of the models into its constituent parts.

The questions asked of a model will usually relate to the values of endogenous variables, that is, those variables which are determined within the system. The endogenous variables will include the aspects of the system which are of interest, as specified in the first step, and also any other variables generated within the system in the course of deriving a final solution. All significant endogenous variables must be specified.

The exogenous variables complete the variables set. These comprise all other variables for which the relevant values are determined by influences outside the system and will be taken to include those variables under the direct control of the decision- maker (sometimes referred to as controllable or decision variables) as well as non-controllable variables. The latter will include not only variables reflecting appropriate aspects of the firm's external environment, but also variables reflecting those aspects of the internal environment that comprise a set of constraints resulting from decisions made elsewhere in the organisation.

It will be seen later that the choice of the set of relevant variables will have a critical bearing on the quality of the model which is eventually formulated. In particular, it is important that no significant variables are omitted, since a mis-specified model which yields misleading results could be of less value to the decision-maker than having no formal model at all. Yet while a degree of realism is important, the cost of building a model means that there is likely to be an optimal level of model complexity beyond which the cost of improving the degree of realism becomes prohibitive, where, in other words, the expected additional benefits do not outweigh the costs of elaboration. In fact, the model-builder can usually ensure at an early stage that unnecessary detail is avoided by differentiating between those variables which are likely to have a significant impact on the behaviour of the model, and those which represent less important items of detail. If the potential impact of a particular variable is uncertain however, it should be included because the sensitivity of a model can be tested at a later date and insignificant variables can then be excluded.

We have already defined the problem as that of cash flow forecasting for specific periods. The method of representing this cash flow is the change in closing cash balances. These changing cash balances are a reflection of the income for the period less any expenditure undertaken in the period. The resulting surplus or deficit can then be matched against any cash brought forward to identify the closing cash balance. The essential elements of the model will therefore be the income, the expenditure, the surplus/deficit, the cash brought forward and the resultant cash position. Whilst this is easily recognisable as a cash flow forecast, we still do not have enough detail of what the relevant variables are or their relationships to enable us to specify the model. In order for us to establish what the variables are and their relationships we must decompose the model.

Specifying the model (decomposing)

Once the relevant set of variables has been defined, the relationships between them must be formally specified in mathematical terms. A relationship may be:

- defined, for example, revenue = volume × unit price;
- empirical, that is obtained by some estimation technique, such as observing the past behaviour of variables (for example, a retailer may observe that the gross margin on sales has, on average, been x per cent of sales value);
- derived, by algebra from some other combination of relationships (for example, if the pricing mechanism in an industry is such that a manufacturer's price to a wholesaler is based on cost plus a fixed mark-up, and similarly the wholesaler sells to the retailer on a cost plus basis, it is clearly quite simple to express the retailer's cost of purchases in terms of manufacturing cost and to ignore the wholesaler).

The requirement to express the relationship in mathematical terms is necessary because simulation is a numerical technique producing output numbers from input numbers in a step-by-step fashion. Whether the computations necessary at each step are to be effected manually or with the aid of a computer, they must be expressed in a form which will allow one number to be derived from some combination of two or more other numbers according to a fixed rule. The rule is, in fact, the mathematical expression of the relationship. The process of decomposing the model is one in which we specify each of the variables and their relationships. This is best explained through the example of the cash flow forecasting model, as follows:

1 Firstly the closing cash balance may be defined as = opening cash balance + change in cash position for the month.
2 The opening cash balance for any period may be defined as = closing cash balance in the previous period. This may be expressed as:

opening cash balance period T = closing cash balance in period T-1.

3 Next, the change in cash position for the month is = the income for the month − the expenditure for the month.

At this stage we have decomposed the original formula into two further sub-formulae, hence the closing cash balance may be defined as being dependent upon the closing cash balance brought forward

from a previous period + the income for the period less the expenditure for the period.
Through decomposing, the relevant variables and their relationships are identified. We shall now follow this process through to identify all the elements within the model.

The income for the month is = receipts from debtors + cash sales + interest on deposits + dividends on investments + cash investments for the month + the sale of fixed assets.
Expenditure for the month is = payments for purchases + wages and salaries paid + expenses + taxation + dividends paid + capital expenditure.

At this stage the model would look something like this.

Income:

1 Receipts from debtors
2 Cash sales
3 Interest on deposits
4 Dividends on investments
5 Cash investments
6 Cash received for sale of fixed assets
7 Total income = line 1 to 6

Expenditure:

8 Payments for purchases
9 Wages and salaries paid
10 Expenses
11 Taxation
12 Dividends paid
13 Capital expenditure
14 Total expenditure = line 8 to 13
15 Change in cash position = line 7 – line 14
16 Opening cash position *T* = closing cash position *T-1* (line 17)
17 Closing cash position = line 16 + line 15

The first problem of the model is now apparent in that lines 16 and 17 apparently refer to each other: in fact this expression requires further decomposition and using our previous statement (see above) i.e. opening cash balance period T = closing cash balance in period T-1, this can be further decomposed by stating that:

> closing cash balance in period 0 be an input variable, then, the closing cash position in period 1 is = closing cash position in period 0 + the change in cash period 1.

This means that, for the initial period, the opening balance is defined by the input variable; thereafter it is a dependent variable. This simple model may now be built.

Encoding the model

Assuming that the model is sufficiently large or complex to justify the use of a computer, the relationships developed and specified must be translated into a computer readable code and organised in the exact sequence in which the calculations need to be made.

Testing the model

At this stage, prior to applying the model, it is necessary to test that it is behaving correctly. The normal method employed is to compare the output produced for some given set of input data against the expected output, probably in the form of actual observations from a previous period. Alternatively, it may be possible to derive estimates of some of the output variables, using other modelling techniques, for example statistical regression. If it is found that the output values indicated by the simulation model are not significantly different from their expected values, the decision-maker should be able to proceed to use the model with a fair degree of confidence. If, however, there appear to be systematic differences between the actual output and the expected output, then the model is probably mis-specified and steps will have to be taken to improve its design. This may involve changing the set of variables assumed to be significant and/or altering the form of one or more of the relationships between variables.

In many modelling situations, the testing process and any subsequent model revisions will be an important, continuous exercise. Whenever the system being modelled contains elements whose nature changes over time, it is important that changes in relationships are reflected in the model immediately. Otherwise serious mistakes could be made as a result of taking decisions on the basis of information from a mis-specified model. Hence the testing process should be regarded by the modeller as a regular exercise in all except the most stable systems.

Cash Flow Forecast Model

Workings:

Sales Revenue	Nov	Dec	Jan	Feb	Mar	Qtr 1
Sales Volume	15000	12000	14000	10000	11000	35000
Price	1.00	1.00	1.00	1.00	1.00	
Sales Revenue	$15,000	$12,000	$14,000	$10,000	$11,000	$35,000
Debt Period % in:	less month		0	0	0	
	one month		0	0	0	
	two/more		100	100	100	
Cash Receipts			$15,000	. $12,000	$14,000	$41,000

Production	Nov	Dec	Jan	Feb	Mar	Qtr 1
Material usage	$4,000	$4,500	$3,500	$4,500	$6,000	
Material Stock change			$250	$250	$291	$791
Purchases	$4,000	$4,500	$3,750	$4,750	$6,291	$14,791
Credit Period % in:	less month		0	0	0	
	one month		100	100	100	
	two/more		0	0	0	
Payments			$4,500	$3,750	$4,750	$13,000

Cash Flow Forecast For Quarter One

Income

	Nov	Dec	Jan	Feb	Mar	Qtr 1
Cash Receipts			$15,000	$12,000	$14,000	$41,000
Dividends Received						$0
Interest on Deposits						$0
Capital Injections						$0
Total Income			$15,000	$12,000	$14,000	$41,000
Expenditure			Apr	May	Jun	Qtr 1
Purchase of Materials			$4,500	$3,750	$4,750	$13,000
Wages			$1,250	$1,000	$1,250	$3,500
Overheads			$2,000	$2,000	$1,750	$5,750
Expenses			$0	$0	$0	$0
Rent and Rates			$0	$0	$0	$0
Repairs and Maintenance			$0	$0	$0	$0
Motor Expenses			$0	$0	$0	$0
Capital Expenditure			$10,000	$0	$10,000	$20,000
Dividends			$1,000	$0	$0	$1,000
			$0	$0	$0	$0
Total Expenditure			$18,750	$6,750	$17,750	$43,250
Cash Position	Nov	Dec	Jan	Feb	Mar	Qtr 1
Surplus/Deficit			($3,750)	$5,250	($3,750)	($2,250)
Cash B/F			$2,000	($1,750)	$3,500	($250)
Cash C/F		$2,000	($1,750)	$3,500	($250)	($2,500)

Sample Listing for Cash Flow Forecast Model done in Lotus 1–2–3

3			
3			
4	*Workings:*		
5	———		
6	Sales Revenue		JANUARY
7	———		
8	Sales Volume		14000
9	Price		1
10			——
11	Sales Revenue	+E8*E9	
12	Debt Period % in:		0
13			0
14		100–E12–E13	
15			
16	Cash Receipts	+E11*E12/100+D11*E13/ 100+C11*E14/100	
17			
18			
19			
20	Production		JANUARY
21	———		
22			
23	Material usage		3500
24	Material Stock change		250
25			———
26	Purchases	+E23+E24	
27	Credit Period % in:		0
28			100
29		100–E27–E28	
30			
31	Payments	+E26*E27/100+D26*E28/ 100+C26*E29/100	
32			
33			
34			
35			
36			
37			
38			
39			
40			
41			

```
42 ______
43 Income
44 ______
45                                                  JANUARY
46
47 Cash Receipts             +E16
48 Dividends Received
49 Interest on Deposits
50 Capital Injections
51                                                  ______
52 Total Income              @SUM(E47 . . E51)
53
54 Expenditure                                         Apr
55 ______
56 Purchase of Materials+E31
57 Wages                                              1250
58 Overheads                                          2000
59 Expenses                                              0
60 Rent and Rates                                        0
61 Repairs and Maint                                     0
 3
62 Motor Expenses                                        0
63 Capital Expenditure                               10000
64 Dividends                                          1000
65                                                       0
66                                                  ______
67 Total Expenditure         @SUM(E56 . . E65)
68 Cash Position                                   JANUARY
69 ______
70 Surplus/Deficit           +E52–E67
71 Cash B/F                  +D72
72 Cash C/F                  +E70+E71
C2   :  'CASH FLOW FORECAST MODEL
C3   :  \=
D3   :  \=
B4   :  'WORKINGS:
B5   :  \=
B6   :  'Sales Revenue
C6   :  U "NOVEMBER
D6   :  U "DECEMBER
E6   :  U "JANUARY
F6   :  U "FEBRUARY
G6   :  U "MARCH
```

```
H6   : "Qtr 1
B7   : \-
B8   : 'Sales Volume
C8   : (F0) U 15000
D8   : (F0) U 12000
E8   : (F0) U 14000
F8   : (FO) U 10000
G8   : (F0) U 11000
H8   : (F0) @SUM(E8. .G8)
B9   : 'Price
C9   : U 1
D9   : U 1
E9   : U 1
F9   : U 1
G9   : U 1
C10  : "———
D10  : "———
E10  : "———
F10  : "———
G10  : "———
B11  : 'Sales Revenue
C11  : (C0) +C8*C9
D11  : (C0) +D8*D9
E11  : (C0) +E8*E9
F11  : (C0) +F8*F9
G11  : (C0) +G8*G9
H11  : (C0) @SUM(E11. .G11)
B12  : 'Debt Period % in:
C12  : 'less month
E12  : (F0) U 0
F12  : (F0) U 0
G12  : (F0) U 0
C13  : 'one month
E13  : (F0) U 0
F13  : (F0) U 0
G13  : (F0) U 0
C14  : 'two/more
E14  : (F0) U 100–E12–E13
F14  : (F0) U 100–F12–F13
G14  : (F0) U 100–G12–G13
B16  : 'Cash Receipts
E16  : (C0) +E11*E12/100+D11*E13/100+C11*E14/100
F16  : (C0) +F11*F12/100+E11*F13/100+D11*F14/100
```

```
G16  :  (C0) +G11*G12/100+F11*G13/100+E11*G14/100
H16  :  (C0) @SUM(E16..G16)
B20  :  'Production
C20  :  U "NOVEMBER
D20  :  U "DECEMBER
E20  :  U "JANUARY
F20  :  U "FEBRUARY
G20  :  U "MARCH
H20  :  "Qrt 1
B21  :  '———
B23  :  'Material usage
C23  :  (C0) U 4000
D23  :  (C0) U 4500
E23  :  (C0) U 3500
F23  :  (C0) U 4500
G23  :  (C0) U 6000
B24  :  'Material Stock change
E24  :  (C0) U 250
F24  :  (C0) U 250
G24  :  (C0) U 291
H24  :  (C0) @SUM(E24..G24)
C25  :  \-
D25  :  \-
E25  :  (C0) "———
F25  :  (C0) "———
G25  :  (C0) "———
B26  :  'Purchases
C26  :  (C0) +C23+C24
D26  :  (C0) +D23+D24
E26  :  (C0) +E23+E24
F26  :  (C0) +F23+F24
G26  :  (C0) +G23+G24
H26  :  (C0) @SUM(E26..G26)
B27  :  'Credit Period % in:
C27  :  'less month
E27  :  (F0) U 0
F27  :  (F0) U 0
G27  :  (F0) U 0
C28  :  'one month
E28  :  (F0) U 100
F28  :  (F0) U 100
G28  :  (F0) U 100
C29  :  'two/more
```

```
E29  :  (F0) U 100–E27–E28
E29  :  (F0) U 100–E27–E28
E29  :  (F0) U 100–E27–E28
B31  :  'Payments
E31  :  (C0) +E26*E27/100+D26*E28/100+C26*E29/100
F31  :  (C0) +F26*F27/100+E26*F28/100+D26*F29/100
G31  :  (C0) +F26*G27/100+F26*G28/100+E26*G29/100
H31  :  (C0) @SUM(E31..G31)
C41  :   ^CASH FLOW FORECAST FOR QUARTER ONE
C42  :  \=
D42  :  \=
E42  :  \=
B43  :  'Income
B44  :  '———
C45  :  U "NOVEMBER
D45  :  U "DECEMBER
E45  :  U "JANUARY
F45  :  U "FEBRUARY
G45  :  U "MARCH
H45  :  "Qrt 1
B47  :  'Cash Receipts
E47  :  (C0) +E16
F47  :  (C0) +F16
G47  :  (C0) +G16
H47  :  (C0) @SUM(E47..G47)
B48  :  'Dividends Received
H48  :  (C0) @SUM(E48..G48)
H49  :  'Interest on Deposits
H49  :  (C0) @SUM(E49..G49)
B50  :  'Capital Injections
H50  :  (C0) @SUM(E50..G50)
E51  :  (C0) "———
F51  :  (C0) "———
G51  :  (C0) "———
H51  :  (C0) \-
B52  :  'Total Income
E52  :  (C0) @SUM(E47..E51)
F52  :  (C0) @SUM(F47..F51)
G52  :  (C0) @SUM(G47..G51)
H52  :  (C0) @SUM(E52..G52)
B54  :  'Expenditure
E54  :  (C0) "Apr
F54  :  (C0) "May
```

```
G54 : (C0) "Jun
H54 : (C0) "Qrt 1
B55 : '———
B56 : 'Purchase of Materials
E56 : (C0) +E31
F56 : (C0) +F31
G56 : (C0) +G31
H56 : (C0) @SUM(E56..G56)
B57 : 'Wages
E57 : (C0) U 1250
F57 : (C0) U 1000
G57 : (C0) U 1250
H57 : (C0) @SUM(E57..G57)
B58 : 'Overheads
E58 : (C0) U 2000
F58 : (C0) U 2000
G58 : (C0) U 1750
H58 : (C0) @SUM(E58..G58)
B59 : 'Expenses
E59 : (C0) U 0
F59 : (C0) U 0
G59 : (C0) U 0
H59 : (C0) @SUM(E59..G59)
B60 : 'Rent and Rates
E60 : (C0) U 0
F60 : (C0) U 0
G60 : (C0) U 0
H60 : (C0) @SUM(E60..G60)
B61 : 'Repairs and Maint.
E61 : (C0) U 0
F61 : (C0) U 0
G61 : (C0) U 0
H61 : (C0) @SUM(E61..G61)
B62 : 'Motor Expenses
E62 : (C0) U 0
F62 : (C0) U 0
G62 : (C0) U 0
H62 : (C0) @SUM(E62..G62)
B63 : 'Capital Expenditure
E63 : (C0) U 10000
F63 : (C0) U 0
G63 : (C0) U 10000
H63 : (C0) @SUM(E63..G63)
```

```
B64  :  'Dividends
E64  :  (C0) U 1000
F64  :  (C0) U 0
G64  :  (C0) U 0
H64  :  (C0) @SUM(E64..G64)
E65  :  (C0) U 0
F65  :  (C0) U 0
G65  :  (C0) U 0
H65  :  (C0) @SUM(E65..G65)
E66  :  (C0) "———
F66  :  (C0) "———
G66  :  (C0) "———
H66  :  (C0) \ -
B67  :  'Total Expenditure
E67  :  (C0) @SUM(E56..E65)
F67  :  (C0) @SUM(F56..F65)
G67  :  (C0) @SUM(G56..G65)
H67  :  (C0) @SUM(E67..G67)
B68  :  'Cash Position
C68  :  U "NOVEMBER
D68  :  U "DECEMBER
E68  :  U "JANUARY
F68  :  U "FEBRUARY
G68  :  U "MARCH
H68  :  "Qtr 1
B69  :  '———
B70  :  'Surplus/Deficit
E70  :  (C0) +E52-E67
F70  :  (C0) +F52-F67
G70  :  (C0) +G52-G67
H70  :  (C0) +H52-H67
B71  :  'Cash B/F
E71  :  (C0) +D72
F71  :  (C0) +E72
G71  :  (C0) +F72
H71  :  (C0) +G72
B72  :  'Cash C/F
D72  :  (C0) U 2000
E72  :  (C0) +E70+E71
F72  :  (C0) +F70+F71
G72  :  (C0) +G70+G71
H72  :  (C0) +H70+H71
```

Applying the model

Once the model has been validated it can be used to produce answers to the questions originally identified by the decision-maker in the first step. The behaviour of the endogenous variables which interest the decision-maker may be observed for given sets of input data, as can the effects on the system of marginal changes in the exogenous variables, thus providing some idea of the sensitivity of the model.

Besides answering 'what if' type questions, it is possible to set up routines based on the simulation model which test the values of various items of output automatically as the input data is changed in some way, for example to represent various decision choices available to the manager. By remembering the 'best' value of an objective function based on values of the output data, it is possible to identify an optimal action from a set of specified alternatives simply by re-running the model for each set of input data. This type of search procedure is sometimes described as 'iterative'.

Conclusions

The foregoing has provided an introduction to building financial models by suggesting a structured method for the task. The method applies both to spreadsheets and modelling systems, however, the former provide greater freedom in the development of the model but in their complex modelling tasks and their reporting capability.

A further characteristic of financial models which should be uppermost in the minds of accountants is that of 'auditability'. In particular, spreadsheets have no inbuilt logic verification and many modelling systems are limited to syntax checking rather than detailed logic verification of the model. The role of models in Decision Support Systems provides the opportunity for 'computer assisted bankruptcy' resulting from valid decisions based on incorrect logic or data handling!

Essentially modelling requires clear identification of what one wants out of the model in output terms and this in turn leads to the definition of the layout of reports (and in the case of spreadsheets the layout of the model) which in turn defines the logic and the input data. This process is similar to the work of systems analysts, operational researchers and other investigative disciplines. It provides a further route to gain insight into how organisations, markets and activities work provided that models are recognised as an abstraction of reality which is subject to repeated verification and refinement. Only in this way is it possible to evolve adequate Decision Support Systems using modelling tools.

Bibliography

The following special reports from Economist Publications provide further coverage of the topics covered in this contribution:

Financial Planning with personal computers

Volume 1 Cash Flow Forecasting
Volume 2 Management accounting reports
Volume 3 Budgeting
Volume 4 Scenario Planning by G.R. Kaye and K.N. Bhaskar

Financial modelling with computers, *Report 120* by K.N.Bhaskar *et al.*

Other texts:

Financial Modelling – A practical guide by Dennis Sherwood. Gee & Co 1983.

4

Control in the Computing Environment

T J Bentley PhD, FCMA, FMS, MIDPM

Introduction

The need for control

Accountants have always been concerned with, and know from their training and experience, how to manage and control the processing of accounting data. The use of computers in no way reduces the stringency of external controls on documents, authorisation, separation of duties, etc. In some ways it is even more important as the data is less visible and more easily erased once in the system. Controls – both manual and computer – are, therefore, necessary in an age of growing dependence upon computers. This necessity covers:

(a) Frauds – as companies' operations become dependent on computer systems the possibility of fraudulently converting cash or goods or of defrauding shareholders and others actually becomes possible by using the computer. A famous securities fraud, the Equity Funding case, might have been detected earlier if there had been adequate controls over the computer systems. The danger of fraud remaining undetected increases when it is perpetrated by trusted management person(s) involving seemingly valid transactions. These could easily escape notice by an auditor under normal auditing procedures where there is no reason to suspect fraud.

(b) Errors – if there is a deficiency in a program, errors will inevitably occur, leading to the expression 'garbage in – garbage out'. Examples of where this has occurred include:

- as a result of changes in a system, goods were delivered without invoices, orders were duplicated without charge, and invoices were not recorded on statements. Substantial losses occurred.
- one accounts payable system drew cheques for debit as well as credit balances on suppliers' accounts!

(c) Security – physical security should have high priority and adequate measures should be taken to ensure equipment protection, backup and recovery, and access control.

Implementing control

The first essential is for proper controls to exist over the completeness and accuracy of input and processing, and to ensure that documentation is valid, authorised and, where possible, leaves a clear audit trail. A second line of defence is a strong internal audit function. External auditors need to plan audits well in advance and will, therefore, be able to contribute to discussions on controls at an early stage.

It should always be understood that management is responsible for maintaining effective and proper controls and cannot abdicate this responsibility, even though aspects of control are delegated down the line, to accountants, systems analysts, and others. In the small business, however, the 'micro-user', does not generally have available the technical expertise or facilities of the larger business. Instead, use has to be made of software packages operated by staff who have not received specialist training. This requires that many routines such as invoicing, debtor and creditor management, and cash books are dealt with by the same person. The attendant higher risks of fraud and error, breaches of security and need for relevant controls are apparent. In such circumstances, manual controls need to be implemented.

The larger, more sophisticated, computer systems will tend to have trained consultants and staff and the programs will probably be written specifically to meet the user's requirements. To a large extent, the computer programs themselves will enable the control and verification of the completeness and correctness of what is being processed at any time in the computer. In such installations the emphasis on control moves from operations towards the planning, specification and implementation decisions.

This contribution provides background information as to how to manage and control computer applications effectively. The reader may typically have had little formal computer training and may welcome an insight into the terminology and an introduction to some of the technical aspects of computer applications.

Control of computer systems

The introduction of computers has led to a number of changes in the normal management and control of data processing. These changes are primarily concerned with:

- rigidity
- visibility
- control

Rigidity causes concern because, when computers are used, there tend to be a lack of flexibility in extending codes, adding additional requirements or 'doing things differently'. The rigidity may be seen in different ways depending upon the type of computer being used. In the case of a mainframe, it might be the time taken to change programs. In the case of a minicomputer the rigidity may be caused by the constraints of the software package. In the case of microcomputers the rigidity could be the size and flexibility of the hardware.
Visibility causes concern because accountants have always been used to seeing their records written in books or on ledger cards. When using computers the records are maintained on unreadable disks and tapes which have to be fed through the computer and displayed on a screen or printed. Identification such as handwriting disappears, alterations are not visible, and the magnetic medium used is liable to damage if not very carefully handled.
Control of manual data processing has been well established with separation of duties, signatures, batch checking, add listings, and so on. With the computer, control becomes somewhat more involved. Several publications on computer control have separated the subject into General Controls and Application Controls. This contribution is somewhat different as the main emphasis is on application, although general controls are mentioned when considered necessary. The four levels to monitor are:

(a) correctness
(b) completeness
(c) security (including authorisation)
(d) 'auditability'

These levels of control depend upon many factors with the use of computers, but these can all be examined by looking at:

- input
- processing
- storage and output
- access

and these will differ depending upon the type of computer used.
This contribution addresses rigidity, visibility and control for three levels of computers, namely:

- mainframes
- minicomputers
- microcomputers

and, for each type of computer systems, suggestions for efficient control are defined.

Types of computers

Before offering guidance it is important to give some broad definition of each of the three categories of computers. These definitions must be read in the context of the degree of overlap that is occurring in current computer developments. Some minicomputers are now referred to as 'super-minis', some are as powerful as mainframes. Equally, many microcomputer systems would now satisfy definitions traditionally applied to minis. Within a few years the boundaries will become so blurred as to be meaningless. These definitions have, therefore, been based more on the organisation and use of the facilities than on hardware criteria.
The above definitions are given as a guide because the practical problems of control differ significantly among the three. There are, however, developments which will link these three types of computers into composite systems with multifunction workstations.

Mainframe computers

Mainframe computers are large machines, housed centrally in purpose-built computer centres. They require special air-conditioning and humidity controls and have many peripheral machines connected to them running a number of jobs at the same time. Mainframes have very large memories and can serve many different users for different functions at different locations. They are capable of dealing with very large volumes very quickly. A typical mainframe might be used to service many users who wish to access information which could be changed by any user, for example in a system such as airline reservations.
Mainframe computers are run by trained operators supported by trained analysts and programmers, who may also have written the special tailor-made software being used. Such computers are usually supplied and installed by the manufacturer.

Minicomputers

Minicomputers are, as their name implies, physically smaller than mainframes. They usually have fewer peripherals and support fewer users. Minicomputers can run several jobs at once, but they are not normally efficient at large batch processing jobs.

While a special environment is not normally necessary, it is often advisable to have some air-conditioning and a separate power supply. Minis are often operated by 'non-computer' people and probably use computer packages written by specialist software companies. Often the applications are not supported by programmers except on call from the software company. They are sold mainly by suppliers who may not be the manufacturer, but who will also supply the software and provide a working system referred to as 'turnkey'.

Minicomputers now have large memories and good communication systems that enable them to be linked directly to mainframe computers and, in this mode, are often used by large companies as part of a network linked to a central mainframe computer.

Microcomputer

Microcomputers tend to be, stand alone, small, single user systems doing one job at a time, although the advent of local area networking (LAN) systems, in which hard disk and printer resources are shared by a number of microcomputers, is changing this view somewhat. They comprise the following elements:

- keyboard
- microprocessor
- memory
- screen
- external storage

They do not need a special working environment, and operate principally with standard packages supplied with the machine. They are mostly sold by suppliers rather than manufacturers and can be purchased 'over the counter'. The buyer is dependent on the packages supplied and on the manuals for installation and use.

Control of input

There are several general points regarding the control of input which apply to whichever type of computer system being used. These are concerned with two types of input, batch and transaction, and two stages of input, data collection and data input.

Batch and transaction input are the two ways in which data enters the system. Batch input is like an elevator, dealing with a batch of items and moving them through the system in a block. Transaction input is like an escalator, receiving items of data as and when they arrive and dealing with them individually. The controls required are significantly different.

The four levels of control, i.e., correctness, completeness, security and auditability can be considered in the form of a matrix for batch and transaction input, as follows:

	Batch	**Transaction**
Correctness	Batch totals outside system checked when input	External transaction log matched to . . .
	Batch codes entered once only for batch.	. . .internal transaction log.
	Checks correctness of batched fields only.	Codes on every transaction.
	Enter/Verify.	Edits for validity.
Completeness	Batch count.	Transaction numbering check, i.e., missing nos.
	Batch record numbering	External transaction log, matched to...
	Batch record sheet.	. . .internal transaction log.
Security	Batch reference.	Transaction reference.
	Authorisation signature on batch.	Authority per transaction.
	Password related to batch type.	Password related to transaction type.
Auditablity	Batch reference codes.	Transaction codes.
	Batch tests on hard copy.	Audit trails retrievable from log file.

The input point in the computer application is critical for control as it is at this point that the vast majority of errors can be made. It does not only apply to the routine accounting data, but also the updating of files such as the issue of new customer and supplier accounts and the payroll procedures for starters and leavers.

Correctness

On input of data, it is normally required to establish the correctness of the data in several ways, covering:

- descriptions
- data coding
- data values

Descriptions can be checked in two ways when input. Firstly, is the field content correct?, i.e. alpha or numeric, and secondly, does the description exist?, e.g. by checking a file of descriptions. A description could, for example, be a customer name.

Data coding can be checked as to the correct number of digits and whether the code exists in the coding system. In addition it can be checked for correct relationships, eg if the batch is one of purchase invoices, then the code should be a purchase code. Check digits can be used to ensure that transposition and other errors are detected.

Data values can be checked by extension, e.g. quantity times price equals value; and by addition, e.g. do the separate values add up to an independently calculated total, as employed in batch control systems?

The above checks and examples are not exhaustive and depend upon the system, the hardware in use and the level of access to files and the appropriate validation routines. The following is a general guide:

Mainframes: Input to mainframe systems may be batch or transaction in type and could be by users or specially trained input staff. Validation could be handled so that the checking at the input stage is limited to field content, field sizes and value checks with the other checks being carried out as the first stage of the processing. This could mean that data is rejected sometime after the data input takes place. In such instances, special controls need to be set up to ensure that the corrected data is subsequently returned to the system. Suspense accounts or dumps for incorrect coding should be avoided wherever possible as they lead to laziness in coding and sloppy control.

Minicomputers: It is more usual for input to be checked at the time the input takes place. This input could be batch or transaction in type, but is more likely to be transaction oriented. The rejection of incorrect data usually stops the input process until the rejected data is corrected.

Microcomputers It is almost certain that input will be checked as it is being keyed in and rejected at this point. This makes it very difficult to input incorrect data though the input process may become rather longer as a result.

Completeness

To ensure that all the data is input it is necessary to know what is expected so that what is received can be checked. This will avoid both missing data and duplicated data. This is usually achieved by transaction count and transaction referencing. If batch input is taking place then the batch will consist of a number of transactions with certain references, for example, 21 transactions numbered from 149 to 169. The system will then check that this is what it has received. A more rigorous method of ensuring completeness is to check, in this way, not only the number of transactions but also their arithmetic total. With transaction processing a log must be maintained of what has been input so that it may be checked against what has been received.
Sequencing of pre-numbered documents can be used as a check, it is not easy, however, to ensure that they are used in sequence, subsequently allowances have to be made for cancelled documents. None of these approaches copes with the problem of knowing whether all batches, or transactions, are ready for input. Purchase invoices can still remain in a manager's drawer awaiting authorisation!

Security

Security of input is essential to prevent corruption of data, caused either accidentally or deliberately. The way security is handled depends once again on the system, in terms of both software and hardware.

Mainframe & Minis: Security of input has to be handled at two levels, receipt of the data from the generation point, and the actual input itself. The first level is dealt with by authorisation procedures outside the system. The second level is effected by passwords associated with the transaction type being input. There is the additional problem that **the security arrangements may be bypassed**, enabling unauthorised access to the system from outside.

Micros: Security here is the password associated with the user who is often the authorisation person. Once again the control here is *who can input what into the system?* In such circumstnces frequent changes to passwords and rotation of the responsibility for initiating and authorising such changes are recommended.

'Auditability'

Auditability refers to the way the system is designed in terms of the audit function. This entails being aware of the auditors' requirements in the initial design phase and incorporating the appropriate codes, validation checks, records and controls necessary for an audit to be carried out effectively. Obviously, one way of ensuring this is to involve the auditors at the initial design phase. They should at least approve the design report, and then comment and make suggestions when the system specification is produced. Auditing is, however, a continuous task and all system changes must be carefully examined in this context.

An auditable system is one in which it is clear who has done what, where transactions originated along with their intermediate and final destinations. This, however, only ensures that data can be audited, and it is also important to audit what the system does, i.e. the programming steps. This means that the auditor has to be able to check what every program does and how it can affect files. The auditor should also be able to print files to check that their content is correct.

When carrying out the audit, auditors will not check every transaction but will want to take a sample which is statistically large enough to give a high level of confidence in the system's performance. They will then check the sample thoroughly to ensure that all is well.

In large computer-based systems, particularly where data base management systems are in use, the auditors will want to use auditing programs to do the work. They may want to input an audit sample and follow it through the complete system, checking every step of the processing. This type of auditing is called **integrated testing** and is being developed by large auditing companies. When a system is originally designed it is a good idea to check with the auditors as to their intentions so that the required facilities can be incorporated.

Control of processing

Data input successfully into the system will be moved around, added to files, transferred, calculated, accumulated, etc. This is generally referred to as processing. Processing involves many different steps which can be looked at in several main categories:

- sorting
- merging and updating
- calculating
- storing

The accuracy with which this processing is carried out depends upon:

- the accuracy of the data
- the efficiency of the software
- the strict control of processing procedures
- the reliability of the hardware

The accuracy of data input has been dealt with earlier. The efficiency of the software depends to a large extent upon the test procedures carried out and on the way the software is protected from accidental or deliberate corruption.

Efficiency and protection of software

The first vital rule is to ensure that, for all software, every processing step is checked. The program should enable three things to be effected:

- decide what will be the result of the program step
- carry out processing
- check that the desired result is achieved

A typical example of a '**Run To Run**' control is as follows:

		Monetary Values
(a)	Opening balance	35,670
	Value of transactions entered	23,115
	Closing balance	58,785

(b) Ad 23,115 of transactions to the file, i.e. merge.
(c) Add the new file and check total equals 58,785.

Another rule that should apply to data movement within the computer is that a log should be maintained of:

- every move that takes place including a record of who enters, who checks, and a printout of who has done what
- the data and its value
- the source from which the data derived
- the destination of the data.

Testing

The efficiency of the software should be checked by testing it with a realistic set of information containing both correct and incorrect data to see if the software responds correctly. Testing of software applies to all types of computers and should cover the following levels:

- program testing
- run testing
- systems testing

Each program is tested when written, and corrected until the test is satisfactory. With modern computer software there are many aids such as, for example, fourth generation languages for the programmer to use when writing and testing programs.

Several programs working together form a run, and this is tested as and when the programs making up the run have all been tested individually. Apart from ensuring that the programs all work together to achieve the objective of the run, it is important to check that the run time and use of the computer agrees with the planned requirements.

Program and run testing are carried out within the systems development environment and do not directly involve the user. The systems test, however, must be carried out with the user and the computer section playing their respective roles. Systems test data should be run by computer personnel and the results should be checked by systems development staff and user personnel.

It is important to prepare a schedule of expected results and to ensure that all features of the system are tested. This is effected at two levels:

- contrived systems test
- real systems test

The contrived systems test contains deliberate faults and errors aimed at testing the validation and control procedures. Every conceivable variation of data should be included, e.g. numeric fields should be alpha and vice

versa, batch balances should be wrong; impossible codes, dates and values should be used. The test should also contain correct data.
Following the contrived test, when errors have been detected and corrected, the real test is run. This comprises a test using a representative period of real data, perhaps for the preceding month, for which actual results are available on the old system. This real test may throw up additional problems caused by the volume of data and errors not previously discovered.

Program maintenance

Once the tests have indicated the efficiency of the software, it is necessary to ensure that there is adequate protection afforded to the master and live program libraries to safeguard against:

- unauthorised amendment
- accidental corruption

Unauthorised amendments are best prevented by a strict procedure for controlling all amendments, for whatever reason. Once the amendment to software is approved and is carried out, the whole of the software involved must be tested rigorously to ensure the amendment has not weakened control. This is equally true for:

- in-house program amendments
- amendments by third-party software suppliers
- issue of updated packages

Accidental corruption should not be an event which is discovered when malfunction occurs, i.e. by default. The reason is obvious since the default might not be noticed and considerable damage can be effected to the quality of the data. Software should be inspected and checked regularly to ensure it is functioning correctly, for example by checking against specially constructed test files with test data. This philosophy holds true for mainframes (particularly so), minis and micros.
Program libraries must be handled with great care. There should normally be three libraries:

- load library
- temp library
- test library

Live programs are held in the load library and all live work is effected using these programs. Programs which have been tested but not yet accepted by operators are held in the temp library. Programs being amended or new programs are held in the test library. Needless to say, transfers between libraries must be handled with care and strict control must be exercised regarding the authorisation and timing of transfers between libraries.

Introducing new systems

When a new system is being installed it is frequently replacing an existing system. This means that existing documentation and procedures have to be changed over to the new system. Changeover can be carried out in four main ways:

- pilot trial
- parallel running
- phased implementation
- direct changeover

Pilot trial schemes are smaller versions of the new system and may operate for one section of the company, or for a subset of the envisaged system, for example a selected number of customers. When the pilot scheme is proved to be effective it is extended to the full scope of the system.

Parallel running, as its name implies, means running the new system alongside the old system until the operation is seen to be satisfactory. This does mean extra work but it is an effetive and safe method of changeover; incidentally, this method often highlights irregularities in the existing system when the respective results are checked in detail!

Phased implementation means bringing the new system into operation in stages. Each stage is introduced on either a parallel or a direct changeover basis.

Direct changeover is when the old system ceases one day and the new system starts the next day. This is the most difficult way in which to implement a new system, but there are situations where the work involved in running parallel is either too much or is simply impracticable.

It is not uncommon for a major system to be implemented in a combination of these ways.

Control of processing procedures

Processing procedures consist of a number of key elements which can be examined under six headings:

- timing
- processing control
- run failures
- file errors
- data losses
- security

and each of these is assessed in the following paragraphs.

Timing

Each job must be processed within a schedule and according to a sequence that ensures that the intended processing not only takes place, but takes place at the right time. For example, certain jobs should not be run before the data is complete; certain jobs must be run at the end of the day, and so on.

Such processing schedules are particularly relevant for mainframe and minicomputers that are used as central processing services. For mini and microcomputers used independently the timing is controlled largely by the user; nevertheless the sequence is still important.

Processing control

This task ensures that what should happen does happen, e.g. that payslips are produced for all 300 people on the payroll; that the total cash paid into the bank is allocated and posted to the Sales Ledger. This means that the software should include the printing or display of control totals for checking by the users of the system. The software should also include processing checks such as '*next file version*' on the file header. This is a control field held by the software which says, '*Last time this program was used the file version was 3/15 so the next file version should be 3/16*'. If the file version does not tally, the software should report it to the operator who can then load the correct file. This information should be held as external control information which will take the form of run instructions and a processing log.

Run instructions should contain details of:

- what the run does
- the files involved
- the file versions
- the controls applying
- action in the event of problems
- run sequence

- relationship of the run to other jobs

On mainframes and large minis this is often part of the job control program resident in the machine which is updated on each run. For micros it is essential that it is in the operator log maintained by the user. The processing log should state what happened during the last run and have space for the operator to record details of what happens during the current run.

Run failure

Run failures occur for many reasons, including loss of power, machine failure, lack of resources, operator error, faulty programs, or missing data. When any of these events happen the operator will have to abandon the run, establish the reason for the problem and take corrective action. This action comprises:

- establishing the reason for failure
- recording what happened
- recording what action was taken to correct the failure
- re-running the job and recording results

Occasionally, operators may by-pass these procedures and just reload and re-run in the hope that all will go well, and sometimes it does. With batch and interactive processing, however, when failure occurs, it could have affected the files held in the system, so a re-run would almost certainly not correct the problem.

File errors

File errors arise from four principal causes:

- loading incorrect files
- machine failure
- incorrect re-run procedure
- incorrect data

Perhaps the main cause of file errors is the loading of an incorrect file or the wrong version of the correct file. This is often not discovered until the control reports are being checked by the data control function and, of course, means that the whole run has been a complete waste of time. This can be overcome if file references are held for the next run, and a check will then register that the wrong file is being used. Prevention is far better than cure.
The occurrence of machine failure, particularly the failure of a tape drive

or a disk drive, can physically ruin a file. A disk '*crash*', so called because the read/write head crashes onto the surface of the disk, not only spoils the file but also the disk itself. This can be coped with only by a re-run to recreate the file that has been spoilt.

An incorrect re-run procedure will often corrupt a file by continuing to use a file that might have been previously affected by the run failure. Files can be transformed into rubbish by careless operating procedures, particularly when an operator wants to hide the fact that a re-run has been necessary.

When incorrect data gets through the validation programs it can corrupt the file being processed, and these errors are usually overcome only by re-processing with correcting data.

Data losses

Data losses are supposedly impossible; unfortunately, this is not true, and data can be lost at every point from creation to final output. Losses can occur through carelessness (i.e. humam error), machine fault and system errors.

Human error covers such instances as quite literally throwing data away by mistake and such transgressions as forgetting to input data but making up the relevant controls!

Machine faults simply cause individual characters or records to be dropped between the point where the fault occurred and the point where correction takes place. Such gaps are normally discovered when the controls are checked, but this may not be until after the run has been completed.

System errors involve the incorrect operation of programs which simply do not handle data correctly, for example, overflow errors caused by numeric data which is larger than the maximum size allocated by the program or operating environment.

Security

When processing data it is perfectly possible for the system to fail: in fact at some time it is certain to happen. It is, therefore, essential that correct procedures are followed to ensure that when the system fails the situation can be recovered so that no data is lost.

Recovery procedures can be handled at several levels:

- full re-run
- partial re-run or continuation
- off-line update
- 'catch-up'

Full re-run, as the term implies, means starting the job again, ignoring the stage that had been reached when the failure occurred. This is quite time consuming and is frequently the method used in batch processing on mainframes and minis. It means that it is necessary to have a copy of the start files and the transactions for the complete run. As this has to be standard procedure for management of files it should present no problem. Partial re-run or continuation is regularly used for transaction processing on all forms of computers, but does require the ability to have control totals at the time of failure, together with a detailed log of transactions accepted correctly, so the processing can be restarted at the appropriate point. This should be possible either automatically or under operator control.
'*Off-line*' recovery is a procedure used in modern network systems, where data is processed on a mainframe via a local minicomputer or controller. If the connection with the mainframe fails, the minicomputer continues and when the connection with the mainframe is restored the recovery from the minicomputer storage facility is carried out automatically.
'*Catch-up*' is the lowest level of recovery, when the processing ceases on the machine and is continued manually. The manual information is then input when the computer becomes available again, either by a summary batch or a series of individual transactions. Once again the computer should indicate the last transaction received.

Performance monitoring

Computer operations need to be closely monitored and this is generally effected in two ways:

- operations log
- computer log

The operations log is maintained by the operations supervisor and records events chronologically. There is a wide variety of layouts for an operations log but, whatever the layout, it should include the following information:

- date
- jobs run
- re-runs
- reason for re-run
- problems
- machine failures

In addition to the operations log a record of files used should be maintained. If the computer centre is large enough, a librarian will manage this aspect.

The operations log is passed from one supervisor to the next, and this is obviously important where shifts are working.
The computer log is the record of processing which is maintained automatically by the computer. This is often referred to as job accounting. Where the feature is available it is very useful, but it does not replace the operations log. Job accounting does, however, provide detailed timing for jobs and shows the use of resources at any particular point in time. Some larger computers will, on request, display a screen showing graphically the current use of the computer resources.

Control of storage

Computer backing storage for business processing is usually held on one of four main media:

- fixed disks
- disk packs (cartridge)
- floppy disks
- magnetic tape

Control of storage for all media covers several activities, which relate to four areas:

- data processing
- databases
- data administration
- physical handling

Data processing

Files of information held on one or other of the media are generated, updated and deleted as part of the processing procedures. Controls must exist to ensure that this is carried out successfully and files must, therefore, be carefully named and numbered and have suitable priority and access restrictions. The quality of the data held on files is in turn determined by the quality of input and processing. In addition, special procedures should be used for ensuring files do not contain redundant data. Such procedures can consist of regular file checks and printouts together with regular deletion of old data onto tape or paper. Files should be monitored constantly to keep them as small as possible and of the highest quality. All principal files should carry control information to enable the following to be established:

- number of records on file
- age pf recprds
- average access and hit rates
- obsolete or slow moving records
- number of additions/deletions – since an earlier date and possibly since generation

Value controls will also be needed where appropriate, together with version number and last run date.

Databases

To operate a database, software called a database management system or DBMS is often used. This software determines how the data elements and their relationships are defined and consequently how the database is structured. The system designer has to understand the DBMS thoroughly and more importantly, exactly how the data is going to be used by all the systems which will have access to the database.
There are two main ways in which the database systems may be designed:

- relational
- hierarchical

Relational databases work in a similar way to related files. They are not, strictly speaking, databases but file management systems which operate by relating the data held in a number of files. It is possible to find data by being directed from the primary file to secondary files, and so on, for several levels of files. Data is given a file address, and this is where the data is held for any system need, depending on its relation to other data elements.
Hierarchical databases work by linking all data elements in a hierarchy which starts with the highest and works down to the smallest elements of data. The data elements are designated owners and members, and data is grouped in sets. Members of one set could be owners of a lower sub-set and so the hierarchy grows. In this form of database every data element is coded with its level and the level of which it is both owner and member. In this way every element of data can be traced, provided it is correctly related to other elements by the system designer.
The success sof the database system depends almost entirely on the efficiency with which this design task is carried out. Therefore the designer needs to use a data dictionary so that he or she can both keep up to date with the current appearance of the database and add additional data elements to it. The data dictionary lists all data with records used and gives its relative place in the database, together with the systems and programs that use the

data. Without a data dictionary the generation of a DBMS is virtually impossible.

Data administration

Perhaps the most significant implication of database systems is the need for careful control of data. It is normal, where a DBMS is in operation, to appoint a data administrator whose job is to maintain the data dictionary. This calls for considerable knowledge and understanding of data flows within the organisation and of the way data is used. The data administrator must understand the following:

- what data flows through the organisation
- the relationships between data elements
- the way data is used by the systems
- the potential for corruption of data by unauthorised access
- who requires access to what data and with what frequency

When data is held on a database stringent controls must apply with regard to who is allowed to change the data, since any change affects all the systems using the data. The advantage of consistency becomes a major disadvantage, however, if the data is incorrect, as it will be wrong in every system which uses it! Data administration is no easy task and, as the quality of the database controls the quality of the output, it is a key factor.

Physical handling

As described previously, it is possible for files to be lost or damaged so it is important to ensure that security copies are maintained. For fixed disks, copies should be taken regularly onto tape or removable disks, which are then stored separately off-site. This is particularly true of mainframe and minicomputers where the copying of '*dumping*' must be a routine part of the processing activity. For microcomputers with small disks and/or floppy disk storage, copies should be taken at the end of each operation so that, if the disk in use at the moment is spoiled, at least one copy of the disk before the present run is available. It might seem wasteful to complete a particular job such as payroll, and then some time copying the new files onto spare floppies for safety, but it will almost certainly save many hours work.
The normal approach for security files is to hold three levels, or generations, as follows:

- grandfather
- father
- son

It is also important to keep copies on file of the transactions that went from grandfather to father and from father to son, so that in the event of loss or spoilage it is always possible to re-run or recover the situation.
It is desirable to ensure the physical protection of the files from fire, theft, damage, etc, by ensuring that they are located in special containers and handled with care. Instructions for handling of computer storage media should be issued to all concerned. All users should also be aware of the need to ensure copies are kept of all software so that, in the event of software being damaged or lost, it can be regenerated.
Many users of microprocessors are not aware of the difference between the ROM and RAM memory in the machine. ROM (read only memory) is non-volatile and remains intact when power is switched off. RAM (random access memory) is, however, volatile and the data actively being processed by the machine will disappear when the power is switched off. It is essential, therefore, that when data in RAM is to be retained, for example a current spreadsheet model, it is copied onto tape or disk before closing the system down.

Control of output

Visible output from all types of computer falls into three principal categories:

- documents
- reports
- screen displays

although output is also possible in other forms, e.g. to disk, tape or computer output to microfilm/microfiche (COM). The management and control of output relates to three aspects:

- layout (format)
- content
- distribution

Documents

This category covers a very wide range of possible output including orders, invoices, statements, remittance advice notes, cheques, etc. Some of these documents will be pre-numbered or will have sequential numbers allocated during printing. Such documents must be carefully controlled within the criteria of completeness, correctness and security mentioned earlier. They must also be designed to carry the addresses and descriptive information required by the recipient.

These documents will normally be pre-printed and require careful set up in the printer with tests for alignment before printing commences. If this is not effected spoilt documents will hinder subsequent sequence checking. Numbering of such documents is important for reference as is the retention of copies held on paper, microfilm or magnetic medium. The handling of large volumes of documents requires careful control but this is normally only associated with mainframes and large minis.

Every computer run (for all types of computer) should provide a printout or screen display showing:

- quantity of documents produced
- total value, if invoices, etc
- numbering sequence, from/to
- date and run reference

The operator or user should then ensure that a copy of the output file (print file) is produced onto tape or disk. This is particularly important on micros as most minis and mainframes do so automatically. Once the controls have been checked and copies taken, the documents can then be distributed according to defined instructions. In the case of value stationery (eg cheques) strict adherence to controls must be observed and, for example, documents wasted by alignment checking must be retained and cancelled accordingly.

Reports

Reports can be produced in three main ways:

- routine
- regular
- ad hoc

Routine reports will be produced automatically as part of the run concerned. They could be control reports, listing documents or statistical reports giving the new position on, say, debtors, following an invoice run. The content and format of the reports will depend on the use to which they will be put, but they will usually consist of text and numbers printed on plain computer paper, rather than pre-printed stationery.

Regular reports will be specially designed computer runs which access files and collect, sort and organise data ready for printing. Such regular reports might be accounting reports, profit and loss accounts, balance sheets, marketing statistics, monthly aged debt analyses and so on. The content and format will be prescribed by the users and they will contain a mixture of text and numbers as required, sometimes on pre-printed paper. Distribution should be recorded on the output log indicating that the reports were produced and despatched. Reports can also be produced in graphical format if the appropriate hardware and software is available.
Ad hoc reports are those required on a random basis, such as a one-off print of details of a particular supplier or customer. This category also covers an occasional special reporting requirement which may necessitate some specific programming effort.

Displays

With modern computer terminals and with the wide use of microcomputers, a considerable amount of information is being presented via displays on screens (VDUs – visual display units). Displays can be simple lists of file contents, specially formatted screens representing documents, or graphical representations of data. There is considerable flexibility in the presentation of information in this way, with the added facility of being able to print it if necessary, or project it onto large screens. With minicomputers and microcomputers the creation of screens is in the hands of the users, within the limitations of the software. Control is, therefore, difficult to enforce, except by the control of access to the system and this subject is dealt with in the next section.

Control of access

With the wide proliferation of computers and computer terminals, together with the telecommunication channels which link them, control of access has become a major problem, becuase the more flexible the system and the greater the range of facilities, the easier it becomes to gain access. Access should be controlled in the same way that the physical access to confidential information and cash has always been controlled, and that is via a complex system of keys. For example, the gaining of access to the cashbox probably requires:

(a) a key to the building
(b) knowledge of the office in which it is kept

(c) a key to the office
(d) a knowledge of the drawer in which the safe key is kept
(e) a key to the drawer
(f) the safe key
(g) knowledge of the combination on the cashbox lock

This mixture of knowledge and keys, seven in all, should be adequate to protect even the most delicate of information. It can apply equally to all types of computers and would work like this:

(a) Personal number to start the system – only issued to authorised users.
(b) Knowledge of which files to access.
(c) Password appropriate to access those files – only specific authorised users.
(d) Knowledge of the access keys appropriate to the file.
(e) The pre-defined password or code to add as a prefix to the key – second level of authority.
(f) The sequence of the key on the file.
(g) Knowledge of the actual key code access the information required – third level of authority.

Though this system might appear complex, it will suffice to protect the majority of commercial systems and the password at **(c)** could be changed periodically while those at all levels would be changed when authorised people resigned.

Software controls

To operate an access system the software must be designed to:

- stop access if the appropriate code is not used
- enable passwords to be changed easily.

Ideally, access systems should limit the number of invalid attempts at entry – e.g. automatic logging off after three invalid attempts to access the system and also when input devices are idle for a specified period of time.

The levels of access control can easily be built into software, but many of the packages offered for use on mini and microcomputers do not have adequate password facilities. The vast majority of codes can be '*cracked*' given time and perseverence, just as most locks can be '*picked*'. The objective is to make access difficult. This can be achieved, but maintenance of security depends as much on personal discipline, as on the facilities afforded by the software.

Password controls

It is preferable for users to set their own personal passwords but where these are provided to them the issue must be controlled with suitable records and signatures. Users should be trained to remember passwords at all levels and not to write them down on paper or on the side of the terminal!
Disclosure of delicate passwords should be a reason for dismissal as breach of contract and passwords should be changed frequently to protect users as well as the system. Special cards containing data can be used, but these can be easily lost or misappropriated.
It must be accepted that it is probably impossible to deny access to a really determined '*hacker*', but it can be made extremely difficult, particularly by denying the opportunity for access attempts to take place.

Ownership of data

The question of the ownership of data is an important one that must be answered if the successful management and control of computer applications is to be ensured. The question can be examined at four levels:

- personal data
- information about people
- corporate information
- sensitive corporate information

In each case it is for the people and/or corporations involved to make the appropriate decisions about what is to be protected, with or without reason. There are, however, some general points to be considered and these are discussed in the following paragraphs.

Personal data

Personal data is private information about the individual which that individual should own and control with only a privileged few being allowed access, and then only with the individual's prior agreement. Such ifnormation might comprise, for example, medical or psychiatric information recorded for the individual's benefit and only available to those whom the individual decides should treat him or her. It might also cover information on personal financial circumstances, etc.
Many people are quite willing to enter an enormous amount of detail on forms they are asked to complete for a wide variety of reasons. If this

voluntary information was brought together with information available in other systems, then a great deal of personal information could be collected, much of it of a highly sensitive nature. This can be illustrated by considering the effect of the combination of data from the following bodies within the UK:

- medical authorities
- banks
- credit companies
- insurance companies
- DHSS
- tax authorities
- police

It is generally recognised that individuals should be protected by legislation to prevent the unauthorised access and accumulation of such data. In addition, people might be encouraged to refuse to give information which is irrelevant to the enquirer. Many consider that individuals should be given the opportunity to access their own rcords and amend them when necessary, deleting whatever they think is irrelevant, although certain constraints in cases such as police records should apply.

Information about people

Organisations collect a considerable amount of data about the people they employ, starting with the application form and continuing with personal appraisals, pay records, etc, during the person's employment. This information belongs to the person and not to the organisation and, on leaving, the person should have the right to delete all that information from the files, or to lock it away with a special password key that only he or she knows.

During the period of employment, only identified authorised personnel should have access to that information. Great care should be exercised in the recording and maintenance of personal records and every individual must be allowed access to such records to see what others might be allowed to see. If there is anything that management would not want the person to see it should not be recorded on the file. This concept applies equally to information which is held in clerical files.

A critical point in this area is the recognition that opinion and fact are two different entities. If an employee is constantly late it is a matter of fact. Someone's opinion that a person is unreliable is just that – i.e. a personal opinion, and one which should not be recorded on the person's files. The passing of the *Data Protection Act*, 1984 indicates the growing realisation of the dangers in this area and the responsibilities which organisations must assume.

Corporate information

Corporate information is available in published annual reports. More detailed information is available within the organisation to those with access to it for reasons of day to day activities. Access varies with job responsibilities and to some extent with position. It is commonplace for corporate information of value to competitors to be accessible not only to top management, but also to clerical and data processing staff at all levels. It is important, therefore, that access to all data is controlled by knowing:

- what is available?
- where?
- how is it accessed?
- by whom?
- for what reasons?

Once this is known, access can be controlled so that any leakage, accidental or otherwise, is identifiable and can be prevented from recurring.
Files of data both within the computer and in filing cabinets should be clearly labelled as to their nature, e.g.:

- open access – operational
- restricted access – operational
- confidential – authorised access
- very confidential – special authority level
- closed – attended access only

Once such a system is established it should be very carefully controlled by the managers involved and subject to regular scrutiny.

Sensitive corporate information

Information of a particularly sensitive nature, possibly about product development plans or new market strategy, should not be held on computer files. It should be kept on paper and held in the most secure area possible. Such '*secret*' information will only be accessible to the very top people, who are generally suitably vetted from a security viewpoint.
This does not, of course, prevent such information from being stolen or

leaked, but as much protection as possible should be provided. If the information is computerised, encryption of the data is possible and, if proper standards are adopted, breaking the code will take a considerable time. People will, however, go to great lengths to break encrypted codes, the danger, therefore, remains, however remote. In addition, coding and decoding slows down processing times, often excessively.

Responsibility for systems integrity and control

Responsibility

Titles of job positions vary considerably between organisations and it is not feasible to specify by title who should be responsible for systems integrity and control. Nevertheless, a single person must be made responsible to the Chief Executive for ensuring:

- systems are designed to rigorous standards
- systems are operated in the defined manner
- access to information is tightly controlled
- regular review and amendment of passwords, etc takes place

For the purposes of the following paragraphs the responsible person will be termed the *Information Control Manager* (ICM). In smaller businesses this may be an additional job for an existing manager but, no matter what size of organisation or computer, the job must be done by someone.

Standards

It is essential that standards for the control of computer applications are written and published within the organisation. It is, after all, difficult to try to enforce standards about which people have not been informed! These standards should cover:

- software design
- control levels and audit trails
- access levels
- categorisation of confidentiality
- operational procedures
- file handling procedures and security

- output control standards
- contingency arrangements

Separate standards should be available for mainframe applications, minicomputer applications and microcomputer operations, The *ICM* should have overriding authority to ensure that people not adhering to the standards are suitably disciplined. It should also be possible for the *ICM* to change passwords at any time and to change authority and access levels.
All new systems developments, purchase of packages and use of computers should be vetted by the *ICM* before they are approved. This is to ensure that they conform to the defined standards. Unless this is carried out, fragmentation will occur and the standards will soon fall into misuse.

Conclusion

This contribution had endeavoured to provide sufficient information for the reader to understand the scope and extent of the work necessary to ensure effective control of computer applications. As organisations become more and more systems-dependent the importance of such control can only increase.
The principles are largely the same for all types of computers, but the level and degree obviously vary as from the mainframe to the microcomputer. These definitions will soon disappear into the '*greyer*' terms of large and small computes. No mattr how they are mxied together in networks, or whether they are used as stand alone machines, they will need to be rigorously managed and controlled to maintain the integrity so essential to successful business practice.

5

Database Systems

R Dixon BA, MA and G Rawlings BSc, MSc

What is a database?

What is data?

Before considering a database, it is reasonable to ask 'what is meant by data'? Data is the raw material from which information is obtained. It comes in many forms; in the business environment basic details are recorded about the day-to-day state of the business. Indeed, an insight into the meaning of data can be gained by considering a company in which three manual systems are in operation, as follows:

Accounts system

The purpose of this system is principally to record the business transactions of the company with its suppliers/customers for the goods and services received/supplied, such that the financial state of the company can be determined.

The data in this system would include the invoices and payments in respect of the goods and services received and supplied. This data can then be processed to provide the information required by the company.

Stock Control

The purpose of this system is to monitor the number of items of each product held in stock to enable the overall level of inventories to be controlled.

The data in this system would include the current stock level for each product, and the re-order level and lead times for orders. This data would then be processed to provide purchase order information and routine stock reports.

Payroll

The purpose of this system is to hold information about individual employees together with their tax and NI details, and from this and other inputs produce individual payslips and cheques as well as maintaining the wages and salary accounts.

Within the payroll the data consists of personal information on the employees and their tax/NI status, and may require additional data such as the number of hours worked, time off due to sickness etc. The information produced from this data is the payroll for that week or month.

In all the systems outlined above the data is processed to provide information; diagrammatically the processes can be represented by:

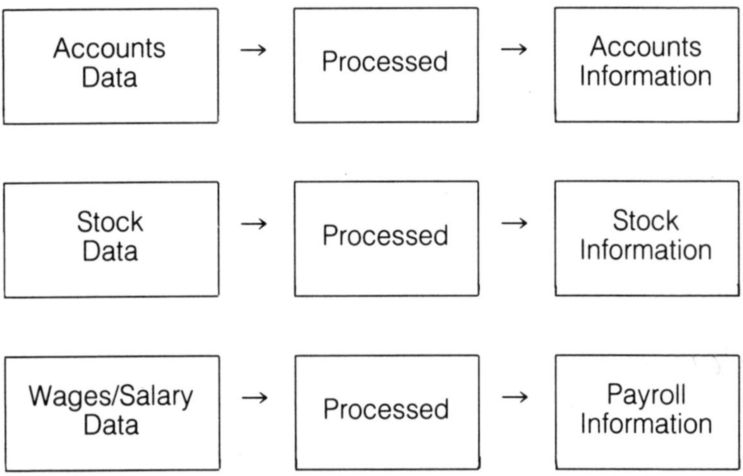

Figure 1 The processing of data

In each case the data may be considered as being kept in a filing cabinet, and as new data or any data amendments arrive they are added to the files contained within the filing cabinet. The processing consists of the extraction and manipulation of the data contained within the filing cabinet to produce the required reports and in this form the data has been transformed into usable information.

Processing data

In the three examples quoted above the data is collected, maintained and updated in the conceptual filing cabinet. This provides the base from which various specific pieces of data are extracted and combined to produce information, for example in the accounts system the data may be processed to produce:

- a sales ledger
- a purchase ledger
- a nominal ledger

from which further reports on the financial welfare of the company can be derived.
Similarly the stock control and payroll systems will use the filing cabinet to develop their reports, the process being as follows:

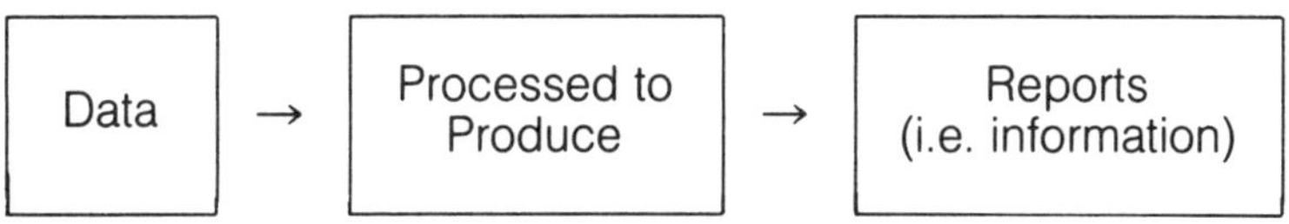

Figure 2

With the advent of computerised systems this manual process was replicated by business applications software. Generally, such software comprises specific programs designed to create, maintain and update the data in a series of dedicated data files together with further programs to process this data to provide the reports required by management. This type of system can be referred to as a traditional file-processing system and is characterised by the lack of integration of data 'belonging' to different systems.
The operation of these computer based systems closely resemble those of the manual system. A computerised accounts system of this type generally follows standard book-keeping practice and, while it is is certainly faster and has less manual operations, it is essentially an automation of the equivalent manual system. Computerisation has added little that is new or unusual to the process, but frees time from routine procedures for the staff and results in quicker processing of the data.
A business will have many such systems, some of which are manual while others are computerised. In general these systems may operate independently in that the data is maintained separately. If, for

example, management were to request a one-off report that drew information from the accounts and payroll files then difficulties would arise. The information required from these files would need to be identified and an extraction program written. This could prove difficult because the file formats may not be the same and consequently the files may need to be converted to a common format. Even in the simplest case, the process of writing this extraction program may prove to be so complex that it is not worth attempting. This is the origin of the '*It's in the computer but we can't get it out*' syndrome. It was this proliferation of different data files for different systems and their relative independence which stimulated consideration of the idea of a central database.

The database concept

Continuing with the example, the concept of a central database can be explained as follows. Assuming once more that the systems are manual, all the data can now be considered to be contained in one central filing department.

The data within this department is organised and cross referenced in such a way that any user can gain access to any specific item of data which they require. In the same way each of the systems, accounts, stock control and payroll, whilst having different requirements, can draw from this central database as all current and historical data is provided and referenced. This database concept can be expressed diagrammatically as follows:

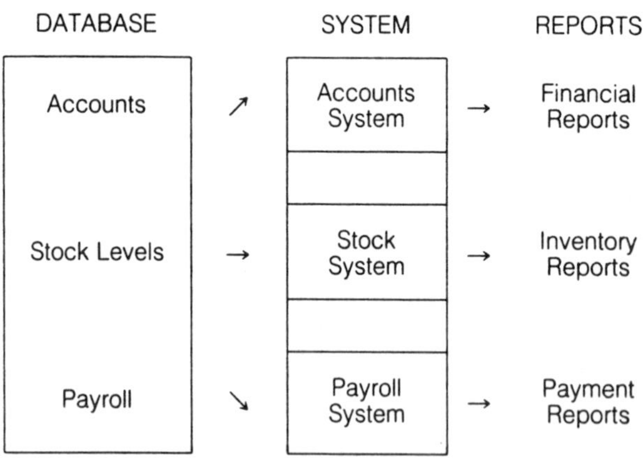

Figure 3 The database concept

The files have been centrally provided and all three systems can feed off the data provided within the database.

This concept of a common base of data provides obvious advantages, including the following:

- any item of data need only be held once within the database rather than being replicated on a number of discrete files.
- this reduction of data duplication overcomes the problem of conflicting reports which are produced where the same item of data has been updated on some files but not on others.

Centralisation also provides problems. Two consequences of the concentration of information in one place are:

- an increase in the complexity of maintaining the central database. A database administration section is usually set up to perform this function.
- an increase in vulnerability, since the database is held in one central place it is more exposed to a 'disaster', whether accidental or deliberate.

In summary a database is a central data store, where data is recorded and maintained in a standard way to allow access to that data. This concept of a database was developed without reference to computers, so how does a computer handle such a task?

Database management systems

A Database Management System (DBMS) is of software used to organise data so that it can be retrieved, modified or updated at will (the equivalent of a good filing clerk!) It is the link between the user and the data, giving access to the data required for the applications programs. A DBMS permits the data of an organisation to be processed as an integrated whole. It reduces the artificially imposed barriers of separate files for separate systems and permits users to access data in a manner that is more natural to them.

In terms of the three example systems, if all three were computerised systems based on a database, then a diagrammatic representation would be as follows:

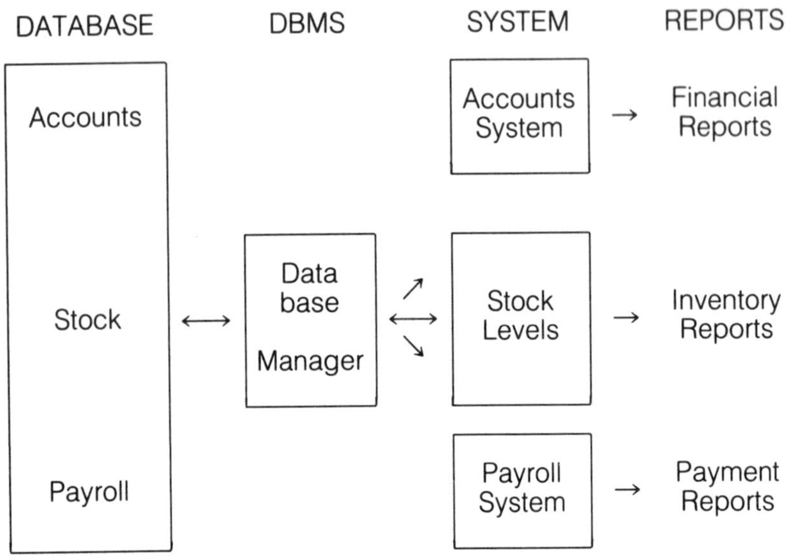

Figure 4 The role of the DBMS

The advantages and disadvantages of database systems

As discussed earlier, the integration of data into a database offers several advantages and also has some disadvantages. Some further points require consideration in relation to a computerised system. The database concept means that data is not only available but is available in a compatible form. As a result of this, more complex one-off queries are generally made easier to handle, and the time needed to develop new systems is usually reduced. In the earlier example a request was made for information which required data to be drawn from the accounts and payroll files. With a central database this request should present few problems. Additionally, the database concept provides the facility to exploit the inter-relationships within the data, e.g. a request for information about stock levels could be made conditional upon specified factors relating to accounts data and even payroll data if required. Potential problems regarding incompatible file formats are removed.

In the traditional computer file-processing environment a particular data item may be recorded in a similar form on many of the system's files. Hence if the data is amended or updated this change may need to be effected on several files. If a particular item of updating data is added to some files and not to others there is a possibility of having basic data items disagreeing and the resultant processed information being incompatible; this situation is not acceptable to the end user, and leads to mistrust of computer output. With a database the data need only be recorded once, and hence any amendments or updates need be effected just once thus facilitating the maintenance of data integrity. A secondary issue is that file space should consequently be less for the full database than for the equivalent file-processing systems.

In the file-processing system outlined on page 157, data is read directly from the data files and thus any structural changes to the contents of the data files must be accommodated by program changes to the system, consequently modification of the data files usually means a reprogramming exercise. In the database structures outlined in Figure 4 each system draws its data via the DBMS so that application programs (e.g. accounts, stock or payroll) interact with the DBMS rather than the database files themselves. Having the DBMS as the intermediary means that the type of data maintained within a particular database file may be more easily changed or modified. Thus the use of the database concept provides users with some degree of program/data independence.

The centralisation of data in this way carries a number of other benefits. It should lead to better data management as standards for maintenance can be defined and specialist functions allocated to ensure the quality of data. Economies of scale may also be available in two forms. By centralising the data management into a database administration function, fewer people need be involved thus relieving other staff of what, to them, may be the peripheral activity of data management. Secondly, the file processing structures, with the inherent data duplication and the loading of independent data and program files, can be expensive in terms of programmer/operator time. A database structure can release these skills for the possible development of systems rather than the maintenance and running of existing systems.

To summarise, the main advantages of a database in a computerised environment are:

- easier implementation of new systems
- maintenance of data integrity
- data/program independence resulting in easier modification to programs

- better data management
- complex one-off enquiries are easier to accommodate

The use of a database in a computerised environment also has some disadvantages. Centralisation makes the data vulnerable; a small failure somewhere can close the system down completely. Allied to this is the problem of data backup and recovery; since the system is more complex these procedures are also more complex, particularly if the system is on-line, in which case data recovery can prove difficult. The computing hardware required to support a DBMS may be *memory hungry*; consequently any existing hardware may need to be upgraded. It may be noted, however, that this is becoming less of a problem as the cost of hardware and software is generally decreasing. In summary, the principal disadvantages are:

- centralisation of data increases vulnerability as the failure of a small component of the system can disable the whole database.
- data backup and data recovery procedures are complex.
- the hardware required to support a DBMS may require upgrading.

Data and data models

Data

In Chapter 1 the database approach to systems was discussed and such systems can be represented as:

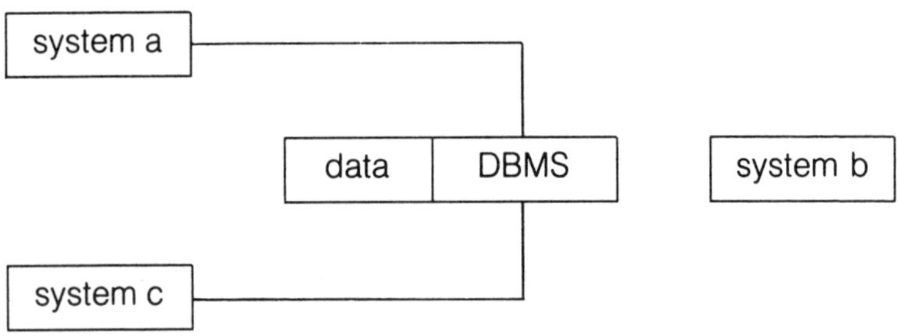

The database approach recognises that certain elements of data are common and relevant to more than one system within an organisation. Rather than think about a system, and the data required to support this system, the database approach concentrates on data as an entity in its own right. This approach can pose problems for an organisation as an analysis of data from this perspective will be required for the following purposes:

- identification of who uses what data, and for what purpose.
- identification of each element of data required.
- identification of the links and relationships that exist between each data element and the other data elements.

This analysis of the data structure is an enormous task for large organisations. In practice smaller units of the organisation, or a set of systems, can be examined to provide a reasonable framework for the development of the database. Even a superficial analysis of the data structure will show occurrences of duplication, and near duplication. This in itself is worthwhile just as an exercise to estimate the extent of the problems associated with data duplication and integrity. This analysis will allow a clearer picture of the data requirements for the organisation and, if a central database is implemented, allow some estimate of the benefits resulting from centralised data management and quality control. One of the aims of analysing the data within an organisation, as discussed above, was to: 'Identify the links and relationships that exist between each data element and the other data elements'. This is the key feature of the database approach; the fact that data is not recorded as a set of unrelated facts, but as a set of related information.

Data models

Currently there are principally three different methods of describing the relationships between the data elements, these are:

- the hierarchical model
- the network model
- the relational model

These are ways of representing the links between the data elements, as such they are a description or model of these linkages and each model has its strengths and weaknesses. Systems using the hierarchical and network models are fairly complex and are predominantly available on mainframe systems, hence they will be described only briefly in this booklet. The principles of the relational model will be described in more detail because the majority of DBMS available for the microcomputer use this model.

The hierarchical model

In this model the association between the data elements is modelled by a parent/child (also referred to as owner/member) relationship. The model here depends on every element being related to other elements as grandparent or child, except for the most *senior*, called the root, which has no parent. The relationship between the data elements can be drawn out like a family tree and, for this reason, this model is sometimes known as a tree model.
For example, the data structure of the hierarchical model can be represented as follows:

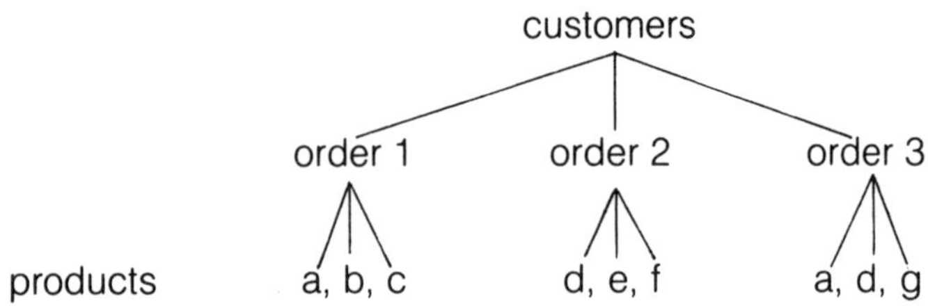

Figure 6 The data structure of the hierarchical model

In this example the root is the customer file, each customer can have an order, so the orders are the 'children' of the customers. Each order is for a product or range of products, these are the 'children' of the orders and the 'grandchildren' of the customers. The relationship between the various files is clear from the hierarchical structure and links between data items are defined by pointers.
The structure of a hierarchical database is predefined and is independent of the actual data contained within the various files; theoretically a change to records in a parent file will also update relevant records in the children files. The critical point about the data structure is that it is defined as a one-to-many relationship and thus no file has more than one parent (or owner).

The network model

The network model may be considered as an extension of the hierarchical model with the restriction that each data element, apart from the root, may have only one parent relaxed. Thus within a network model a data element may have many parents and many children, i.e. a many-to-many relationship. The network model is fairly complex and has its foundations in the mathematics of set

theory. This complexity, however, means that this model is able to represent a large number of real-world data structures.
CODASYL (Conference on Data Systems Languages) is a body that makes recommendations as to how computer software should be developed. In the area of DBMS they have defined the facilities that constitute an 'ideal' DBMS. CODASYL based systems use the network relationship between the data elements. Since hierarchical relationships are a subset of network relationships, these systems are equally applicable to the hierarchical model.

The relational model

Because of the need to define data relationships in advance, the hierarchical and network models may be subject to frequent reorganisation of data and are generally considered to be 'unfriendly' in terms of use by non-specialist personnel. An alternative approach to database management, the relational model, was first described by Edgar Codd of IBM in the early 1970s. One way of thinking about the relational model is to think of the data set out in a table; for example consider a simple stock monitoring system, this might be constructed around three databases, as follows:

a Database 1

The 'Customer File' which contains the names and addresses of the customers.
For example:

Account Number	Name	Address
F-4564	J GREEN	COVENTRY STREET, BRISTOL
M-4632	R BLACK	AIDEN TERRACE, NEWCASTLE
F-9832	T WHITE	ST JOHNS AVENUE, SKIPTON
M-9564	A BROWN	OAK HILL DRIVE, LANCASTER

Before describing the other two databases the above example will be used to describe how a database is set up using the relational model. The information presented in the database example above is presented in the form of a table, the columns being a specific piece of information, for example column 1 is the account number. Each row represents information about one particular customer, the data items in each row are all linked in the sense that they are attributes of the one customer.
The columns are called fields, and the rows are called records. (In

more purist database terminology the rows are termed tuples and the columns attributes, predicates or classes). A relational database therefore consists of a series of unique records, each record within the database having the same fields. A further requirement is that there is at least one field which can be used uniquely to identify each record; this field is called the key field. The field Account Number is a key field for the customer database as it can be used uniquely to define any record. It is possible to define key fields that are combinations of the fields within a database, for example if a database consists of surname, address, telephone number, and other information, a key field could be defined from the combination of the fields surname, address and telephone number.

b Database 2

The 'Order file' records information about the items ordered. For example:

Transaction Number	Account Number	Item Code	Number Ordered	Date of Order
8631213	F-4564	8754	2	21/03/86
8631214	F-9832	9834	1	21/03/86
8631215	M-4632	7685	4	24/03/86
8631216	M-4632	8754	3	24/03/86
8631217	M-4632	7876	1	24/03/86
8631218	F-4564	8987	1	24/03/86

Transaction Number is a key field for this database.
Note that customer M-4632 purchased three items on 24/03/86

c Database 3

The 'Inventory file' which contains details of each item and the current stock level.
For example:

Item Code	Description	Number in Stock
8754	Screw Driver	21
9834	Hammer	42
7685	Pliers	16
7876	Tenon Saw	28
8987	Set of Chisels	15
9761	Electric Drill	9

Item code is the key field for this database. In the example above it may be required to produce a transaction statement for a particular customer. If the customer's name is known then the customer file could firstly be searched to obtain the relevant account number and address. Using the account number the orders file could then be searched to obtain a list of orders placed by that customer. The orders file only gives an item code so, by accessing the inventory file with the item code as the reference, a description of each of the items ordered could be obtained. All the information required to complete the account has now been obtained so the statement may be constructed and rendered.

In the process outlined above information from different databases has been linked and this linkage is accomplished by using common fields. For example, the Customer and Order files are linked through the common field of Account Number. In the customer file M-4632 should uniquely identify R Black as it is a key field whilst M-4632 in the order file identifies the orders placed. Note that the Account Number in the Orders field is not a key field.

In generating the account in the example above procedures have been used to process and select data from the databases. In the relational model there are three critical ways of processing the contents of databases. Any database which is purported to be relational will have these three processing procedures, or operators as they are more formally called. The majority of DBMS's available, however, offer these three processing options and a range of other processing options to increase the power of the DBMS.

The relational operators

The first processing option is known as SELECT, and enables a subset of records to be chosen according to some criteria. In the preparation of the statement SELECT was used on the order file to select the set of orders for a particular customer.

The second processing option is known as PROJECT, and allows the selection of certain fields. In the preparation of the account PROJECT was used, in conjunction with SELECT, to choose the description from the inventory file.

The last processing option is called JOIN and enables two databases to be joined together to form a further database.

A summary of these operators and examples of the way that they may be used within a database management system, together with their effect, is given below.

a SELECT

This is an operator on one table that enables a subset of records to be selected.
An example of the use of the Select operator to pick out all the records where the surname is BLACK, this would produce:

Account Number	Name	Address
M-4632	R BLACK	AIDEN TERRACE, NEWCASTLE

To use the SELECT operator the following information must be provided:

- the name of the database from which to choose records.
- the selection criteria.

b PROJECT

This is an operator on one table that enables a subset of fields to be chosen.
An example of the use of the PROJECT operator would be to pick the fields name and address from the customer file, this would produce:

Name	Address
J GREEN	COVENTRY STREET, BRISTOL
R BLACK	AIDEN TERRACE, NEWCASTLE
T WHITE	ST JOHNS AVENUE, SKIPTON
A BROWN	OAK HILL DRIVE, LANCASTER

To use the PROJECT operator the following information must be provided:

- the name of the database
- the names of the fields required.

c JOIN

This is an operator on two tables that enables a new table to be formed. The tables are joined on the basis of a common field name. An example of the use of the JOIN operator would be to join the order file to the inventory file using the item code as the field on which to join the two databases, the fields Account Number, Item Code, Date of Order, Description and Number in Stock defining the structure of the new database. The following database would be produced:

Account Number	Item Code	Number Ordered	Date of Order	Description	Number in stock
F-4564	8754	2	21/03/86	Screw Driver	21
F-9832	9834	1	21/03/86	Hammer	42
M-4632	7685	4	24/03/86	Pliers	16
M-4632	8754	3	24/03/86	Screw Driver	21
M-4632	7876	1	24/03/86	Tenon Saw	28
F-4564	8987	1	24/03/86	Set of Chisels	15

To use the JOIN operator the following information must be provided:

- the names of the two databases to be joined
- the name of the common field on which the joining is constructed
- the names of the fields from either database that are required in the new database.

True relational database management software must, by definition, have these three operators, however they are insufficient to define a full DBMS so software houses add other processing options to increase the flexibility of their products. There has been much debate about the 'purity' of implementations of relational database systems but there is little doubt that some of the relational database packages have had a major impact on systems in recent years.

Design of databases

Why is it necessary to design a database?

In considering the data requirements for a system, data needs can be described in a number of different ways, some of which will be more efficient than others. An ideal would be a database that is logically constructed, has no unnecessary data constraints, data duplication or data redundancy, and in which every required piece of data is recorded precisely once in a known location. Such an ideal can often be brought about by common sense and good planning, however a technique known as 'normalisation' is available to provide a framework for developing workable and robust relational databases. Referring back to the example in the previous section the required information about each sale to each customer could have been recorded in a ledger format, as indicated below:

Name	Address	Date	Items ordered	Number ordered	Number in stock
J GREEN	BRISTOL	21/03/86	SCREWDRIVER	2	21
T WHITE	SKIPTON	21/03/86	HAMMER	1	42
R BLACK	NEWCASTLE	24/03/86	PLIERS	4	16
			SCREWDRIVER	3	21
			TENON SAW	1	28
J GREEN	BRISTOL	24/03/86	SET OF CHISELS	1	15

(Number in stock being the number in stock at the beginning of the day.)

Figure 5 Sales information in ledger format

This form of recording the data would not be as suitable for a database because of the following problems:

- Repeating Fields The field 'items ordered' can be a repeating field, as it is for the customer R BLACK.
- Duplicate Data The field 'number in stock' contains duplicate data, the number in stock for the item screwdriver appears twice.
- Redundant Data The customer J Green appears twice in the example, if his address were to change then, possibly, a large number of records would require changing.

Constructing the databases

Taking a common sense approach it would seem reasonable to have a database of customer names and addresses, a database of the items held in stock and a transaction file recording each transaction. Within this system the customer name and address is held on one database, so if any address changes then the address may be changed on the one record of that file, this change is all that is required. The number of items in stock can be recorded in one place on the inventory file, if the stock level changes then this change can be recorded for that item on the inventory file. The transaction file records all transactions, each sale of one item being recorded on one record. Any relational database requires a key field, so the fields, customer number, transaction number and item number are created on the customer, order and inventory databases to meet this requirement. The table shown in Figure 5 can be constructed using the SELECT, PROJECT and JOIN operators as discussed earlier. The benefit of constructing the databases as above are that any changes to the customer file are automatically adjusted for in the ledger as shown in Figure 5.

Normalisation

Normalisation is a technique that has been developed to ensure that the database design for a relational database management system is efficient. The precise mechanics for the procedures of normalisation are beyond the scope of this booklet, however a brief indication of the process is given below for the interested reader.
Normalisation (due to Dr E.F. Codd), is carried out in three stages to obtain databases that are in:

- the first normal form
- the second normal form
- the third normal form

(There is also a possible fourth normal form due to R Fagin.)
Each stage is progressive, and cumulative. A database that has been normalised to the second form must, by definition, satisfy the conditions of the first form. Similarly a database in the third normal form must be in the second normal form.

The first normal form

The first normal form seeks to structure the databases such that there are no repeating fields. Thus in our example we would devise databases such that the repeating field 'Items ordered' was made non repeating.

The second normal form

The second normal form, seeks to ensure that each field within a record is dependent upon the key. The simplest way to describe this process is to construct a database that is in the first normal form but not in the second. Suppose in our example we had constructed two databases, the customer database as before, and a transaction data base consisting of the fields:

Account Number	Item Code	Number Ordered	Date of Order	Description	Number in stock
F-4564	8754	2	21/03/86	Screw driver	21
F-9832	9834	1	21/03/86	Hammer	42
M-4632	7685	4	24/03/86	Pliers	16
M-4632	8754	3	24/03/86	Screw driver	21
M-4632	7876	1	24/03/86	Tenon saw	28
F-4564	8987	1	24/03/86	Set of chisels	15

Here the key is a little more complex, it is the combination of the fields Account Number and Item Code. (This still may not be sufficient uniquely to identify each record, in which case we could add the Date of Order to the key.) In this case the Account Number is completely independent of the description, thus the key is only partially dependent upon the fields within the records. The solution is to divide this database into two databases as in our example.

The third normal form

The third normal form, refines the second form to ensure that each field within a record depends only on the key field, in this form within the database there are no fields dependent on non-key fields. The reader who is interested in pursuing the detail of the process of normalisation further will find a very readable chapter, with reference to simple examples, in the book by Tony Shaw. *dBase II Developing Applications*.

What is a database management system?

Does a database need a computer?

In the earlier chapters it was noted that a database is in essence comprised of groups of data with each group of data stored in a similar way. The concept of a database makes no reference to the medium of storage, the database could equally well be stored in a filing cabinet, as within a computer file. The database concept is a model of data structure and, as such, is independent of the storage method and processing medium. Given the size of most databases, manual systems would be impractical and, therefore, most databases rely on computer file handling and computer processing power to produce workable systems.

The Database Management System (DBMS)

As noted previously, a Database Management System (DBMS) is a suite of computer programs that enables data to be organised into a database according to the ways in which the original groups of data had been designed and enables the subsequent modification and interrogation of the database. Using a DBMS thus enables new data to be entered at a keyboard, or any other computer input device, and the information within the databases retrieved, modified or interrogated accordingly. The DBMS may thus be described as an 'intelligent filing cabinet' as it performs the functions of an efficient filing clerk. It is the medium by which a data model may be converted into an accessible database system.

The types of database management systems

Database Management Systems are available for the:

- hierarchical model
- network model
- relational model

Whilst this booklet relates principally to the relational model many of the features described in the following paragraphs relate to all types of DBMS.

Components of a DBMS

Generally DBMS, particularly those aimed at the microcomputer market, provide certain common features. As there are many different systems available on the market, however, there is no such entity as a 'standard' DBMS.
The components which are generally available are:

a Enquiry Language

At the heart of the software comprising the DBMS are programs which handle the storage and retrieval of data. Within this part of the program there is usually an 'enquiry language' facility which is provided to enable the user to interrogate the contents of the database. In the earlier example a series of databases that recorded customer information, transaction information and inventory information were discussed. The DBMS handles the setting up of these databases in the required form, and enables particular records to be accessed and modified if necessary. The enquiry language would be useful in several situations; for example a manager wishing to investigate stock levels could ask for a list of all records in the inventory database where the 'Number in Stock' is less than say 5 or greater than 50.

b Screen Form

A program that allows the user to design and use on the visual display unit a 'screen form' that is similar in construction to the forms used by the user so that data may be entered, and searched for in a familiar way. In terms of the example a customer with a particular query about their outstanding transactions could be answered by drawing onto the screen a picture designed to look like the statement the company sends to its customers, containing all the current outstanding transactions. In this way the results of a database interrogation may be presented in a form appropriate to the user.

c Report Generator

A report generator that allows the user to construct reports according to some previously defined criteria or to summarise the information contained within a group of records from a range of databases according to the user's requirements. In terms of the example a report could be produced giving the total sales of each item on the inventory file, together with the opening stock level over a given period of time.

d Interaction with a word processor

An interface between the database and a word processor is frequently found so that personalised letters can be sent using the mail-merge facilities common to most word processors. Using the example, if a customer's invoice remains outstanding after a certain period it might be deemed necessary to send out a reminder letter to the customer utilising this facility.

Data manipulation facilities of a relational DBMS

The above features allow the user of a DBMS to generate, maintain and manipulate databases. If the DBMS is relational then the procedures available for manipulating the database include SELECT, PROJECT and JOIN as described in the previous chapter. Software houses usually include a range of processing options to increase the flexibility of the package. The following is a brief indication of the types of procedures (operators) usually provided:

a Procedures involving the maintenance of the database

A relational DBMS will provide procedures for creating a new database, entering new data into the database, adding additional data or editing the existing data within the database. A procedure for removing redundant records will also be provided.

b Operation on a database

As noted, a relational DBMS must, by definition, provide the operators SELECT, PROJECT and JOIN. Within a particular package these operators may have different names or be invoked by the style of the software but their function will be as described earlier; they may however be enhanced and include an 'enquiry language' facility to make them more versatile. For example, the SELECT operator may contain a condition where the SELECT command could have been used in the following format:

Select from the inventory database all records where 'Number in Stock' is less than 5 or greater than 50

In addition to these three operators, sorting procedures are usually provided to enable the records on a database to be sorted and held in some pre-defined way. When working within a system the records contained in a particular database may require sorting according to several different criteria during the preparation of reports. For example, from the inventory database a report to the management for stock monitoring purposes may require the selection of all stock records where the 'Number in Stock' is under 5 or over 50, it would be useful to give this information with the 'Number in Stock' in ascending order. A report to the purchase department would probably be better provided in 'Item Code' order. Sorting is usually quite expensive on computing time, consequently another way of sorting the records within a database is usually available, this process is called indexing and does not entail the physical relocation of records but instead creates index files in the required sequence. Not

only is the creation of such files faster than a sort exercise but they can also be used to enable rapid retrieval of information on specification of the required index key value.
Further facilities are usually available in the form of report generators which facilitate the production of reports from within a database according to user-defined criteria. Database systems often also include a high-level programming language (or command language) which enable the user to write a series of programs, and hence generate systems in which the operations required are all preprogrammed. In terms of the example a series of programs could be written to:

- receive input or edit data in the databases and produce a monthly statement of transactions to the customer
- produce a series of management reports

All this could be pre-programmed with the user being presented with, for example, a series of menu choices. The fact that a DBMS is being used would not necessarily be obvious. In this form some DBMS may be regarded as Fourth Generation Application Generators.

Conclusion

The management of database systems

The management and administrative problems associated with operating and maintaining a large database are frequently under-estimated. The database concept regards data as a resource which implies the need to manage this resource effectively. This task is tackled by the function of the Database Administrator.

The Database Administrator

Much has been written about the management of databases and the role of the Database Administrator, which may be a group of people taking responsibility for this function. The main functions of the Database Administrator are:

a The design and organisation of the databases

This usually includes the determination of the overall data requirements, providing data structures and standards for all the database applications. An important function is the maintenance of the data dictionary which is an index of the data contained within a database and information about the cross-references and data structures within the database.

b The user interface

The Database Administrator should provide documentation and advice to all users about the means of access to the databases and how to make the most effective use of them.

c Security, Integrity and Confidentiality

The procedures for maintaining data security, integrity and confidentiality should be administered by the Database Administrator.

The overall function of the Database Administrator is to provide central control over the data resource and, where required enforce standards in terms of data security and maintenance.
From the discussion above the decision to adopt the database approach is not simply a question of 'which DBMS do I purchase?' but rather a change in the attitude to data as a resource. If a database is implemented without due regard to the management of the process and allowed to grow without control then many more problems will emerge than were solved by the adoption of the database. The decision to go along the database route is an important one and requires a high level of control in carrying out the change but, if properly implemented, will be of lasting benefit.

Bibliography

Date C J	*An Introduction to Database Systems*, Addison Wesley (1981)
Elbra T	*Database for the Small Computer User*, NCC Publications (1982)
Laurie P	*Databases*, Chapman and Hall/Methuen (1985)
Lewis C	*Managing with Micros*, Blackwell (1983)
Shaw T	*dBase II Developing Applications*, Addison Wesley (1984)
	Computer-based Information Systems, Course M352 Blocks I II & III The Open University Press (1980)

6

Systems Analysis

R Dixon BA, MA

Introduction: What is systems analysis?

A dictionary will typically define '*system*' as being a number of activities united by some form of regular interaction or interdependence. In a business sense a system represents all the tasks that must be done in order to provide information required by the people who have been given responsibility to run respective portions of the business. Everyone in an organisation is either directly involved with a system or is in some way affected by it. The introduction of a computer will often involve major changes in the organisation's information systems and, as a result, there may be changes in the organisation and management's decision-making responsibilities.

The principal objective of systems analysis is to ensure that an optimum decision regarding a business system is made and is then properly executed. While systems analysis can apply equally to clerical systems, for the purposes of this contribution relevance to computer based systems will be assumed.

The role of the systems analyst has been described as:

> '. . . the investigation of a system and the design and implementation of a computer based system to produce the required output from the necessary input whilst minimising the sum of computer cost and related manual cost, yet allowing flexibility and ensuring accuracy commensurate with the job to be done.'

Four stages can be identified in systems analysis as follows:

(a) The investigation and recording of the requirements and performance of the existing system.
(b) Analysis of the recorded investigation in the light of new requirements.
(c) Design and documentation of a new system to meet the new requirements.
(d) Implementation and effective maintenance and review of the new system.

Systems analysis involves a quality and breadth of knowledge and experience which is so high that it is unlikely that any one person can meet all of the requirements. In any large systems project a team of analysts will be used for the various aspects of investigation and design.
It should be emphasised that, whatever cost or time or technological pressures may prevail, systems must be designed for use by people. In the final analysis, it will be people that make a system work.

Investigation and analysis

Establishing systems objectives

Clear objectives for a particular project must be set before any team of analysts can begin their investigation. It is the responsibility of senior management to set these objectives, which then act as terms of reference within which the systems analysis function can operate. In order to set these objectives senior management form a '*steering committee*' comprising representatives of the computing, user and strategy functions.
The setting of objectives involves the following tasks:

(a) Identification of areas for systems study. This involves identifying the '*purpose*' and '*scope*' of the project, indicating the existing procedures to be covered and the departments involved. A time-scale is also usually defined.
(b) Identification of management requirements for information. It is important to give careful consideration to this area. Any statement of management information requirements must begin with an analysis of what the information is for and what decisions will need to be taken.
(c) Assessment of benefits and costs. It is unlikely at this preliminary stage that there will be any accurate indication of the costs involved and potential savings; although other desired benefits will already have been identified. Detailed indications of costs and benefits will only come through the work of the analysts at the feasibility study stage.
(d) A formal definition of purpose and objectives. If the steering committee decides to initiate a project then a final assignment brief will be issued stating the aims of the project and the overall timescale involved.

After establishing systems objectives, the steering committee will pass the project to the systems analyst and will monitor events during the research and development stages.

The feasibility study

The function of systems analysis commences with the feasibility study. The aim of the feasibility study is to assess the computing requirements of the system under review, to investigate and recommend possible solutions and to provide management with information on which a decision can be based. In addition the study should quantify the disadvantages of the existing system so that a true comparison of costs and benefits can be made with the proposed solution.

The feasibility study is conducted by an appointed team which is normally directly responsible to the steering committee.

Fact finding

The first stage in the feasibility study is the systems investigation, or fact finding, process. This is undertaken to establish procedures and constraints under which existing systems operate in the area under review. There are three methods of fact finding normally employed:

- interviews
- questionnaires
- observation

The process of the individual interview provides the systems analyst with the best opportunity of promoting confidence in the potential user as to the possibilities and benefits of change from existing procedures. This confidence is a very important factor in the successful design and introduction of a new system. The analyst will, therefore, take great care in planning initial interviews and will recognise that the primary object is as much to promote an atmosphere of trust as to establish facts about procedures. Analysts will also appreciate that they are dealing with individuals, with their own positions in the organisation and in society and with different attitudes and personalities. Rather than follow a standard routine, the experienced analyst will be able to adapt the approach to suit the individual interviewee, a task which requires considerable behavioural skills.

It is essential for the analyst to be well briefed on the interviewee's job position and to prepare the introduction and a plan of the questions to be asked. It is also important for the interview to be conducted on a one-to-one basis and in a relaxed atmosphere. The analyst should therefore seek to guarantee that there will be no interruptions.

It is important that some sort of rapport is established between the analyst and the interviewee. The background to the systems project should be carefully explained to ensure that any misunderstandings about its purpose are removed. The analyst should aim to ask questions appropriate to the level at which the interviewee is positioned in the organisation. In general the analyst should aim to lead the interviewee into the specific areas about which knowledge is required or confirmation is sought.

Questionnaires may be useful whenever a limited amount of information is required from a large number of individuals, or where the organisation is decentralised with many '*separate entity*' locations. It should be noted that, even with a well constructed questionnaire, the quality of response is likely to be poorer than may otherwise have been obtained through interviewing. It is still the case, however, that questionnaires can be useful when it is required to confirm facts about existing systems such as volumes or frequencies of particular transaction types.

The use of observation can be invaluable in providing an insight as to the real constraints and bottlenecks experienced in existing systems. Normally, critical points in the system will be observed and many '*informal*' procedures may be identified which would have been unlikely to have been discovered through the conventional interviewing or questionnaire techniques. Observation is particularly useful in monitoring the actual physical progress in the area under review, a useful example might be the receipt of goods into stock. In many instances, breakdowns in the current system may be readily identified, for example through goods obviously not having been dealt with for some time or where documentation fails to reflect deviations in terms of physical quantities.

Documenting the existing system

The task of documenting the existing system, whilst not an end in itself, provides the basis upon which the recommendations regarding any new system can be made. It also ensures that the analyst has obtained a complete understanding of the current procedures in operation. During this process, weaknesses in the current system may well be identified and these will be of interest to the relevant line management, who might wish to implement improvements in advance of any new system.

The documentation produced at this stage will normally comprise four principal sections.

(a) Description Section – describing the system under view in outline terms, detailing the parts of the organisation which are affected and tracing the flow of information through the various departments.

(b) Document Section – comprising copies of all the forms used in the system, together with notes of regular letters and telephone messages

which play their part in the system.
(c) Interview Section – containing notes of the interviews conducted.
(d) Chart Section – including graphical depictions of the system in terms of flow charts, decision tables, block diagrams or whatever other means are appropriate.

Analysis of recorded data

The second phase of a feasibility study involves establishing the requirements of a new system; i.e. analysis. This analysis stage is vital as it acts as a specific break between the investigation and design processes. It also enables the weaknesses of the existing system to be analysed and provides the opportunity of evaluating alternatives and ensuring that the weaknesses are not repeated in the new system.
The analysis of the existing system should suggest:

- methods of improving control over routine applications
- methods of providing better information for decision-making
- changes in the system necessary to achieve the above requirements and new forms of input and output
- possible alternatives: i.e. an examination of possible data processing methods that would ensure efficient operation of the new system.

The feasibility study report will form the basis for decisions made by the steering committee in determining the appropriate course(s) of action to be taken. Frequently this decision will be to proceed with the computerisation of the particular function (although this may not necessarily be the case) or to change the method of computing from that which is currently used.

Systems design

If the recommendations of the feasibility study report for the computerisation of an application have been accepted, the role of the systems analyst will be to prepare systems documentation from which programmes can be written (assuming, that is, that it is not the intention to purchase packaged software) and revised procedures adopted. The process of detailed system design may take a considerable time and, in major projects, an interim document, often termed '*Outline System Specification*', may be produced in advance of the '*Detailed System Specification*'. It is often beneficial for the user department to be involved in the review of such documents, at least on an overview basis, so that the user management can keep in touch with the way in which the project is progressing. Indeed, the active co-operation of the user department should be encouraged throughout the detailed development stages as this will almost certainly help with the smooth implementation of the final system.

The nature of change caused by new systems can vary considerably. Traditionally, systems analysts were assumed to be principally involved in the change-over from a manual system to a computerised system. Today, this may only exceptionally be the case and the nature of a project is more likely to involve upgrading from an existing computer system in association with a centralisation or decentralisation of various elements of processing.

There is a large number of areas which will be covered by the detailed design phases and the principal of these are identified in the following paragraphs.

Computing environment

A fundamental design decision will be the computing environment in which the proposed system is to operate. It is crucial that this is properly researched as it will be extremely expensive, if not impossible, to change course once system development is under way. Close contact will need to be established with the vendors of the equipment and operating environment to ensure that timescales and precise facilities are defined. Among the principal areas of consideration will be the following:

(a) Hardware (processors and memory) – the specific computer(s) required for the application. Speed and capabilities of specific processors will be of interest here, together with the ability to support the envisaged number of users.

(b) Hardware (storage devices) – normally magnetic disk or tape. The amount of storage available on-line at any time will be critical when assessing envisaged volumes, while access speeds will be of interest when evaluating likely performance.

(c) Hardware (peripheral I/O devices) – for example, input terminals such as visual display units (VDUs) and output devices such as printers. Data preparation considerations will influence the selection of input peripherals.

(d) Operating software – the software environment in which the system is to operate. Where a multi-user or network system is envisaged, the security and locking facilities provided by the operating system will be of interest as will the presentation of the user interface.

(e) Software language – the language to be used for the development of the applications software. This will largely be dictated by the hardware and operating software selected and by the level of in-house expertise for development and maintenance.

(f) Communications – if the new system is to involve data transfers between locations or other systems the use of relevant modems, lines and communications software will need to be considered.

In assessing the requirements, the analyst will wish to be aware of current and envisaged technological developments, although there are obvious dangers inherent in developing a system which is to run in an environment which has not been proven and tested.
The importance of making the correct decision in this area cannot be overemphasised. In arriving at this decision the analyst must consider all likely requirements of the envisaged system and match these requirements firmly against the selected environment.

Stages in systems design

The design of a system involves the accomplishment of the following basic tasks:

- establishing output requirements
- file design
- input requirements and format
- procedure design
- design and specification of controls

and the principal elements of these tasks are described in the following paragraphs.

Establishing output requirements and format

It is essential that the output requirements of a system are firmly established from the outset. A system has little intrinsic value in its own right; it is the information which it produces that justifies its existence. Systems analysts need to design outputs so as to give the users control over the functions for which they are responsible; in order to achieve this they must consider the:

content
volume
timing and
format

of the information to be supplied.

Obviously, in terms of content, the output should contain the information required by the user. Generally the content will be determined by the system.

Considerations relating to the volume and sequence of data are fundamental to good systems design. For example, when a stock-controller is expediting existing orders on suppliers it is not necessary to list all the orders that have been placed; only those which are overdue should be listed, the aim being to use exception reporting to minimise the volume of records that the user needs to examine. In addition, the stock-controller will probably need to contact suppliers and will hence expect to see all overdue transactions arranged in supplier sequence.

The individual data elements in output reports are the means by which information is conveyed to users. By identifying these elements, the systems analyst is beginning to specify the data that must be held or generated within the system. Information, however, is only of value to the user if it is supplied at the right time, thus enabling the user to take action relevant to particular goals. By analysing the neds of particular users, it is possible not only to identify what data is relevant but also when it is required.

Users' output requirements should be verified in detail before specific output formats are finalised. It is also important to check the formats against the aims defined in the original project brief.

File design

Computer files cannot be designed in isolation, their content and structure being linked to input, output and intermediate processing requirements. Three considerations are of principal importance:

(a) File Types. In general files can be divided into three types as follows:

- Transaction files. These contain operating data, i.e. details of the various transactions in which the organisation is involved.
- Master files. These include some information which is of a permanent nature and also data which is continually updated by recent transactions.
- Reference or standing data files. These contain information used for reference purposes. They are also sometimes referred to as master files.

(b) Methods of access. There are two ways in which information can be accessed:

- sequential access – data can be presented to a program only in the sequence in which the records are stored on the file

- direct access – any record can be extracted more or less directly without the necessity for reading all preceding records.

The requirements regarding access to records will be noted by the analyst as this will affect the choice of media for the storage of files.

(c) Choice of storage media. The principal forms of storage media used in business systems are magnetic tape, hard disk (fixed or removable) and floppy disk. The choice of storage media may well influence the selection of hardware for the proposed system, particularly where specific performance criteria must be met.

File organisation

A file is divided into a number of records, each record containing various data fields and each field comprising a number of alphabetical or numeric characters. A typical file will contain:

- a header record, holding identification details about that file, e.g. file name, generation number
- a number of data records, e.g. transactions or customer details
- a control record (or trailer record) containing control details about that file, e.g. record counts, value totals.

Records may be fixed or variable in length and each record will have at least one key by which it is identified. Where there is more than one key the file might be organised in principal key order. Much of the skill in systems analysis lies in optimising record and file structures before detailed programming work commences. Once files have beens pecified, modifications to file or record structures can rarely be accommodated with ease.

File update and maintenance

The terms file update and file maintenance are often used interchangeably although there is a distinction in practice. File updating involves the alteration of records in a master file so that they reflect the current position; normally this is achieved by passing a transaction file against the master file. File maintenance is the process of adding, amending, or deleting standing data on a reference or master file. The main difference between update and maintenance relates to the frequency of occurrence; update refers to regular, expected changes to data on the file, whereas maintenance refers to infrequent change.

File security

Files are valuable assets and, therefore, the systems analyst must provide for their security. Usually several copies of current files are maintained and some of these may be held off-site or in fire-proof cabinets to protect against physical disaster to the building in which the computer is located. The analyst must also provide for the protection of files and/or functions from unauthorised users. This can be affected by the allocation of user identifiers which can in turn be associated with passwords. The operating systems or applications program can then control access and ensure that only authorised users are permitted entry to given files or facilities.

Input requirements and format

Input requirements are dependent upon output, file structures and the type of application involved. The analyst will examine the following aspects:

- data collection methods and controls
- input mechanism
- data volumes.

Input document formats can then be designed, bearing in mind the logical sequence of entry and the structure of the files.

Data collection and input

The collection of data and subsequent entry to the computer is one of the most important, and often one of the most problematic, areas of data processing. The computer will only accept data which is in '*machine-sensible*' form, and if its original form is unacceptable it has to be transcribed. As a result, data collection and preparation is often a very expensive stage of systems operation. In addition to the expense, the collection of data is also prone to serious or numerous errors up to the point of input to the computer. It is essential, therefore, that adequate controls are maintained; these controls must be designed to ensure that all the data collected, transmitted, prepared and entered into the computer is correct. The problem arising from this, however, lies in determining the optimum balance between the cost and time of data collection and validation in context of the degree of control and accuracy required.
Some systems may lend themselves to the entry and validation of batches of transations whereas others may require on-line entry and validation.

Whatever method is used, the same principles apply regarding the integrity of the data.

Input mechanism

The selection of input devices will be critical to the success of a system. Inc arrying out the selection process, the analyst will consider suitability under the following headings:

- the nature and timing of inputs to the system
- the degree of validation which is required at the point of input
- suitability for the application, considering the physical location and conditions under which input is to be made
- current developments in terms of input device hardware (e.g. in the case of bar-code readers)
- data volumes, together with peaks/troughs
- cost

Data volumes

The procedures developed to deal with data collection, processing and storage must be capable of expansion to meet an increased volume over current or envisaged levels. Failure to recognise the possible growth in the overall size of a system is one of the most common reasons for systems failing to last their projected lifespan with the consequent detrimental effect on payback calculations. It is frequently the case that a good computer system will be instrumental in accelerating growth in its application area and such systems often become unwieldy because the actual volumes were never envisaged at the design stage. Given the problems and costs associated with changes/upgrades to hardware and software, it is wise to allow from the outset a good contingency, particularly in terms of backing storage and, if applicable multiple access possibilities.
In addition to future growth, the implications of sudden or periodic peaks in activity should also be considered carefully when assessing the data volume requirements.

Procedure design

Computer procedures provide the means whereby input and file data is processed to produce the required output, whereas clerical procedures deal with the provision of this input and the processing of the output. Both will require careful consideration and documentation at the design stage. Flowcharts will normally be used to depict the sequence of events projected by the systems analyst and a number of levels of chart may be drawn up as follows:

- system flowchart
- computer run chart
- clerical procedures flowchart
- computer procedures flowchart.

A system flowchart will provide an overview of the whole system showing, both for clerical and computer elements, the principal documents, files and processes involved and the department in which processing will take place. A computer run chart will show, at computer file and process level:

- all principal programs/processes
- input to and output from each program
- use of files by each program

The concept of flowcharting will extend also to the clerical and computer operations procedures and these flowcharts will indicate clearly the responsibility and timing of the various manual functions surrounding the computer system.
Decision tables may also be used for recording processing paths, particularly within complex procedures. Decision tables record information in such a way as to enable a number of conditions to be related to required actions clearly and unambiguously and hence are an invaluable aid to programmers during the development stages.
In addition to the documentation of flows through the system, the analyst will also record the points of control which are to be provided in the processing cycle, i.e. hardware controls, input controls, processing and file controls, output controls etc and these are discussed further below.

System controls

Systems controls should be designed in co-operation with management and should take into account the conditions that will prevail when the system is live. The analyst should ensure that the control procedures are written into procedures manuals produced for use by line departments and the computer operations staff.
Computer system control can generally be divided into three main areas:

(a) administrative controls, which can be sub-divided into:

- organisational controls, relating to specification and division of responsibilities within and between personnel and departments;
- operational controls relating particularly to procedures in the computer environment concerning the physical security of data files and program libraries:

(b) systems development controls, relating to the adherence to proper standards in such areas as documentation, programming discipline, maintenance provisions and system review during the development cycle.

(c) processing controls, relating to controls exercised over a particular application in terms of input, processing and output procedures.

Implementation and review

As mentioned previously, no system, however well designed and intentioned, can operate successfully without the active participation and co-operation of the users. It is therefore, in the interests of all concerned that user management and staff are kept informed of developments and are involved in the planning stages for testing, implementation and live running. The implementation stage, and the periods immediately before and after it, are critical in determining the success of the system and their importance cannot be over-emphasised.

Once the decision to proceed with a computerised system has been made the systems analyst has still, therefore, much to consider regarding various aspects of the system before it can become operational

User participation

User participation is important at all stages in the development of a system and particularly so at implementation. The essential ingredient of the success of any system lies in the attitude of the people who are either users of the system output or who are creators of the system input. In essence, if the user is not happy, the system will not work, or will work inefficiently! It is important that the analyst has built a good relationship with users in the earlier stages of systems development, for this relationship is vital at the implementation stage. User management and staff may well be satisfied that the system works in theory but will require confidence that this is matched in practice and that their requirements are in fact satisfied.

The assistance of the user is required in four principal activities:

- definition of revised clerical procedures
- supply of test data and review of test results
- planning for pilots or parallel running
- training of management and staff.

User participation should be maintained throughout the changeover to the new system in order to ensure a smooth transition and the minimum of disruption.

Installation planning

As with any major project, the need for careful planning is paramount. The following activities may be involved in installation planning:

(a) selection of a site – this may be in an existing or a new building.
(b) preparation of the site – for example, installing protection devices, air-conditioning, furnishing etc.
(c) standby equipment – this is needed to ensure continuity of processing in the event of a power failure or computer failure.
(d) planning for delivery.

Obviously, the scale of these activities diminishes with smaller computer systems but the same considerations apply; for example, the siting of a VDU screen or a noisy printer may be critical when planning for the introduction of an office microcomputer system and the problems regarding power or equipment failures apply equally to all computerised systems.
A Gantt chart, which is used to plan the timescale for a project and to estimate the amount of resources required, is a useful aid to planning. Other project control techniques (e.g. PERT) may also be used as appropriate.

Training/staff selection

During the planning of the systems implementation the analyst will estimate the staffing requirements for the different activities involved in the new system. Invariably, the implementation of a new system will require the education of users in the operation of the system and the extent of this will depend upon the complexity of the procedures being introduced. A program of training should establish the following:

- the categories of staff requiring training

- the timing and timescale of training
- mode of training (e.g. on-the-job, seminars, courses).

The timing of training is a particularly important aspect which is frequently overlooked. Interest and enthusiasm may be lost if there is too long a delay between the end of training and its application. The training should not be rushed nor should it be arranged during holidays or periods of peak work loads.

Systems testing

System testing is probably the most important aspect of system development and may well be the most expensive in terms of time and resources. Failure to recognise this, however, will almost certainly result in even greater penalties being incurred during live running. It is unfortunately the case that system testing is often carried out against a background of tight time pressures resultant from slippages during the earlier stages of development and this can promote a tendency to conduct testing superficially, ignoring all but the most obvious of fatal errors. Construction of test data should be effected on a controlled basis with attention being paid to both valid and invalid eventualities. Both the user and systems analyst will contribute to the development of a test pack and the objective of providing an ongoing basis for the testing of later amendments and upgrades should be borne in mind. Saturation testing, in terms of high volumes, should also be effected as this frequently exposes weaker points of systems and will also enable benchmarking against envisaged processing times to be established. It is also important that systems test data should not be designed and constructed by programming staff who will, of course, have previously carried out their own program testing procedures. Procedural testing may also be effected to ensure that all the non-computer parts of the new system are practicable. As procedural testing involves manual procedures such as input document coding control checking and use of computer output, test data must simulate operating conditions rather than be specifically designed to cover every abnormal occurrence.

Changeover

Once system testing has been successfully completed it will be possible to consider implementing the new system. The timing of this changeover and the method adopted will depend upon a variety of factors including the compatibility of new and old inputs and outputs, the volatility of movements and the necessity to meet deadlines. The method of changeover can be effected in the following ways:

(a) Direct changeover. In this method the old system is completely replaced by the new system at a point in time. This will usually be the case where two systems are incompatible or where there are insufficient resources to effect parallel or pilot running. This means of changeover is inexpensive but it also carries a high risk and requires complete confidence in the new system. Direct changeover should be made during a slack period and, in large systems, it may be effected application by application (i.e. a phased implementation), allowing several months between each stage to ensure all problems are resolved before the whole system becomes operational.

(b) Parallel running. As the term implies, old and new systems are run in parallel for a period of time, both processing current data and enabling cross-checking of results. This means of changeover provides for a degree of safety but it also involves some delay in implementation and a strain on staff resources. If this method of changeover is effected, a time limit should be recognised from the outset and the criteria on which successful parallel running is to be judged should be defined. Procedures for recording and dealing with discrepancies between the two systems should also be established.

(c) Pilot running. Pilot running involves a direct or parallel run changeover in part of the organisation which is to use the new system. Typically, pilot runs would be carried out in say, a couple of local offices of a large organisation for which it is intended that the system should eventually be operational in a large number of such offices. This allows the new system to be proven with the minimum of disruption and, at a later stage, may provide useful facilities for the training of staff at other locations.

File conversion

File conversion involves the transfer of existing records, which may be manual, machine-held or on disk or tape on an existing computer, into a medium which can be read by the new computer system. Once a file has been converted, it must be checked comprehensively and control totals of number of records, values etc should be agreed between the old and new files. As with other aspects of system development, it is essential to plan for file conversion exercises and to be aware of such problems as the provision of extra staff, timings and the possibilities of re-runs being required.

Systems review

Once a system is fully operational it is important that it is reviewed periodically, perhaps at six monthly or yearly intervals. The analyst will examine all aspects of the system together with the users, and any suggestions for modification and improvement should be discussed.
The first review, generally termed the post-implementation review, should be made soon after the changeover, and a comparison between predicted and actual performances established. This review will include an examination of the timings and input and output, use of computer storage, the number and type of errors, the cost of processing and any savings which are being realised.
In general terms reviews should cover the following areas:

- staff and organisation
- ongoing suitability of equipment
- internal controls
- operating procedures
- implementation of individual applications
- timing and volume considerations
- cost/benefit analysis.

Documentation

Proper documentation is necessary to ensure communication between the systems analyst and any other interested parties at all stages of the systems activity. The analyst will wish to adhere to the documentation standards applying within the organisation for the analysis, design and implementation of business systems. Additionally, by following these standards from the outset, the analyst creates a complete record which will be readily understood by all concerned with the development of the system. Good documentation also provides essential continuity over the period of existence of a system, so that however a system may develop, there is always a clearly documented link of the changes which have been effected.

NCC documentation standards

The NCC have a valuable method of organising, filing and retrieving documents collected during, or generated by, the system development process. This comprises a scheme of files for containing the documents, document references for deciding the order of the documents within the files and cross-references which allow the standards to be used in a top-down approach to system description or definition. These are categorised into two files:

(a) Old system file – containing all documents relating to the old system, such as sample forms, present system clerical document specifications, grid charts and procedure descriptions.
(b) New system file – containing all documents relating to the current state of an implemented or proposed new system, such as reports, new system forms, new system clerical document specifications, grid charts and procedures specifications. Only the current edition of a document is maintained in this file. Rejected proposals are removed and placed in a system history file.

Some documents may relate to more than one system and these can be dealt with by the following:

(c) Shared database file – containing specifications of any database which is used by more than one system.
(d) Library programs file – containing documentation of programs used by more than one system.
(e) Component file – containing documentation of program components used by more than one program.

Each of these files contain a number of pockets which hold a particular type of document. The document reference is entered on the top right hand corner of each document, the complete reference determining the sequence of documents within the file. Cross-references may then be made from one document to another by quoting the document reference.

Documents

A number of documents are prepared during the course of systems initiation, design, development and implementation. While terminology and level of detail may vary between organisations, the following documents are typically involved:

- assignment brief
- feasibility study report
- system specification
- program specification
- user/operator procedure manuals.

Other documentation, such as working files, are also normally produced during the course of a project. In large projects, specific documentation may be produced to cover the system testing and file conversion procedures.

The assignment brief

The assignment brief is an important document which serves to identify the problem area and to agree the bounds of a particular project. The assignment brief is, in effect, a request for systems activity.

Feasibility study report

The feasibility study report will be drawn up following the initial fact finding and review exercises and will include the following topics:

- problem definition and suggested solutions
- overview of envisaged new system(s)
- outline flowcharts depicting principal computer and clerical procedures
- file information – changes in files and new files
- input information and methods
- principal output and its nature
- processing timetable
- time and resource estimates for development and implementation
- file conversion considerations
- proposed implementation method
- staffing implications
- costings and tangible benefits for the projected lifetime of the system
- intangible benefits
- proposed implementation timetable
- recommendations.

System specification

This document is the definitive statement of the computer and clerical procedures which are to form the new system. It is used primarily to specify the files, documents, programs and procedures needed for the system when it is in live operation, and may also specify routines and procedures yet to be adopted. The completion of the system specification normally forms a review stage in the development of the system and the user department will be involved in this review process.
The system specification will include:

- system objectives
- system description
- computer procedures
- clerical procedures
- data preparation and data control
- source documentation
- input procedures
- screen layouts
- file specifications
- record layouts
- data volumes
- detailed processing requirements at program level
- processing timetables
- output specifications
- print layouts
- implementation procedures
- file conversion and data set up requirements
- equipment utilisation.

The system specification is of fundamental importance and will be used as the basis for programming work on the system. All amendments to the system, however small, will need to be recorded in the system specification which will thus retain its value throughout the lifetime of the system. The detailed program requirements will be recorded in flowchart or decision table form and will clearly identify input, output and reference files to be used by each program together with processing to be effected at a field/record level.

Program specification

Unlike the system specification, the program specification will be of interest only to the programming personnel who will use it to record, at a program level, documentation relating to the specific program coding. Such documentation will include, for example, the use of variable names within programs and the values of internal indicators which may be set during program execution. A detailed representation of the flow of logic through each program will also be included. Some programming languages are now considered to be 'self-documenting' and this has given rise to some debate as to how much detail needs to be recorded outside of the actual source code. From a maintenance viewpoint, it is vital that the program specification, in whatever form, should be updated to reflect amendments as and when they occur.

User/operator procedure manuals

User instructions for computer operations staff and for user management and clerical staff also form an important part of system documentation. These instructions should provide staff with clear instructions for dealing with both normal and abnormal occurrences (the list of error messages is often the most well-thumbed page of a user manual!) and are particularly useful when new staff come to use the system in the future as they provide a supplement to initial training.

Conclusion

Systems analysis is a complex and often prolonged activity. Time limits are often set for changing systems, but where the system and organisation involved are particularly large and complex, the completion of any one project may take as long as five to ten years.

The stages in systems analysis which have been outlined in this contribution will always apply, as will the various tasks facing the systems analyst, although the approach of the analyst will vary according to each situation and its particular demands and problems.

Even after a system has been implemented and reviewed there still remains a constant need for maintenance. No system is immutable and neither will it be perfect, no matter how thorough the design, testing and documentation. A well designed system, however, will provide a firm base for changes to be incorporated as new requirements and amendments are identified.

7
Stategic Control of Information Technology

T J Bentley PhD, FCMA, FMS, MIDPM

Introduction

Computers have been a significant part of business life for the past 25 years and, like all innovations, they have had their ups and downs. Nevertheless, most companies of medium or large size have now established quite substantial computer operations and seem to be using them successfully. The average budget for expenditure on computer and communications equipment has probably risen to some 3 to 7% of turnover and appears still to be rising.

So why is a chapter on this subject necessary and why now? Many reasons will become apparent as we progress, but the principal reasons can be summarised as:

- despite the apparent success the majority of computer users are only exploiting a small proportion of the potential of information technologies.
- management appear to have done a good job of staying distant from the complexities of information systems. Unfortunately this is based on a misconception of the topic and a misjudgement of the contribution of information systems to the performance of the company.
- the trends in technology now point to an increasing need to involve the management of organisations in the strategic and development control of information technology (*IT*). Without this involvement the strategies cannot be effective.
- *IT* is now effecting the very process of business, the expectations of our suppliers and customers, and the market boundaries in which we operate. Change, and the ability to accommodate it, has become a life-sustaining factor in business and commerce. The message is becoming clear – *adapt or decay*. In order to adapt, management must grasp the *IT* nettle and ensure that the service provided by the technologists is in response to their defined needs and is directed at

areas of greatest profitability in the company.

All of the above arguments are business arguments. The decisions required can only be made at the most senior level within a company. The responsibility for realising the benefits offered by the new technologies can only rest with line management. This contribution is aimed, therefore, primarily at business managers and discusses largely business issues. There is little point in clouding the issue by presenting too many technicalities and a strategic level perception of the issues will be maintained.

Finally we shall be positive and forward looking. There is a lot which can be learned from the experiences of the past 25 years. Our objective, however, is not to encourage feelings of inadequacy or guilt. We are looking to the strategies for the next decade and the role of senior managers in the direction of those strategies. The rapidly changing face of technology means that you cannot afford to have one eye over your shoulder. What is needed is a positive and progressive way of assessing where you are today and plotting a way forward which will result in the profitable exploitation of the technologies available – what we call *Information Power*.

Information technology in perspective

The current revolution

To many managers Information Technology (*IT*) is simply the latest and most fashionable term by which to refer to computing. Their views of computing have probably changed little over the past five or six years (and why should they?) and computers will only have affected their management decision making in that some information is now available in computer-produced format. If this does not sound like you then you are in the minority.

Yet the changes taking place on the technical side of the *IT* fence are nowadays almost as dramatic as the changes made when the computer was first introduced. At the same time the business and commercial world is beginning to take up the challenge of information technologies in ways which have not been seen before – ways which do not represent technological miracles but business revolutions. Industry boundaries are being eroded by competitors who have an 'information' edge. Markets are being driven by technological practicalities.

Look at the battle lines being drawn between the High Street Banks and the Building Societies. Who can hope to prosper in that battle without the latest heavy armament from the *IT* arsenal? It is perhaps obvious that such large rich organisations will invest heavily in technology, but even here the way in which they have invested has been extremely variable with some companies leading the way and gaining commercial advantages from that lead.

Similar commercial advantage is being gained by the retailers in the grocery business who have had the imagination and management commitment to stick with electronic point of sale (EPOS) systems. The technology has for some years not been strong enough to pose a serious business challenge. Now the technology is good and the business practices are in place it is the first in the field who will gain the advantage. It has been claimed that in this area the use of EPOS has also changed the supplier/retailer relationship with the 'high-tech' retailer taking the upper hand. This is information being used to generate business muscle, i.e. a good example of information power.

These are two examples of very public companies and markets where the technological battle can be seen by us all if we care to look. You may feel as you read this that it has little or nothing to do with you. This is quite wrong. Had you read in the 1960s of the early applications of stand-alone minicomputers for business applications you may also have said that it had nothing to do with you.

Just as the minicomputer has now reached into most corners of business so the fierce competitive application of information is going to affect all of us in one way or another over the next decade. This is not an idle technological ball-gazing exercise but a sound prediction of a business trend based on fact and very little hypothesis.

The management perspective

Although information technologies are now intruding into the activities of most business managers it is not generally true that the computer is a welcome intrusion. Nor is it true to say that the computer has often improved the actual efficiency or performance of the manager.

Nowadays it is relatively easy for a manager to surround himself with computer-generated information. In fact it is often quite hard to avoid being surrounded by the stuff! How is this information used? Sometimes the manager becomes fascinated by the new tool and excessively interested in manipulating information at the expense of other aspects of his job. More often the result is that the information goes unused and the management process is largely unchanged. Certainly there is little evidence to suggest that the information opens up new management opportunities.

Few managers would argue with the need for accurate, timely, relevant information. It is perhaps a truism to say that the best informed manager has the best chance of making the best decision. Having said that, how many managers devote time and imagination to trying to improve their information systems? Many managers would find it difficult to define their information needs in relation to their decision making process. They would find it even more difficult to relate these to the opportunities offered by information technologies.

The most common management view of information technologies is perhaps that they offer vehicles whereby their staff can produce information more quickly and more accurately – but in practice the technologies cause restrictions and problems.

Computers, therefore, take on a negative perspective – they represent a problem which will not go away. Computers waste time as often as they save time. They are basically expense items which are very difficult to cost justify. They frequently fail to achieve their potential either because the software specialists cannot deliver the goods on time or because the computer performance is not up to expectation. The terms used by the information technologists are far removed from the business language of the accountant and this does not help communication. To make matters worse, many financial managers, for historical reasons, find that they are responsible for the DP community. Not only do they have difficulty relating to the use of computers in the financial community, they have all the other members of the Board on their backs because the computer systems are giving them trouble!

Because computer technology has had a chequered history and no one wants to be associated with failure there has been a tendency in some companies for line managers to divorce themselves from the application of information technologies. Too often the buck has been passed to the specialists. The inevitable result has been misdirected projects and wasted resources. This is only the beginning of a slippery slope down which have slide the *IT* investments in many companies.

If line management are not involved in the strategic planning of *IT* the justification is unlikely to be adequately scrutinised at a Board level. Professional analysis of the original need and linking of the *IT* strategy with the other business plans cannot have the credence it requires unless the exercise has the full involvement of those managers responsible for the business plans.

At first sight it is surprising that an *IT* strategy should not receive the consideration it deserves. Would any senior executive allow total delegation of a new product design, a major investment programme or a marketing campaign? If not, why do such people allow their information systems to be completely redesigned without insisting that their needs are fully understood? Perhaps Information Systems sit in the same unfortunate category as Quality, i.e. everyone wants it and says it is very important but nobody will take the time to make it happen until it is too late.

The effect of inadequate senior management involvement at the critical early stages will shadow the development and implementation to its bitter conclusion. The solutions will be deemed to be inappropriate. The usual cry from the DP Department is *I don't know why they are complaining, the system does everything that was specified*. The problem, however, is that nobody really associated with the specification.

In companies where this has happened *IT*, and the DP Department, have had a tough time. Many Departments have been split up and users have been given their own budgets for computing. Certainly many *IT* budgets have been cut back and applications restricted to the operational necessities of life. This has come at a time when such a view of *IT* could prove fatal to the company.

Just as the slippery slope begins with the failings of senior management, so the successful ascent to Information Power requires some initiatives from senior management. The first change is largely attitudinal. Management have to become *information aware* and let their people know that this is the case. They have to put energy into identifying the major business information needs and areas of profitability.

Once this happens the management hierarchy will also become involved. The *IT* strategy will be owned and driven by the people who are going to make use of the solutions. Inevitably targets will have to be realistic and expectations will be based on a clearer understanding of the potential. The ascent to information power is not too difficult once the attitude is right at the top.

Why now?

If computers have been around for 25 years then why is it so important to make these changes now? Information Technology has certainly progressed at a revolutionary pace, constrained partly by the inability of the software specialists to keep pace and control costs, but constrained mainly by the adaptiveness (or, rather, lack of it) of the people who run the business. Most innovations of a scientific nature have taken many years to achieve their full potential. We are probably only half way through the computer revolution and the second half will certainly be driven by the skill and imagination of those who can profit from the technology rather than by the technical advances of the engineers. Certainly the technologies will continue to change and the rate of change may even quicken but the ability of managers to live with that change and make it work for them will be the critical success factor.

The economic signs are that information is going to be a crucial factor in business growth. This is already evident in many areas of the economy especially in the financial services sector. The spread of information power is likely to cover many more sectors of the economy as people grasp the implications. If you do not see this now but wait for the next technological miracle to raise its head then your competitors will steal an advantage over you.

The need today is to take a realistic view of your company and the exploitation of information. You need the tools to be able to assess your performance and to identify the priorities. Only then can a practical way forward be planned and the process of change managed.

Success factors

The need for a strategy

When considering a strategy for Information Technology we start with the disadvantage that it is already misnamed. Success in the application of technology can only be measured in terms of the success the organisation has in utilising that technology. A strategy for technology, therefore, can only be derived on the basis of an agreed strategy for information and its management.

The success of an information strategy will be measured in terms of the ability of the organisation to capitalise on the opportunities, either by operating more efficiently and more effectively, or by deriving some competitive or business advantage from the technologies. Managers will be able to support their decision making by having accurate, relevant and timely information available to them. In addition, since it is recognised that technologies are changing rapidly and new opportunities have to be seized quickly it is essential that the business has an organisation and culture which is adaptive and able to respond to these challenges.

The first and most significant prerequisite to derivation of this type of strategy is that management recognise the scope of the subject and begin to think in terms of management technology. A major obstacle in this process of awareness is that many information strategies today are conceived, described and classified in terms of the technology itself, e.g. computers, communications and software. They need instead to be described in terms of the management processes which they are intended to serve.

Rather than just learning how to use databases, word processing, electronic mail etc, managers need to know what technology is available for getting work out effectively, handling various kinds of information, communicating, making decisions or planning.

An information strategy which is driven by the technological opportunities is typically the type of strategy which produces systems which are operationally effective but ineffective in terms of achievement of business benefit. Typical results are computer terminals with advanced capabilities sitting in an undisciplined and unprepared production environment, reports lying unused on the desks of unreceptive users, people who regard *IT* as a threat and sales forecasts and schedules which lack credibility because the information is inaccurate or unrealistic.

For a quarter of a century we have been trying to put computers to work successfully. How much can we learn from this experience? The answer is not obvious. Certainly we have learned a lot about the conflict between technological revolution and business system evolution. It is questionable, however, whether the experiences of implementing major mainframe projects, involving large teams of specialists and taking months or years to realise, can be directly applied to the problems we face today. We are dealing with a different technology, a different scale of investment, and much shorter realisation times. If we concentrate too much on the mistakes of the past, we are in danger of tackling the wrong problems, of taking a conservative and cautious investment approach, and of missing the main objectives which we are seeking to achieve.

The strategy needs to be derived with the information objectives mentioned above in mind. This leads to the introduction of some factors which, historically, have not received the management attention they merited.

Information Power requires the right blend of technologies, information structures, business systems and people skills. The key to success is to recognise that all these aspects need to be assessed and balanced to constitute a receptive environment and to capitalise on the opportunities.

The technology factors

The word *technology* encompasses all of the technical aspects which impact information processing. Nowadays this means the combination of computers, communication devices and the software which drives them. There is also a need for adequate technical support in terms of provision of guidance in the selection and implementation of the equipment and the back-up needed to maintain operational performance. Finally, an essential task of the technology specialists must be to maintain a watchful eye on the changing markets and to assess the opportunities as they arise.

Perhaps the most obvious sign of a successful technological operation is that the *IT* Department has come to be regarded as a consultancy service to the company offering information and advisory support to the management. The other side of the coin – the bad news – is where the IT Department has either become an *ivory tower* handling all the complexities of major operational systems and usually having to be accountable for the success or otherwise of their ventures, or a much reduced operation which has divested itself of the role of systems analysis and project management and offers a technical computing service to anyone who requests it.

If line managers can grasp the totality of information processing and accept accountability for the end products they will also recognise the need for the support of information specialists in achieving their goals. *IT* specialists will be asked to do that which they are capable of doing but not be given the '*mission impossible*' of trying to enlist the support and commitment of an unreceptive user community.

This may require a move from the traditional specialist roles as *Doers* and *Prescribers* towards those of Trainers, Advisers, Educators or Counsellors. *IT* specialists will also have to provide independent advice on purchase and use of both hardware and software, as well as continuing to help with installation, some aspects of system design and user support. They also need to establish suitable electronic communications and information structures (see below) to provide the skeletons onto which users can put the flesh.

Information factors

Although the need for accurate and relevant information has always been recognised, the realisation of the ideal has been severely restricted by the pure limitations of volumes, communications and accessibility. Technology now offers dramatic opportunities in that these restrictions have largely been removed. Unfortunately realisation is proving rather more difficult than might have been anticipated. The release of these limitations has in many cases only served to reveal a new set of limitations. These relate to such issues as:

- how does information in one area of the company relate to information in another area?
- how can our information be structured to avoid duplication, ambiguity and inconsistency?
- who owns the data and controls its use?
- how can we define the information needs of different groups and ensure that each group has the appropriate degree of access?

Even when these questions have been answered there are further problems ahead if the people who own the data and use the systems do not recognise the importance of accurate processing and general information discipline.

An information environment, therefore, has to be created which provides an information structure which is commonly agreed and supports individual applications. The information has to be comprehensive in that as much information as possible is available to contribute to decision making. There need to be mechanisms for controlling the integrity of information and people have to be *information aware.*

In assessing the performance of your information structure at present you should be looking for high levels of data accuracy and an acceptance by the users that the computer information is reliable, proven and relevant. The opposite effect is that alternative sources of information spring up and begin to assume equal importance. Regular re-runs to clear data discrepancies, continual reconciliation failures and lengthening error reports are all symptoms that the information environment is on the sick list.

Information awareness among the people who use the system means that they not only maintain the accuracy of their computer data but that they also refuse to allow inaccuracies to multiply. Typical cases of information anarchy are the stores controller who may be told there is a shortage but knows very well that there are some parts available which the computer does not appear to have registered. The crime is not the fact of knowing this but to allow the situation to continue without bringing the computer record up to date and asking *why did this happen?*

Systems factors

Business systems evolve through the influence of a variety of factors. Anyone who has worked for more than one company will know that the environment and way of working is always very different and there is not always an obvious reason why this is so.

This very environment can in itself cause people to seek out employment in the company or actively to avoid complete sectors of the economy. It is perhaps doubtful that a Financial Manager from a Bank for instance would be attracted to the idea of taking on a similar role in a high pressure Marketing company. Even companies within the same markets may differ radically in their management styles and conventions and, in this day of the *managing director superstar*, there are many examples where the perception of companies' environments is directly related to a superficial knowledge of the people behind those companies. Of course this does not necessarily mean that the success of one company and the demise of another derives directly from these presumed cultural differences.

What has this got to do with Information Power? In fact this is one of the most common causes of systems failing to meet expectations. Computer systems are, by their nature, rigid and disciplined. There is a long way to go in the development of expert systems before the computer can be as adaptive as it would need to be in some of the chaotic environments which can be seen in some businesses. Assessment of your strengths and weaknesses in this area, therefore, can prevent trying to achieve the impossible task of imposing a discipline and a culture by means of the technology. This is doomed to failure.

A business system is a mixture of formality and informality, normal practice and exception, people, paper and machine. In some companies there is a great deal of formalisation and stability whereas in others change and innovation is the order of the day. This is not to say that systems which are subject to changes are not suitable for computerisation – on the contrary there is usually increased benefit in this environment if *IT* is used successfully. What it means is that the technology has to be applied quickly and great effort has to be put into guiding the company into a different level of integrity. In more stable environments the very stability is likely to prove an obstacle since the new systems will challenge the status quo and innovation is not seen as necessary.

The management challenge is to make an objective judgement of the systems environment in which they work and to identify those aspects which need to be nurtured through the ascent to information power. This will demand an assessment of the organisation, the policies and procedures, business skills and professionalism, management style, and the physical environment.

People factors

A number of issues arise from planning information strategies which can only be classified as human issues. Since we have recognised that we depend on skilled people with the right attitudes to make the systems work, to maintain the information integrity, and to be opportunity-seeking in their jobs, we must recognise that this raises new challenges in motivation, training, management and working relationships.

The issues in motivation and attitudes can be summarised as:

- some people are afraid of computers, do not want to touch keyboards, think they are too old to learn and will avoid the technology.
- others are over-enthusiastic and spend too much time experimenting with new systems to the detriment of their job objectives.
- people need to develop a sense of *ownership* of systems they are using.
- people need to overcome blocks to thinking about new uses of *IT* which go beyond the previous manual systems.

The challenge then is to recognise these points and prepare the user community for the changes ahead. Education and training will be needed not simply in the application software to be used but in a wider context, as follows:

- how can managers and staff get an awareness of the potential of *IT* to enhance effectiveness?
- how can they be helped to cope with the sheer complexity and rapid changes in the *IT* scene?
- there may be problems of re-orientation and adjustment from manual to electronic systems. The latter have neither the ambiguity, redundancy nor supporting context upon which people have come to

rely. This makes it difficult for people to find their way around the system.

- the extent of the user skills to be learnt is still unclear. They may range from typing to being able to understand packages and even perform high-level programming. The emphasis may be switching to using the computer as a tool to achieve given goals rather than as a device which has to be operated according to prescribed instructions.

In the area of working relationships, managing staff who are users of technology creates a new set of questions and requirements with which most managers are unfamiliar. How can you ensure, for instance, that your staff use the available technology neither too little nor too much for effective performance? and that their performance becomes more visible when using common systems. Managers are at risk of interfering at a lower level.

A lot of publicity has been given to the needs for computer literacy. If this is interpreted as the need to *appreciate computers* or to use a keyboard with confidence then the training is wide of the mark. Again we are suffering from a nomenclature problem. If the people can become information aware then computer awareness will follow. Keyboard errors and mistakes caused by misunderstood applications can be corrected. Incorrect attitudes and inbuilt resistance to the changes causes wasted years, lost investment, and spoilt opportunities.

Selecting a systems approach

The position of the IT strategy

Having discussed the success factors and wider implications of information technology it is now clear that, in tackling information strategies, many companies are taking too narrow a technical view. The plan for the technologies is only part of the plan for the development and exploitation of information. This section discusses, therefore, not simply the *IT* strategy but all the aspects of information and information systems. By a systems approach we mean a business orientated derivation with the objective of producing a systems strategy which is driven by the business needs and controlled by the user management.

Just as an information technology strategy can only be created in relation to an overall information strategy so the information strategy has to relate to other company strategies and planning cycles. Since these vary widely from one company to another it is not practical to present an information strategy *technique*. The most we can do is identify the relationship with other strategies, the general requirements for deriving and working to an information strategy, and the potential sequence of events in its derivation. Later we shall review some organisational issues concerning management of the information strategy.

The preliminary requirement for deriving an information strategy is that management accept the role and value of information systems and agree on a common information view of how the business is structured. Every manager will have a parochial view of the business – the financial manager sees cash flows and profit margins, the sales manager sees sales performance and so on. Any experienced manager will know that this can cause conflict and confusion. How many Board Rooms have seen battles between a Sales Director who wants to sell *MORE* and a Financial Controller who wants to sell *MORE PROFITABLY*? Equally, different views of information can cause disruption and confusion. The first step is to define an information model of the organisation which is understood and agreed by all concerned. In addition, this model has to be a useful aid to analysing information needs and formulating a suitable strategy.

Information analysis techniques

This chapter is not the place to describe tools and techniques. The manager who is concerned to initiate new thinking in information strategies is not going to be personally concerned in the understanding of these techniques. It should be sufficient to say that *the techniques are available and your management team can apply them*. Unfortunately this is not strictly true. The techniques available have not been created with management analysis in mind and there is no one commonly accepted method.

Several methods for the construction of an information picture of organisations have been developed in recent years. The early attempts, based on clerical and document flowcharting, have several major disadvantages which make them unsuitable as management tools. In particular they are all drawn at a single detailed level which makes them voluminous and confusing, they are a reflection of the present physical environment and they do not help to bridge the gap between the old and the new.

The introduction of data base concepts has brought with it techniques for documenting and analysing data structures and relationships. These are rigorous, relevant and often revealing. They are again quite complex, however, and will not appeal immediately to a manager who is trying to come to grips with the information flows in his area. A further analysis of function is also needed.

The techniques of *Structured Analysis and Design* have been hailed as a major breakthrough by many professional Systems Analysts. Certainly they have provided a more rigorous analytical tool than the old flowcharting methods and tend to lead to more effective system solutions. They are also relatively easy for managers to understand and use without extensive and inappropriate study. The biggest drawback to this technique as a management aid is that although the data flows are levelled, even the highest level charts can become very confusing because there is no distinction between strategic levels of information, control (or performance) information and operational information.

The authors have developed a documentation technique for managers which recognises these levels of information and distinguishes between them. There is also a clear distinction made between functions and data which also simplifies the picture. In effect the most appropriate parts of the data analysis and structured analysis techniques have been put together in a package which is geared to identifying information needs at a management level and helping to define an information strategy. (For those interested in pursuing this, the technique is described and taught in the CIMA course *Design and Development of Information Systems*.)

In general, what is required is an analysis of the information flows throughout the organisation showing the use of this information for operational needs, performance and control requirements and management decision making. These are usually linked in that most information used for control or decision making is derived and summarised from operational information. Nevertheless the distinction needs to be made if managers are going to be able to use the output in a constructive analysis and placing priorities on their information needs.

It is clearly impossible to conduct a full and thorough information analysis of the entire organisation before embarking on the business of deriving a strategy. In practice the analysis will be confined to key business decisions, major company functions and key data elements.

Deriving the strategy

Those organisations which have an *IT* strategy have usually developed it on the basis of immediate need and short term priorities, bearing in mind the in-place technology. In other words the approach is *where are we at and where do we want to go?*

Although this is perhaps the obvious method and the approach taken in most planning exercises it may not be the best for information strategies. Since we have recognised the increasing rate of change and the need to seize opportunities as and when they arise, an alternative approach which could yield additional benefits is to begin by painting a theoretical picture of the ways in which information could be exploited. Start with a vision of Information Power and withdraw to a practical reality. The techniques of information analysis will provide a good framework to investigate the potential and to construct this theoretical picture.

To illustrate this point let us go back a few years and imagine we were constructing an information strategy which had identified a priority need to increase management and office efficiency. The rather lengthy process of writing and typing a report has often been analysed by the O & M specialists who produced various physical solutions to organising the office, the typists and the managers in the cause of increased efficiency.

When word processing came along there was a tendency to see this as a typing efficiency tool but not as a management tool. Only recently have managers begun to use word processing at their own workstations, principally in order to improve the quality and quantity of their output. Had we attempted to draw a picture of information power at the outset then this vision would perhaps have included a manager communicating with a device which would create documents, allow for amendments and communicate the results to the recipients. We would then have pulled back to the reality of the typewriter but would have been prepared for the opportunity about to present itself.

If you are reading this as a manager who has never used a workstation and cannot envisage doing so, we would ask you to consider whether your attitude would change if you were able to talk to your terminal instead of using the tiresome keyboard. If your answer is *maybe*, then the follow up question is why and for what? Answering this question will be the first stroke of the brush on the canvas which will eventually display your vision of information power.

How then does one pull back to a realistic information strategy? In effect you have to apply certain constraints which you know have to be applied and to weight certain aspects of the picture according to priorities.

The constraints will come from:

- the capabilities and limitations of technology
- the weaknesses identified in the performance assessment mentioned (see page 205)
- the impositions of the company business plan and, in particular, the financial plans

The prioritisation will be driven by:

- recognised business priorities
- opportunities which have arisen from the analysis which show greater profit potential

From this it should be possible to prepare a business orientated information plan which reflects the company plans and priorities and capitalises on the opportunities offered by technology.
Based upon this strategy, up to four lower-level plans will be needed:

- a technology plan, to create a technological environment
- an information plan, to create an information base to support the applications
- project plans, required for new systems
- education and training plans, to ensure that human factors are taken into account

The last three of these plans, and occasionally the technology plan as well, may be wrapped together into a project plan for a major project. If this is done at this stage, however, it should be done in the full knowledge of the overall information needs. This is not the same as creating a project plan to meet a specific problem or as the result of a specific feasibility study.

IT in the organisation

Creating an Information Strategy is beginning to look like a rather formidable task. Who will be accountable for it? Who will lead the way?
There has been speculation in some informed quarters that the information technologies could present the next source of power in the Board Room over the coming years. The Financial Director has had his day, the Marketing men have reigned supreme, now the technologist will rise to power on the back of the increasing potential for exploiting information in business. If so, then the champion of the Information Strategy is clearly identified.
This is not the case, however, in most companies. Very few have an

IT Director. The Data Processing Manager is not usually in a position to perform such a role and it could be argued that he or she does not have the skills or track record to perform the task.

The Finance Director is perhaps the one most closely associated with Information Systems and therefore the one best poised to assume the role. The strategy needs, however, to encompass a much wider field than the financial interpretation so often given by the accountants. So the motivation, awareness and skills of the management accountant have to be updated before the information crown can rest comfortably on his or her head.

In the end it may have to rest with the Chief Executive Officer to initiate the programme and control its execution. If so, then he or she will certainly need the support and commitment of the Board and will probably need an advisory management body to keep the programme under control. This may take the form of an Information Steering Group.

At this point you may be saying: *Ah yes, we have one of those so all is well* – beware – many groups with names like this are serving the very different function of steering projects and prioritising project requests. In many cases this amounts to sanctioning the best guesses of the IT Department. If so, then this is not taking a step towards information power. Projects need management control and a steering group may be an effective way of maintaining a high level monitor, but the group which guides the information strategy will, in some respects, have finished its job when a project is given the go ahead.

There is no one answer. All organisations are different and the organisation of information has to reflect all the in-place organisational complexities. In assessing the options the final and most relevant advice would be to remember that the overall objective is to create a mechanism whereby a comprehensive system strategy can be established which is driven by the business needs and controlled by the management who have to live with the results.

Managing technological change

Management of change

The essential challenge of managing technological change is balancing the revolutionary effects of new technologies with the evolutionary processes of business changes and the even slower processes of change in the attitudes and practices of the people who make the business tick. The ultimate target is information power but the planning horizon for individual projects may have to be short if any degree of certainty is to be maintained.

Managing change with respect to the computer projects of the 1970s was essentially a long term investment involving complex risk assessment. Many of the technological risks have now been reduced through the availability of cheap hardware and instant software. This makes it technologically feasible to implement in weeks solutions which previously would have taken months. Unfortunately the associated changes related to the business, the environment and the human factors, are no less complex and the very speed of the changes serves only to increase the problems which can occur.

The management of change is therefore as much a man-management exercise as it is a task-orientated project management exercise. All the factors in successful implementation mentioned in this chapter have to be recognised, assessed, and planned for. This means education and training. It may demand modification of business practices and even changes to the very scope and nature of the business. It will mean building a consistent and reliable information base. All these are additional to the design and production of the software solutions. In some cases they assume such importance that they become separate projects in their own right.

Manufacturing companies which have implemented modern material control systems have had to recognise this challenge or have suffered as a consequence. It has been known for companies to instigate major stock clean up exercises before conversion to a new system. In one case the introduction of a new product was rescheduled to fit in with a new material system. Had this not been done the changes in the purchasing department would have been too dramatic and the workload would have been unacceptable. Far from benefiting from the new system disciplines, the new product would have been jeopardised by its introduction.

Some projects may be driven by specific business needs and may fit comfortably under the management of a functional manager – e.g. a personnel records system has a clear ownership. Others may cut across organisational boundaries and the ownership of the system will have to be clearly designated at the outset – e.g. integrated material systems usually impact many line functions. Others may be driven by a technological innovation where the departmental boundaries may not represent a problem but everyone is involved e.g. Office Automation projects.

For each project a suitable management structure is needed which will ensure the right level of commitment, adequate monitoring facilities, and a means of recognising and managing the inherent risks involved.

Programme for change

The move to information power is not based on a single management directive or even a new approach to management of change. It requires a cultural reappraisal and a programme for change which encompasses all the aspects mentioned in this paper. The programme may take many months to complete even in its first cycle and, like so many programmes of this type, once this has been completed it will be necessary to start all over again.
The following is a suggestion as to the typical steps which may be needed to implement a suitable programme:

1. Assess the present level of information performance in your company to highlight the strengths and weaknesses of your systems and environment.
2. Introduce an awareness programme for senior management. The best place to start is at Board level.
3. Investigate suitable steering mechanisms and management accountabilities.
4. Organise middle management workshops to encourage them to assess their own performance and to create the outline for information power.
5. Analyse the information view of the business and identify the key areas.
6. Prepare an action plan which prioritises the needs, recognises the business plan and drives the technology plan.
7. Agree the necessary project development methodologies and the tools of project management.
8. Organise and implement an education programme aimed at increasing information awareness rather than improving computer literacy.
9. Establish the objectives, targets and expectations of the information environment and define performance measurement criteria.
10. Monitor progress and seek new opportunities to improve and expand the information base and its utilisation.

IT in the management process

The importance of information

That information has a direct effect on power is not disputed. The sheer scale of the international investment in information gathering clearly shows that governments believe information is crucial to ensuring the balance of power between nations.

This is no less true of the corporate environment. Information can radically alter attitudes and opinions about everything to do with corporate success. Managers need information to help them make effective decisions. They must receive information related to their jobs, their responsibilities and the decisions they make.

Some of this information will be available, some will not. It can be obtained from both internal and external sources. However, getting exactly the information that is needed is never easy. Peter Drucker put the problem into its true perspective when he said:

The manager will never be able to get all the facts he should have. Most decisions have to be based on incomplete knowledge – either because the information is not available or it would cost too much in time and money to get it. To make sound decisions it is not necessary to have all the facts; but it is necessary to know what information is lacking in order to judge how much of a risk the decision involves, as well as the degree of precision and rigidity that the course of action can afford. For there is nothing more treacherous – or alas more common – than the attempt to make precise decisions on the basis of coarse and incomplete information.

The task, then, is to ensure that the manager ceases to be misinformed and instead becomes informed by the *MIS* (Management Information System). This is far from easy.

Information is a peculiar thing which varies depending upon when it is received, how it is received and who receives it. The same piece of information may be interpreted differently by different managers depending upon their attitudes and approach to the decisions concerned.

Like management itself, management information has vital human implications. To demonstrate the point, consider the implication to various people of a train whistle penetrating the evening dusk.

To the saboteur crouching in a culvert it might signify the failure of his mission because the whistle indicates that the train has already passed his detonating charge without causing an explosion. To the playboy it might presage the imminent arrival of a transgressed husband. To the fireman in the cab of the locomotive it indicates a drop in steam pressure and the need for re-stoking the furnace. To the lonely wife it means the return of her travelling husband. To the man with his foot caught in the switch down the track it foreshadows doom, for another (preparing to retire) it signifies time for prayer. In brief, the nature and significance of any information are fundamentally and primarily functions of the attitudes, situations and relevant responsibilities with respect thereto of the people involved with it.

The need for business intelligence

Information is management information only to the extent which the manager needs or wants it; and it is significant only in terms of its relation to the accumulation of relevant knowledge and plans and to his or her personal responsibility.

Establishing the information manager's need has never been easy. The problem of knowing exactly what data to collect and which to tabulate is not new. In 1914 Edward T Elbourne recognised this when he wrote:

It is possible for the management to collect more information than it can use to advantage, or which is more costly or hinders production more, than the information is worth. This is a real danger that has to be guarded against continuously, for routine that serves a valuable purpose when initiated may cease to be useful by some later changes in conditions.

It is interesting that over seventy years later, after massive investment in computer based systems, management are served by even more rigid and unresponsive systems than in Elbourne's days. Traditional accounting systems have not helped. Information is far too often seen as the spin-off from some *necessary* accounting or administrative system. Much information is produced too late to be effective or is not directly relevant to the manager's decision making needs. The technology has so far not solved the problem.

There is a frighteningly common desire today to prove that incredible amounts of information can be developed with electronic devices by preparing business reports that are increasingly long, incredibly dull and, all in all, just plain incredible.

Information alone is not enough. Try visualising, for example, one of our big daily newspapers if it was presented straight off the wire in continuous columns, with no headlines, no attempt to avoid duplication, and no simple means of judging the relative importance of the various news stories or putting them in proper perspective. Would you even attempt to read such a paper? I think not. Yet management is frequently forced to hunt through a haystack of irrelevant information in its reports in order to find for itself the needle of pertinent fact. What is needed, obviously, is a planned system of business intelligence which selects, rejects, edits and headlines business information – in short, which turns it into business intelligence.

The sources of management information

Management's real information needs have not been clearly identified by those seeking to build information systems. There has been no real understanding of the way information is used by managers. The research that has been carried out has concerned itself with the more academic mathematical techniques than with aiding the managers' choice of alternatives.

The fundamental basis for the design of a manager's information systems is a clear identification of management's information needs. This is no easy task. Each of us seeks information which we know will improve the decisions we make. Sometimes the information is related to past events and will hopefully provide answers to why results differed from our predictions. Alternatively the analysis of past information may lead us to re-appraise problems and perhaps re-define them. But the most important information we gather has to do with the future. People are frequently heard to say *if only I had known*, indicating that they would have acted differently. We all refer to hindsight in the sense that if we had had the information that we now have we would have made a better decision.

There is also the information which is gathered almost accidentally from our contact with other people. Such information forms our opinions and affects our actions in an instinctive way that cannot often be explained. One often hears managers say *I can't explain it, I just have a feeling about it.* These feelings or hunches stem from experience, collected knowledge and intuition. This form of information is often the manager's main source and one which he or she seeks to protect. Unfortunately, other sources that could be of value are often overlooked. Information is quite often available in the organisation, but frequently it is not available to the other people who could make the best use of it.

There is a certain degree of privilege and status to be catered for in the design of the information system. Any system designer who ignores this is taking his career in his hands. Some organisations have formalised this in their carefully developed procedures for the circulation of information. Some use different coloured documents; others have predetermined lists of recipients depending upon their classification, the higher the classification, the greater the power. To be *in the know* is a sought-after position, and such people will not forfeit their exclusiveness by letting anyone else into the secret.
Information systems in the widest sense deal with all the ways in which information flows to the decision maker. Many of these flows can be considered informal where there is no planned structure for collecting, processing and storing the information. These informal systems are often developed over the years and can be extremely effective. Many managers rely very heavily on these informal systems which have served them well in the past. It is not surprising therefore that they resist the move to more formalised methods, especially if these interfere with the informal systems.
The idea that all information flows can be formalised and built into a comprehensive data base is preposterous. Such an idea can only stem from someone who does not understand the decision making habits of management. The answer lies in the design of information systems that complement the informal systems and that directly feed managers with the information they need to take the decisions their jobs require. The design of such systems calls for a knowledge of the business, an understanding of the manager's decision-making needs and an ability to analyse these needs so that the system produces the necessary information for decision making.

8 Micro Multi-User Systems and Networks

R V Franks BSc, MBCS, FCMA, MIDPM and A D Kitcher MA, FCA

Introduction

The concept of running serious multi-user systems on microcomputers would have been viewed with some scepticism only a few years ago but, such is the rate of advancement in the microcomputer market, these systems are now becoming widely accepted and are instrumental in changing the structure of information processing in many organisations. As with previous developments in the microcomputer field, however, the inexperienced user is often exposed in the face of unfamiliar terminology and concepts. Many systems have failed as a result of the extravagant claims of suppliers or the unrealistic expectations of users.

This chapter provides a starting point for those considering the introduction of multi-user microcomputer systems and examines four specific areas in this field:

(a) developments in hardware which have enabled multi-user systems on microcomputers to become viable
(b) considerations applying to processing in a multi-user environment
(c) implementation of local area networks (LANs)
(d) related topics in the communications field.

The latter subject is included as the implementation of multi-user systems is often regarded as a step towards the 'office of the future' with its implication of automatic links with other computing environments and equipment both within and outside the organisation.

Obviously this chapter can cover only the broad principles involved in these subjects and the application of these principles to specific circumstances and products will require considerable effort in terms of time on the part of the user. Indeed, this effort should not be underestimated as incorrect decisions or assumptions during the selection process may have consequences far beyond the cost involved in the acquisition of hardware and software.

A basic knowledge of computing terms and concepts is assumed throughout this chapter and emphasis is placed upon the importance of systems from a user's viewpoint.

Hardware concepts

A brief history

The early generations of business microcomputers were developed around '8-bit' processors such as the 6502, Z80 or 8080 CPU (central processing unit) chips. Such systems typically provided for:

- single-user, single-tasking systems
- floppy disk storage (progressing to hard disk as technology advanced and prices fell)
- 64K as the maximum directly addressable RAM
- CPU clock speeds of around 4MHz.

Computers which incorporated these features rapidly became accepted in the office environment and, it is fair to say, revolutionised the traditional view of business computing. For the first time the actual users of computers could gain direct control over their applications. Software packages which provided a framework for the user to define and solve particular problems became increasingly popular and, for example, the use of spreadsheet packages accounted for the sale of many microcomputer systems.

As the users' expertise on such systems developed so their level of expectation increased. It became frustrating to have to queue for '*machine time*' when a number of users wanted access to the microcomputer. Often the solution was to buy more and more discrete microcomputer systems, together with printers, to satisfy the growing needs of active users. While this may have been only marginally punitive in cost terms it was obviously an inefficient and unwieldy approach towards developing the microcomputer functions. Additionally a critical appraisal of the disparate systems which developed resulted in identifying many advantages which would arise if, for example, user A could have ready access to data processed by user B with the resultant output being passed directly to another user for output through word processing software. Such reactions led rapidly to a demand for systems that facilitated multiple access to programs and data with an overall integrated approach. It is this demand which has led directly to the technically advanced products which are

available today.
Some brave attempts were made to implement multi-user systems on 8-bit microcomputers. Such systems were, however, limited in their true degree of multiple access and it has only been with the development of what are termed 16-bit (and, following on from this, 32-bit) microprocessors that the explosion in the use of multi-user microcomputer systems has taken place.
Multi-user systems are, by the very nature of their complexity and the requirement for them to perform several tasks '*simultaneously*', much more intensive in the use of hardware resources than single-user systems. Systems with limited hardware capability would simply lack the power to enable multi-user operation to be effective. Even if there was sufficient hardware resource to run the operating software there may be nothing left to run any applications!
In addressing this, the new range of microcomputers have typically provided the following important features:

- 16-bit, and 32-bit, as opposed to 8-bit, CPUs
- faster clock speeds
- increased RAM addressability
- hard disk storage as a standard design feature
- the availability of virtual RAM disks.

The combination of the above has provided the gateway for the development of multi-user systems, including networks.

16- and 32-bit vs 8-bit CPUs

There is often some confusion as to precisely what is meant by the term '*16- (or 32-) bit*'. The following may help to clarify the situation.
There are three principal attributes used when comparing the relative processing capabilities of particular CPUs:

- width of internal transfer bus
- width of data bus
- number of address lines.

The internal transfer bus relates to the amount of information which can be operated upon (ie processed) within the CPU in any one operation. In 8-bit processors, as their name implied, eight bits (or one byte) of information could be processed. This has increased to sixteen, and subsequently, thirty-two bits in later processors. As more information could be processed at any one time it followed that the speed of processing could accordingly be increased. It is this attribute which is normally taken to describe a processor as being '*x-bit*' although it must be said that interpretations of this phrase differ.

The width of the data bus relates to the number of bits of data which can be read into, and written out of, the CPU in any one operation. In 8-bit processors, and even in some 16-bit processors, an eight-bit data bus is incorporated. Again, subsequent development has led to sixteen and thirty-two-bit data buses appearing.

The address bus relates to the number of discrete lines available to the CPU for describing the address of a particular memory location, each line being capable of adopting the binary values 0 or 1. An address bus of size *n* lines would thus enable 2 to the power *n* memory addresses to be described. The more address lines available, therefore, the greater is the amount of memory which will be directly available, resulting in fewer (time consuming) disk accesses.

The overall point of the above is that a 16- (or 32-) bit computer will be able to process more information in any one operation and will have a larger amount of directly addressable memory available to it. This is not, however, merely to say that a 16-bit microcomputer system will be twice (or any factor) as fast as its 8-bit equivalent as there are many additional elements to be taken into account.

Clock speeds

One of the elements referred to above is termed the clock speed of a computer. All computers use an internal clock to synchronise operations throughout the computer's circuitry. In simplistic terms, the computer carries out an operation each time an electronic pulse is issued by the clock. Thus the faster the clock operates, the more operations will be performed in a given period of time. This speed of the clock is measured in millions of cycles per second (megaherz – MHz). The clock speed of most 8-bit computers was around 4MHz, that of many 16-bit computers is around 8MHz. A speed of 8MHz corresponds to an element of processing every 125 nanoseconds so it is performing more instructions in a given period of time than its 8-bit counterpart.

Increased RAM addressability

The increase in the number of address lines available in modern CPUs was mentioned previously. In 8-bit chips the number of address lines was 16, enabling 2 to the power 16, or 64K (actually 65,536), memory locations to be directly addressed at any one time. Techniques, such as bank-switching, were devised to make it appear that more was available but this in turn

introduced processing overheads. Most 16-bit and later processors incorporate at least 20 address lines making 1 Mb of memory directly available – many processors have capabilities in excess of this. This has resulted in the feasibility of developing many sophisticated programs for microcomputers.
This RAM availability is crucial to the operation of multi-user systems which, by their nature, tend to have a heavy memory requirement for the complex operating software which is required. This, coupled with increasingly sophisticated (and frequently memory-intensive) applications software and the concept of multi-tasking (concurrency), has made the size of available RAM a critical factor in establishing powerful systems.

Hard disk systems

Hard disk drives, with storage capacities of between 5 and 120 Megabytes (Mb), are standard components of most modern microcomputers. The fast access time and high capacity are mandatory for building multi-user systems and, while individual terminals within a particular configuration may have local floppy disk drives, or even no disk storage at all, there will always be at least one hard disk device within a multi-user environment.

RAM disks

While the concept of virtual disk drives in RAM has been used for quite some time, these have usually been available as additional products to a system. Recent operating systems, however, have been designed with RAM disks as an integral part with consequent optimisation. RAM disks are particularly useful for locating programs during a processing session, especially as the computer does not then have to access disk drives for program overlays. While RAM disks can be used for data, great care should be taken to ensure that files are written back to physical drives at frequent intervals.

Conclusion

It is the combination of the above which has made the advent of multi-user microcomputer systems feasible. The microcomputer industry is extremely fast moving and technological developments continue apace. Multiple terminal systems which, only a couple of years ago, would have been regarded solely as the domain of mini computers or even mainframes, are now available on microcomputers. Of course, the hardware is only part of the picture and it is the software which has to take advantage of these developments, as will be seen in the next section.

Multi-user systems

If a computer system is to offer '*multi-user*' capabilities, all three elements of that system, namely:

- the hardware
- the operating system
- the applications software

must be suitably configured. The hardware aspects were dealt with in the previous section and this section is therefore devoted to a review of the latter two elements. Again it is appropriate briefly to consider the history of the development of microcomputer systems. In the early days, operating systems were designed to be limited in their memory requirements and, as a consequence, afforded little in terms of sophistication. In particular, the microcomputer user was only able to run a single program or task at a time. For business use, this was often considered to be unsatisfactory and, in response to demand, the first multi-user operating systems were released for microcomputers. In general, there were three drawbacks to these systems:

- performance was slow, often degrading to a totally unacceptable level when more than two users were on the system;
- facilities were still very limited, in view of the need to conserve the use of memory for application programs;
- faults were commonplace, users found themselves restoring from security copies following a system crash on too many occasions.

The arrival of 16 and 32-bit chip offered the opportunity for the first two of these problems to be overcome with faster execution speeds and increased memory addressing respectively. The passage of time has, for the most part, enabled the systems houses to fix the faults in their operating software although it must be admitted that this process is still continuing in many cases, particularly in respect of the newer products. It is now true to say, however, that fully viable multi-user operating systems are available for microcomputers.

Turning briefly to applications software, the development of multi-user capabilities has, in general, followed that of operating systems, although almost inevitably one step behind. In the same way as operating system development was only possible given a suitable hardware environment, applications software was initially constrained by the limitations of the operating systems. Two classes of software are considered in this section:

- software which permits each user to work with an exclusive set of data files at any point in time within a multi-user environment e.g. spreadsheets, word processors etc where it is not necessary for two users to update a single file simultaneously
- software which permits and controls the use of a common set of data files by a number of users simultaneously e.g. integrated accounting systems.

Considerable caution must be exercised when reviewing software to identify firstly the user's needs and, in that context, the classification of the software required to fulfil those needs.

Definition of terms

This requirement for definition in respect of software prompts a closer examination of a number of terms which are liberally scattered around by computer 'buffs' and in advertising literature. It is more or less possible tow rite down '*multi*' followed by any computing term (user, tasking, programming, processor etc) and thereby to derive another perfectly valid term. Definition of the meanings attached to these terms is often difficult and probably not too helpful – different people attach different meanings and, frequently, the definitions overlap or vary dependent upon whether they apply to hardware, operating systems or applications software! Because of this, these terms will be defined during the course of this section, so that their meanings can be explained in context. Terms which are specific to manufacturers or software houses will be avoided as it is the intention to give a general review of this area rather than to point out the good or bad points of particular products. Whether or not a particular system or piece of software is suitable will depend so heavily upon the application to which it is to be put that generalisations are not appropraite.

Operating systems

The operating system has become even more important in the multi-user environment. Applications software will generally only operate under a specific operating system, thus the need to run a particular application will often dictate which operating system is required and, as a consequence, will limit the range of hardware from which a user's selection may be made. This limitation is being broken down at present with the availability of hybrid operating systems capable of running products formerly specific to different families of operating systems. These new systems will be of particular value in providing users with the widest possible choice in terms of software.

It is useful at this stage to review the functions which the operating system should be expected to perform in a multi-user environment, in addition to the basic function of interpreting application program requirements in hardware terms. A multi-user operating system will perform the following:

- memory management
- CPU utilisation and prioritisations
- peripheral device control
- utility programs
- security.

and each of these aspects is considered in the following paragraphs.

Memory management

The memory available within a microcomputer must be allocated to different users or tasks. Firstly, the operating system itself will often require considerable areas of memory for its own functions. A RAM capacity of 128K used to be viewed as evidencing a good-sized computer when 48K or 64K were the norm – nowadays this may be inadequate to permit even the operating system to be loaded. Secondly, each user of the system will normally require an area of memory in which to work, although this may be small when all users are running the same program and the software has been designed to be code sharing, i.e. one copy of the program is loaded to which all users have access. Multi-tasking describes a computer's ability to run two or more different tasks simultaneously; obviously code sharing is not possible in such circumstances and the operating system must ensure that memory is partitioned and allocated such that different tasks cannot interfere with each other.

A special form of multi-tasking has recently been introduced, namely, concurrency, which provides the user with a number of virtual consoles which can be attached to or detached from a single physical console at '*the press of a button*', enabling multiple tasks to be controlled by a single user console. Thirdly, or more properly, an extension of the second aspect of memory management, the operating system may permit and allocate memory to background tasks which are initiated by a user (in the foreground) and then detached to run without intervention – a good example would be the print spooler, which is discussed later. The operating system must manage the allocation of memory efficiently and keep all programs or tasks to discrete areas.

CPU utilisation and prioritisations

In most hardware configurations, the CPU must be shared by a number of tasks. The CPU actually executes programmed instructions and without service from the CPU nothing will happen in the computer. The operating system will determine which tasks are waiting to use the CPU by a process known as polling whereby the list of tasks present is interrogated on a constant cycle basis. The operating system allows each waiting task to use the CPU in turn. Of course, some tasks may be CPU intensive and would bring all other tasks to a standstill if allowed to retain the use of the CPU until they had finished with it. To avoid this the operating system will allocate maximum periods of time (typically one tenth of a second) for which a single task may run uninterrupted; if at the end of the period the task is still running, the operating system '*expresses its regrets*' and suspends the task until its turn comes around again.

In more sophisticated environments, different priorities may be attached to tasks such that they receive longer time slots than other less critical tasks. It should always be remembered that the operating system itself is made up of a number of programs which require CPU services, particularly in a multi-user environments; this drain on the CPU resource is generally referred to as system overhead and in the days of slower, less powerful processors, this was primarily responsible for the poor performance of multi-user systems.

Peripheral device control

In addition to memory and CPU requirements, all user tasks will need access to peripheral devices for input and output purposes. The range of devices available is always expanding and includes floppy and hard disk drives, keyboards, screens, printers, tape drives, modems, network ports, etc. The operating system will receive requests from tasks running on the system for access to these peripherals and must translate them before passing on to the firmware of the device controller. A procedure equivalent to that described for the CPU is necessary in respect of each peripheral device to ensure that no two tasks are allowed access to the same device at the same time. In respect of direct access devices, primarily the disk drives, sharing is possible while in the case of a serial device such as the printer exclusive use is obviously essential and another task calling for that device will simply have to wait until the task in control has been completed.

Utility programs

Although not strictly part of the operating system, a number of utilities will be available to the user, providing for directory listings of the contents of a disk, the copying of files etc. Such utilities are initiated by the user as required and run effectively as application programs.

One particular utility associated with multi-user environments warrants specific mention, namely the print spooler. The difficulties arising when two tasks wish to use a printer at the same time have been mentioned previously. One solution would be to acquire a printer for each task but this is generally unrealistic; furthermore, printers are slow devices and even when a task has control it is generally idle for most of the time whilst it waits to send the next block of information to the printer – meanwhile the user is probably sitting in front of a screen which reads '*Report in Progress*' and is unable to proceed with other work! The print spooler solves these problems very effectively; a background task is initiated which intercepts all information sent to the printer by application programs and re-routes the data to temporary files on the hard disk. A further task will scan these files and once the 'print' has been completed will cause them to be printed as soon as the device to which they were originally addressed becomes available.

These utility programs vary in terms of complexity and the facilities afforded to the user, however, they are of fundamental importance in maximising the use of computer resources and removing the constraints otherwise inevitable with printers.

Security

There is an obvious need for the operating system to manage memory, the CPU and peripheral devices in such a way that users do not interfere with each other's work. The need for security extends beyond these internal functions, particularly where routines or data files are to be restricted to particular users. The Finance Director may object to the Sales Ledger clerk having access to his correspondence, the budget proposals for the following year or the salaried staff payroll. The operating systems now available have improved dramatically the facilities available for security, generally through the implementation of password control on routines and/or data files. Since the problems associated with security are generally greater in a networking environment, detailed discussion of this aspect is deferred to that section.

The effect on the user

While the above description of the functions performed by the operating system is not exhaustive, the principal aspects have been explained and it is obvious that the operating system in a multi-user environment must be a highly sophisticated piece of software. Equally it will be apparent that, if a multi-user system is to be used to maximum effectiveness, a more knowledgeable user is required to manage the system. Users must understand these concepts and how they are implemented on their own systems such that workloads can be scheduled properly, files assigned to relevant devices, priorities established, print spoolers used appropriately and security procedures implemented. Users must also understand why 'log jams' are arising and identify solutions – to buy more memory, reschedule the workload, upgrade the hard disk unit, change the printer or whatever the correct course of action might be.

It has also become apparent that a different level of computer dealer will be required, to ensure that the operating system is efficiently installed and to provide ongoing technical support – selling microcomputers in today's environment is very far removed from shifting cardboard boxes as around 25 per cent of dealers per annum find out to their cost, and to the cost of their existing customers, when the winding up order arrives!

Applications software

As identified previously, software for use in a multi-user environment should be classified as to whether or not data files are to be shared by users operating contemporaneously. In many cases, the user will only require that the software operates 'as though it were single-user' in a multi-user environment. For example, a number of word processing users may be required, however, no two users will be working on the same letter at any point in time, indeed the results could be rather disastrous if this were permitted! In other cases, data files must be shared by a number of users with a consequent need for controls to be applied to prevent such occurrences as '*deadly embrace*'. An explanation of this phenomenon will instance the problems which can arise. When data is written to disk, it is read back again to verify the accuracy of the write operation. If two users are trying to amend a single piece of information at the same time, the following may arise:

(a) User 1 writes version 1 of the data to disk.
(b) User 2 writes version 2 of the data to disk.
(c) User 1 reads disk, compares with version 1 and finds error, rewrites version 1.

(d) User 2 reads disk, compares with version 2 and finds error, rewrites version 2.
(e) Go to (c).

This cycle is perpetuated and cannot be broken.
The considerations which should be borne in mind when acquiring software in the first category are more straightforward than those for the second, and are as follows:

(a) Will the product run under the multi-user operating system? It must not be assumed that software designed for use with a single-user operating system will always run under the multi-user equivalent. This aspect must be checked with the supplier for each specific product.
(b) Will the operating system or the applications software prevent simultaneous update of a single file by two users? Protection is essential to ensure that two users do not accidentally work on a single file although simultaneous reading may be acceptable. Such protection may be afforded by the operating system, however, if this is not the case, users must look either to the applications software or, more commonly, to their own disciplines and restrictions to avoid problems from this source.

In respect of the second category, where file sharing is essential, the user must look solely to the applications software for control responsibility. A specifically multi-user version is required which will apply 'locking' either at the file or record level to prevent access conflicts.

Locking

The most straightforward technique applied for control of multiple access to common files is for the system to '*lock*' a data file (i.e. file locking), denoting that its use is temporarily restricted to a single user. On completion of that user's update, the lock is released and the file once again becomes available to other users. While the lock is in force, other users attempting to access the file will be advised that they must wait for the file to be released. This technique is obviously effective but is also excessively restrictive in most cases – in the case of a stock file, for example, the update of a single stock line by one user will lock out all other users from access to all stock lines. It will often be found that software written originally for single-user environments and subsequently '*upgraded*' to multi-user operation will lock only at the file level.
A more sophisticated and far less restrictive technique is to lock at the record level (i.e. record locking) such that only the actual record, instead of

the entire file, is locked out during updates. In the case of the stock file example, a number of users will be able to update the file simultaneously provided they are accessing different stock lines.

It will be seen that for both locking methods some degree of communication between different users of the same software is required. This may be effected through the use of operating system facilities, if available, or by routines within the applications software. There are many different implementations of locking techniques and the potential user will be well advised not to assume that a product which is defined as '*true rcord locking*' is automatically to be preferred to a '*file locking*' system. Record locking may be implemented but can lead to general inefficiency, while file locks may only last for fractions of a second and be imperceptible from the user viewpoint. An assessment must be made during a full demonstration of the system with particular attention being paid to the consequences of simultaneous update.

Multi-user management

As stated in the context of operating systems, an increased level of management on the part of the user will be required for multi-user applications software. The timing, for example, of ledger updates will be crucial since, firstly, this will generally degrade the performance for other users on the system due to the high leel of processing and disk activity implied, and, secondly, the access restrictions imposed during such routines will normally be of a high level. Managers of multi-user systems must ensure that they are aware of the full implications of that system and plan its use accordingly. This theme is returned to in the next section.

Networks

There is little doubt that the introduction of local area networks (LANs) into the office environment has revolutionised the use of business microcomputers and has changed radically the way in which they have been perceived as serious computing tools. The concept of networking is that a direct communications path is established between a number of computers such that resources (e.g. disk storage or printers) which are part of a particular computer are available on a shared basis.

As many experts have pointed out, making the decision to adopt a networking strategy is easy, however, acquiring the correct tools in terms of hardware and software is much more difficult. Part of the reason for this is that networking products for microcomputers are still developing (and very rapidly at that!) and, as has been the case in so many instances in the computer field, it is difficult to find standards which are adhered to or any form of 'guiding hand'.

Local area networks (LANs)

Local area networks are a specialised form of communications in which the task of linking computers within geographically limited distances is optimised in a cost-effective manner. The principal advantages of networking can be summarised as follows:

- cost economy through the sharing of physical system resources among many users
- improved processing facilities through the sharing and exchange of data files between users
- convenience of selection of alternative resources (e.g. printers) if a particular resource is unavailable at any point in time
- facilities for the use of internal mail and for communicating directly with other users (termed 'chatting')
- flexibility in terms of expansion and, to some extent, reconfiguration.

Prcise hardware configurations vary considerably but, the essential ingredients of a typical microcomputer networking system can be categorised as:

(a) At least one microcomputer with a hard disk storage device and RAM from 256K upwards to act as a server (i.e. provider and controller of resources) to other machines on the network.

(b) A number of other workstations which will be microcomputers, possibly with their own hard or floppy disk storage devices. These workstations may be merely requesters (i.e. requesting resources from server) or may be both servers and requesters. In addition, these computers will normally, but not necessarily, have access to their own local resources.

(c) Network circuitry within the above computers to provide the physical control of network communications.

(d) Network cabling and points to provide the connection between computers within the network. Cabling may be twisted-pair but, in more advanced systems, coaxial cable or even fibre optic cable may be used.

(e) Network operating software. The software that provides the network with its individual characteristic and presents the interface between the user and the hardware.

Each device which is directly connected to the network is termed a node.

Network planning and selection

When considering the implementation of a network system it is easy to become sidetracked into investigating the technical concepts of network operation rather than concentrating principally upon the actual requirements of the proposed environment. In many ways, acquiring a network is like purchasing any other type of system – it is what it does which should be fundamentally important rather than how it does it. There are now a large number of network products available on the market ranging from the single concept of linking machines to provide each with a separate work area on a shared hard disk to those providing true capabilities for file sharing. The capabilities are, of course, reflected in the broad spectrum of costs which apply in building a network.

Given the above, it is essential to define in some detail the immediate and medium-term requirements from a network system before investigating actual products in detail. While networks are usually flexible in terms of expansion it will be neither easy nor inexpensive to change products if the wrong network has been acquired in the first place. As the expenditure on a network system may run into tens of thousands of pounds it is well worth investing some time in the planning stage.

With reference to the user's requirements the following type of questions will normally be applicable:

- how many workstations will be required and where (in terms of location) will they be?
- what physical resources in terms of disk storage and printers will be required by each workstation?
- which applications are to be run at each workstation? Will these applications require multi-user operation and, if so, will they support it?
- which data files, if any, should be capable of access by multiple users? Should these accesses be available to more than one user at any one time? If so, how many of these users will need to write to, rather than merely read, these files?
- what internal arrangements will be required for the system manager function (i.e. who will oversee the system, set access controls, supervise backup arrangements etc)?

Having considered the above and drawn up a list of requirements together with a '*map*' of the envisaged installation, the following type of questions should be addressed to the prospective network supplier:

- what is the precise nature and cost of all of the hardware and software elements which will comprise the network? In particular look for additional RAM requirements, special boards, network software and any specific requirements for servers.
- what are the costs and arrangements for cabling and initial installation of the network?
- what facilities are available (and what restrictions are there) in terms of the sharing and multiple access to drives/files/records?
- similarly, what facilities exist for the sharing of printers and is print spooling incorporated?
- what electronic mail and '*chat*' facilities are available?
- how will the network appear to the inexperienced user?
- what training facilities are available to the user in terms of network operation and management?
- what security features are available at logon/drive/file level?
- what arrangements apply for security archiving of data?
- what facilities exist for defining the resources which workstations can access (commonly termed '*resource mapping*')? Are these easy to redefine?
- can a workstation use facilities from more than one server at any one time?
- what is involved in expanding the network in terms of ease, cost and effect on the existing network?
- what is the maximum number of (a) stations which can be supported by each server and (b) nodes which can be supported by the network?
- what is the maximum distance between nodes that can be supported by the network?
- what happens if a node goes down?

In addition to the above it is useful to get some idea as to the overall speed of the network. As noted previously, the use of a network may entail an operating system overhead which, in some cases, can have a noticeable detrimental effect on processing speeds in comparison with simple single-user operation. A visit to an existing site using the proposed network is normally helpful in this and other respects.

Lastly, and perhaps the most difficult aspect, is attempting to assess the experience and expertise of the dealer in the installation and maintenance of networked systems. The configuration of these systems can be complex and require a thorough knowledge of operating system generation together with network utilities and circuitry. Problem diagnosis and solution is also correspondingly more involved than with single-user machines. In these respects many network users will become heavily reliant on their suppliers and should take this into account during the selection process.

Only when all of these factors have been considered is it then appropriate to look into the technical aspects of networking in some more detail. It is important to remember, however, that the following paragraphs consider the subjects in general terms and that specific techniques will vary considerably between products.

Servers, requesters and resource mapping

As noted previously, servers are computers on the network which provide resources for other workstations on the same network. The term is normally associated with the provision of hard disk resources such that network users can store and access files contained on a common hard disk – hence the term '*file server*'. In some networks, computers used as file servers are not available for other uses and these are termed dedicated servers – in other systems, servers may also be accessed as workstations in their own right. Requesters are workstations on the network which, as the term implies, request the use of resources from servers. A network may comprise a number of servers and requesters and some servers may themselves also be requesters (termed server/requesters) of resources from other servers. The terms server and requester may vary between networks (servers are frequently termed '*network managers*' for example) but the principles will be the same.

In terms of operation, the network software running on a requester will typically intercept a call from an applications program and determine whether it requires resources contained on another station in the network (i.e. a server). If so it sends a message to the server which will then, subject to whatever constraints apply in that particular network, make the resource available and return a message to the requester to this effect. The requester will then pass the relevant signal back to the calling applications program and processing continues with access to the remote resource just as though it is a local device.

With the use of servers and requesters the concept of resource mapping is fundamental to network operation. Essentially this involves the definition of what resources are available to a particular user (requester) in the network and where these resources are physically located. In its simplest form, a requester workstation with no disk or printer resources of its own will be '*mapped*' to the resources of a server in the network. In such a case, drive A of the server may become drive A to the requester and so on. In more complex cases, a requester may be using the resources of more than one server at any time together with its own local resources. Normally, the standard resource map for each workstation is installed with the initial implementation of the network but this mapping may be subsequently changed on a permanent basis or even temporarily for the duration of a particular process.

Network classification

Local area networks are normally classified in one of three principal ways:

(a) Topolog – the '*pattern*' of the network, the most common being:

- star; or
- bus; or
- ring

(b) Means of transmission of data – principally whether baseband (digital pulses) or broadband (using radio frequencies) is used. While baseband has been the most prevalent in early network systems, there are now a significant number of broadband systems appearing. Broadband has added sophistication in that sub-networks can be created of workstations which are tuned to a particular frequency and that external signals (e.g. TV signals) can be carried. This is normally, of course, reflected in additional cost elements. Typical throughout (i.e. speed of transmission around a network) is between 1 and 10 million bits per second (Mbps).

(c) Access protocol – essentially the method used to ensure control over transmissions on the network, the most commonly used being Carrier Sense multiple Access (CSMA) with Collision Avoidance (CSMA/CA) or Collision Detection (CSMA/CD) and Token Passing.

Although all of the above elements will normally be somewhat transparent to the user, the topology aspect is described in some detail in the next section as it is frequently referred to in sales literature.

It is also worth noting that the International Standards Organisation (ISO) has established a framework for categorising network attributes into seven layers. This is termed the Open Systems Interconnection (OSI) model and one of its purposes is to enable compatibility to be achieved at particular levels of network operation even where there are differences in the implementation at higher levels. The lowest level (level 1) is physically related to the hardware and network medium whilst the highest level (level 7) deals with the application functions available to the user.

Network topology

Star network

In star network configurations all data is transmitted through a central point and it is commonly used for switched circuits such as PBXs.

Bus network

The bus topology involves a central cable to which all nodes are directly connected. Each node continually scans the central cable and removes any messages or data which are destined for it. Similarly it outputs to the bus information for other nodes. The highway analogy extends to the manner in which data is merged on and off the central bus as it proceeds from source to destination node.

Ring network

The ring network, as its name implies, joins together each node with its two neighbours to form a continuous circuit. Each node accesses the ring for messages which are ciruclating. To control matters, a protocol convention known as the '*token*' is used to denote whether a node may be permitted to transmit information at any point in time. This token can be imagined as continuously circulating the ring. When it is '*empty*' a node may place information destined for another node on the ring and '*seizes control*' of the token. The recipient node reads the token and removes the information attached to it. When the originating node receives the token back again after its journey around the ring, it '*empties*' the token and then releases it for access by another node.

Security

In conjunction with the advanced facilities brought about by networks a considerable number of points regarding system security procedures become essential items for consideration. In order to ensure that these are properly defined and are effective it is important to nominate someone as the '*System Manager*' for the whole area of the network operation. This person should be responsible for the definition of the facilities and physical resources which are available to any authorised user of the network. It should also be impossible for an unauthorised user to gain access to the network or to cause any form of damage from a terminal while the network is in operation. All of this sounds fairly trite, but many users are not aware of the responsibility which they have in this respect. Most network software provides '*system supervisor*' utilities to assist the system manager in carrying out these various functions.

The security facilities offered by networks differ between proprietary products, however, the types of protection which may be available included:

User identifiers (IDs)	each user attempting access to the system is allocated a unique identifier – this in turn will relate to a table of defined access for that user.
User password	associated with the user ID.
Resource mapping	definition of which disk drives may be available to a particular user or application. In this context only certain applications can be made available to particular users.
Drive protection	whole drives may be designated RO (read only) to particular users. Alternatively, RW (read write) access to the drive may be available only by password.
File protection	similar to drive protection, only at file level.

Most networks provide for a user-defined '*menu*' to be presented for each user and the user is barred from access to any function which is not available on his/her menu. This technique has the following advantages:

- the facilities available to each user are clearly defined
- housekeeping tasks, such as copying files or formatting floppy disks, can be automated for the user from the menu
- the user can be prohibited from accessing certain facilities within the resident operating system.

In addition to the above, many applications software products provide password protection on critical facilities providing a further level of access control.

While all of the above may make the network sound like '*Fort Knox*', it is worth stressing that a poorly designed or poorly managed network may have little or no security and may also be very inefficient in operation. The network is a complex tool and requires good management to obtain the best results.

Conclusion

At the time of writing, many microcomputer LAN systems are clearly passing through development or early stages although there are some which have become established. In many ways it is the user who is required to change as many users still have a '*simple single-user micro*' mentality when considering or even operating a network. As mentioned in the previous section, network systems have also placed a heavier burden on microcomputer dealers who are now expected to accumulate a large amount of technical expertise in order to make and support each sale. It will be interesting to note the overall effect of networks on the microcomputer marketplace in the years to come.

Communications

The principal method employed for the input of information to computer systems remains the keying of data by an operator. In many circumstances, this will represent a duplication of clerical effort since the data being keyed has already been input to and is held in a magnetic form on another system or machine. Much frustration is experienced when the magnetically encoded data cannot be communicated between different systems. The microcomputer industry has not helped as standards for information interchange, disk formats etc have only been loosely applied. In this section the following aspects of the need for communications will be considered:

- one micro to another
- micro to mainframe and vice versa
- micro to external databases
- electronic mail
- format conversions.

As in other sections, references to particular products or services will be avoided wherever possible, however, this cannot be rigorously applied and, whilst certain trade names are mentioned, there is no intention to express a recommendation or otherwise.

Micro to micro communications

As an illustration of the pitfalls in this area, it is not even certain that difficulties will not exist in the communication of data between microcomputers from the same manufacturer. Floppy disks written under one operating system may not be readable under an alternative operating system. Furthermore, there is frequently no compatibility between old and new ranges of machine. These difficulties are exacerbated when data is to be communicated between microcomputers from different manufacturers. One of the benefits arising from the significant market share taken by the IBM PC has been that many other manufacturers have considered it appropriate to provide an IBM PC disk read/write option with their machines. This has certainly eased problems in this field provided that the machines concerned have access to a 5.25″ disk drive and an IBM disk option; no matter how hard one tries, a 5.25″ disk will not fit in a 3.5″ disk drive! An additional consideration is the speed with which transfers to remote locations can be achieved – even Datapost implies next day delivery; furthermore, such transfers are costly.

An alternative solution is to link the output port of one computer to the input port of another enabling the transmission of data between them. For this purpose, it is necessary to acquire a software package for each machine which provides a protocol for the transmission. A protocol, in its simplest form, is a signalling system between the sender and the recipient ensuring that the former only sends when the latter is ready to receive. Error checking is also generally built in such that a corruption in the connection between the machines giving rise to data errors is detected by the receiver which then requests a retransmission from the sender. This method for data transfer depends on the availability of suitable ports on the two machines in question, the preparation of a specific cable and the availability of the communications software. Many '*mixed microcomputer*' sites have established communication links in this form.

When the microcomputers are sited at different geographical locations, the transmission method described in the preceding paragraph may still be employed, however, it is necessary to introduce modems as the means for providing the physical link between the machines via a telephone network. A modem is essentially a device which is capable of converting (MOdulating) the digital information output from the computer port into signals which can be carried over a telephone line for receipt and reconversion (DEModulation) by a further modem at the other end of the line. In this field, at least, there are standards, specified for the most part by the governing body (CCITT). A number of terms are associated with modem communications, as follows:

Full Duplex	transmission of data in both directions simultaneously.
Half Duplex	transmission of data in both directions but not simultaneously.
BPS	bits per second, used to specify the speed of transmission of the modem which must be matched at the receiving end.
Baud rate	also used to denote the speed of transmission. The baud rate is broadly equivalent to bits per second.
Acoustic coupling	the provision of a facility within the modem whereby indirect connection to the telephone system is effected through conventional handsets.

V21	300 BPS full duplex, a transmission standard commonly used by acoustically coupled modems.
V22	1200 BPS full duplex, a transmission standard commonly used by directly connected modems utilising the public telephone network.
V23	a standard which gives 1200 BPS half duplex or 75 BPS send 1200 BPS receive full duplex, the latter being used, for example, by Prestel.
V24, V25, V26 etc	higher speed transmission standards generally used for leased lines rather than the public network.
Auto-dialling	a modem facility which enables the computer to send dialling information to a directly connected line.
Auto-answer	a modem which enables automated activation on detection of an incoming call.

There is now a plethora of modems available and the user must ensure that the device acquired is suitable for all intended purposes. One particular variant is the '*on board*' modem which may be installed within certain microcomputers.

A further intermediary may be introduced into the micro to link micro through the availability of public access electronic mail facilities such as Telecom Gold or Easylink. Whilst this aspect is covered in a later paragraph, it is useful to note at this stage that the use of such intermediaries will often avoid the necessity to synchronise the availability of the sending and receiving computers.

Micro to mainframe communications

The considerations which apply in setting up a microcomputer to mainframe link are essentially identical to those discussed in the preceding paragraphs. The most important aspect in this case is the communications protocol which must be used for mainframe access and the availability of suitable software to emulate that protocol on the microcomputer. Many packages are available to emulate, for example, IBM 3780 or ICL C02, C03, however, installation is often complex and is definitely not for the amateur! Dirct cable connections are often affected, however, if the microcomputer is located more than about 30 metres from the mainframe, the use of line drivers which boost the signal will be required. It is more common, perhaps, to find modem links to remote mainframe installations and indeed many microcomputers are sold as remote data collection/output points for mainframe-based systems.

Communications packages generally enable the micro to emulate a terminal under the mainframe's time sharing system and provide file transfer facilities to and from the mainframe. It must be remembered when assessing the viability of data transfers that transmission speeds, even directly cabled or over a leased line, are relatively slow – 9600 BPS, approximately 1K per second, is the normal high speed rate. If high volume transfers are to be effected, some other medium for data exchange, probably floppy disk or 0.5″ reel to reel magnetic tape, may need to be considered.

Micro to database communications

Thus far only communication links between the computer resources within an organisation have been considered. There are now an increasing number of database and bulletin boards which may be accessed by subscribers via public telephone line connections. These require merely a suitable modem and the software for the microcomputer enabling it to emulate a standard terminal (plus the small matter of the subscription to the service). Prestel, the British Telecom (BT) viewdata service is available to the microcomputer user together with many other databases dealing with specific areas of interest, for example, bibliography, medicine and financial data.

Electronic mail

The facility to send messages or extended text files to other microcomputer users has been a recent major development area. This facility may be established at the lowest level between the users attached to a local area network. Further extension may be achieved through the use of communications equipment and the appropriate software; the software may still be restricted to users within an organisation or may be broader in scope through attachment to one of the commercial public mailing services. These public services are generally linked to similar services on an international basis e.g. BT's *Telecom Gold* is part of the global *Dialcom* network. Users of public electronic mail are allocated a '*mailbox*' number which they can pass on to their business contacts who may then dial up the service and send messages or files to that mailbox. Recipients will typically clear their mailboxes once or twice a day to read the mail which has been left for them. In almost all cases, telex messages will be an additional option and many users are finding this facility to be a low cost method for access to telex when their requirements would not otherwise justify an individual connection. In other cases, those who have already installed telex lines are acquiring the interface hardware and software to permit use of their telex line from, perhaps, a network of microcomputers.

Format conversions

Thus far only the physical problems and solutions associated with the linking to other computers and services have been considered. Unfortunately, this may only be part of the story – having communicated data from one point to another, it may still be found that the data cannot be used or even read intelligently by the recipient. It may be necessary to translate that data through the use of further software before it can be used effectively. A few examples serve to illustrate this point:

- text files written by word processing packages may contain embedded control codes which are specific to the creating package and may be unreadable by another package
- data files written by a nominal ledger package will almost certainly be of little value in their standard form as input to a spreadsheet and vice versa
- mainframe files may be written in EBCDIC character code instead of the ASCII code more or less standard for microcomputer use; furthermore, the storage of numeric data in a computational or packed form may cause problems.

Software solutions will almost certainly be specific to the problem and will quite probably be costly to acquire. It is to be hoped that the applications software industry will reflect an increasing need for information exchange within their standard products, however, progress to date in this respect leaves a little to be desired.

The ready availability of communications facilities to the microcomputer user has already opened up many opportunities. Inevitably this will be an area for continuing growth in the progression towards the much publicised 'electronic office'.

Conclusion

The subjects covered in this chapter illustrate the exciting developments which are taking place in the microcomputer field and the possibilities which are opening up for the users and managers of information within organisations.

Even by the standards of the computer industry, the microcomputer environment is developing rapidly and the rate of introduction of new products will doubtless increase. The availability of more computing power raises the level of expectations of users and frequently provides solutions to long-standing information problems. Users should remember, however, the underlying messages contained in this chapter in that:

(a) the increased level of responsibility when running more sophisticated systems must be accepted seriously, and
(b) they should not be '*blinded*' by technology when determining whether particular systems will fulfil their requirements.

As with all computerised systems, the need for careful planning and control remains paramount.

9
Expert Systems in Context

R Dixon BA, MA, K Hood BA, MPhil and
S Priestnall BA

Expert Systems – an historical perspective of artificial intelligence

The term *expert system* is often referred to in many subject areas and yet a few years ago it was an obscure term. Yet we can ask 'Is the concept behind the term so very new?' An expert system is sometimes superficially defined as a *machine that does anything an expert does*. Analogies can be made from pre-computer days with traditional depositories of expertise. For example, a field book for identifying wild flowers [*1*] may involve searching down a hierarchy until a particular flower is arrived at. This *pre-expert system* consists of several methods of identification. Perhaps one method is by classification according to botanical features, another by classification based on type of plant (woody; non-woody; water) followed by obvious features like size or scent, and so on. There may be a classification based on general appearance and colour of flowers, which are represented by coloured drawings in the field book. Thus, the expertise of the professional botanist is encapsulated in the field guide and is available to users from novice to proficient amateur.

In order to understand the phenomenon of the expert system, the root of its development must first be examined. It was the field of *artificial intelligence* (or AI, a phrase coined around 1956) which provided the research enabling progress to be made with expert systems and consequently is the area to be covered by the first section of this chapter.

Ultimately, artificial intelligence exists when an artefact can collect, assemble, choose, understand, perceive and know; to a greater or lesser degree, that is what various knowledge processing machines have been doing since the late 1950s. The seed that gave life to AI as a science was the realisation that the 'computer' was badly misnamed. An implication of counting and calculating does not show the true potential of a capability to manipulate any sort of symbol.

Early developments

The earliest examples of artificial intelligence in the late 1950s reflected the personal interests of the researchers involved. Such work would have seemed to the outsider to have little relevance or potential for real world applications as typical programs of the time may have played chess or proved logical theorems in subjects such as geometry. However, the principle of reasoning implicit in both chess playing and logic construction is unchanged when applied to human intellectual behaviour. Scientists of the day reasoned that whether the principle was isolated in chess playing or anywhere else, it could be applied to any other modes of action that required intelligence.

A problem arises, however, in that whatever the underlying principle, any particular action involves specific intelligence, or 'knowledge', in greatly varying quantities. Knowing that digital computers respond not to principles nor generalisation but to a binary code involving a two-way decision rule, this problem becomes even more complex. Intelligence, with its inherent combination of messy details, facts, rules of thumb, intuitive judgement and knowledge based on experience must be broken down in specific domains and translated into a program that can be understood by a computer.

It was also during this period of time that, the general field of AI having been established, individual aspects of this field aroused interest from different bodies. These included such areas of research as speech recognition, robotics, machine vision and also expert systems. Much industrial interest was aroused in the field of robotics, the results of which can be seen in today's motor car assembly plants. Speech recognition and machine vision, meanwhile, were seen as potentially useful in the context of education and security, in addition to a pure research mode.

Each of these fields demand independent consideration if they are to be adequately dealt with, but all can be linked to the development of expert systems by the all encompassing genre of AI. The early research, however, on which we shall concentrate, will be that applied particularly to expert systems, although the reader should recognise that other divisions of AI were undergoing similar pioneering work.

Expert system research history

The research undertaken in the early 1950s to solve the problem of enabling a computer to deal with intelligence reveals an over-optimism. This over-optimism was evident in PERCEPTION (Rosenblatt 1957[*2*])–a typical system of these early years. It attempted to simulate a system of neurons in the human brain, but an under-estimation of the complexities of the human brain on the part of its creators limited the system to an ability to recognise a very limited class of patterns.

The shift from this search for broad, general laws towards an appreciation of specific knowledge became pronounced with the completion of DENDRAL, an expert system that was able to infer chemical structure from data available to physical chemists. The effort on DENDRAL, which began in 1965 with Professor Feigenbaum at Stanford University, was succeeded by work on MYCIN by Shortcliffe, culminating in 1976[*3*]. This system was even more influential and spawned several medical diagnostic expert systems of similar type, many of which are still in routine clinical use.

MYCIN introduced some new features that will be explained subsequently within the context of the 'mechanics' of an expert system. The significance of developments at this stage in expert systems history can be noted in that Shortcliffe was the first with MYCIN to devise a scheme based on *certainty factors*, which allowed the system to reach plausible conclusions from the available evidence. This reasoning under uncertainty is known as *fuzzy logic*, a term invented by Kafti Zadels (1965) who extended classical Boolean logic to real numbers[*4*]. In Boolean logic, 1 represents truth and 0 is falsity. The same principle applies in fuzzy logic but, in addition, all the fractions between zero and one are used to indicate partial truth. As will be shown in our own review of one of the currently available *expert system shells*, this is a crucial element when dealing with any application area where certainty is limited; thus any aspect of accounting and business falls into this category.

A phrase recognisable to every potential microcomputer system buyer – 'user-friendliness' – was also an important aspect of MYCIN. The user–in the case of MYCIN, a medical person–could interrogate it in order to determine various points. For example, the system would have reasons for asking particular questions and reaching particular conclusions that could be derived via questions from the user. Perhaps the most obvious evidence of a major breakthrough having been made was the fact that MYCIN was a working system with a real life application area. Its diagnosis of bacterial blood infections and subsequent prescription of suitable drug therapy may be very limited in scope when compared with a typical general practitioner, but the job it does would, nevertheless, take years of training for a human.

Perhaps the greatest outside interest in this generation of machines was aroused by PROSPECTOR; this system followed lines of knowledge and representation similar to MYCIN. It was designed to predict mineral deposits from certain data, and not only did it simulate human decision-making, but it actually found a previously unknown deposit of the valuable mineral molybdenum. Thus a combination of experts' knowledge in geology within a machine enabled a superior performance of the machine over any humans.

It is these types of machines that have provided the intellectual capital for the compact systems in existence today that are available to the business world. However, to depart from the present capacity and focus on the developing potential in AI, a further concept has come to the fore of present research. A system called EURISKO, demonstrated by Lenat in 1982[5], improves and extends its own body of rules automatically. It constitutes a machine-learning system, and as such is the key to this decade's development of AI. As information processing and evaluation has become the focus of current office technologies in the business environment, so the commodity of knowledge and its manufacture will be applied to the research field.

Summary

The subject of expert systems is a branch of AI–the latter being the collection, understanding, perception and knowledge of information taken by a computer program.

Research in expert systems started in the early 1950s on a rather optimistic basis, but progressed with greater success as systems were designed for the application of specific knowledge, e.g. DENDRAL and MYCIN, which included the explanation of reasoning used (by means of a *log* of the actual rules employed) and also the development of fuzzy logic (using uncertain data). In recent years, a new concept has entered expert systems–that of the machine-learning system.

Artificial intelligence theory applied to expert systems

From the previous chapter it should, hopefully, be clear that the knowledge-based approach to expert systems design is distinct from the conventional data processing computer programs. One way of representing this distinction is:

Traditionally: DATA + ALGORITHM = PROGRAM

Knowledge-based: KNOWLEDGE + INFERENCE = SYSTEM [*6*]

where

an *algorithm* is any process of calculation
knowledge is a body of rules plus facts
inference is any process for manipulating the rules.

Although similarities are apparent in the two concepts, the differences have profound consequences. To clarify this principle further by reference to non-technical terms, an example can be shown in the context of computer aids for taxation.

A typical data processing system, used by a tax consultant, would be able to provide software to compute the advantages of alternative investments to a client. An expert system would, in addition, use rules of thumb to determine (i.e. *infer*) which planning alternatives are feasible considering such items as refinement planning, covenants, etc. (i.e. *knowledge*). This corresponds to the tax consultant using the results from the data processing system and combining it with his or her own knowledge of any legal or intuitive considerations to advise a client on a particular project.

On this basis, an expert system would provide a summary of recommendations, together with reasoning if required, leaving the expert free to explore any specific problems, attributes or areas of disagreement shown up by the system.

Components of an expert system

This simplified example illustrates the components required within an *intelligent knowledge-based system* as twofold:

(i) The knowledge base
(ii) The inference engine

These actually comprise only the core of a full expert system but allow a conceptually simpler aproach.

(i) The knowledge base refers to the type of information storage an expert system uses, this differs from conventional databases in that it lacks a pre-determined structure. It will contain a few facts that may emerge during the course of operation of a system and permanent rules that determine how to generate new facts applicable to whatever is the current problem. These rules, such as an *if–then* clause act as data for a high level interpreter known as the inference engine. The rules are *stand alone*; in other words a rule is not dependent on any context other than when it is explicitly referred to by other rules (the rule itself may also explicitly refer to other rules). This is quite unlike the sequential ordering of instructions in a traditional program.

(ii) The inference engine is the program that drives an expert system. Basically, it attempts to match known facts about a particular program with its existing knowledge. The combination of the two allows the system to make deductions and conclusions about knowledge fed in by an expert and formulate an effective rule.

Human interaction of expert system components

Having established the 'working parts' of a basic expert system, two more components must be described.
Firstly, in setting up the knowledge base, knowledge of a subject area (*domain*) must be transferred into the knowledge system. Many fundamental concepts and techniques in a domain are evolved from a natural language understanding that is alien to a knowledge base. At present, and for our practical purposes, the process of codification that is required is achieved by consultation between a *domain expert* and a *knowledge engineer*; the former supplies knowledge in the form of expertise, whereas the latter translates this expertise into the rules acceptable to the knowledge based system. Such a process may be very time consuming and also requires a very skilled knowledge

engineer able to interpret correctly the rules used from many almost 'intuitive' expert judgements. Technically termed the acquisition module, the parallel technology of the future involves Doug Lenat's EURISKO program (1982), which is the forerunner of a new generation of machine-learning systems as described above (see pages 251). Secondly, there must be a human window or *user interface* for there to be natural communication between the system and the user. The user should be able to pose problems and also ask at any time why the system has made a deduction or sought information from the user. The importance of this explanation facility should be stressed, because if a reasoning method cannot be explained then it is unsatisfactory and such a system can never be relied upon in the business or any other environment. A full expert system, therefore, contains the components as in Fig.2.1.

Fig 2.1 – Components in an expert system

	Component	
	Domain of knowledge	Expert procedures and facts
	Acquisition module	Knowledge engineer
Core of expert system	Knowledge base	Representation of knowledge
Core of expert system	Inference engine	Methods of plausible reasoning
Core of expert system	Natural language processor	Human window
	Problem specific data	Designated by user

Technological developments–natural language processor

Some people believe that by applying the current rate of technological progress, the human window or user interface will eventually result in the use of a natural language processor. A situation will be reached where the computer could respond appropriately to anything typed at the keyboard in a natural human language.

Alternatively, a form of speech recognition could be utilised, but this introduces many different problems and complexities.
A genuine understanding of natural language requires an extensive knowledge of syntax, semantics and common sense pragmatism. Some commercially useful systems, such as Logos and Weidner, require some editing by someone who knows the computer language to be used, though it can be argued that human translations themselves frequently need editing. Speech recognition is a field of artificial intelligence that demands its own research and needs a great deal of development to approach the human level of performance. Speech recognisers will probably have to use all the knowledge displayed in natural language systems plus a specialised knowledge of phonetics.
It should be noted at this point that Professor Alan Turing envisaged a test for a computer whereby the ultimate conclusion to be drawn would be that, when matched with a human, performance would be indistinguishable given a certain activity. An example would be the composition of a report or a letter using natural language communication, the user being unable to determine that the result was computer produced. Such a system, however, can still only be envisaged owing to the complexity of problems involved.
Some systems can currently cope with large vocabularies, unfamiliar speakers or continuous speech, but no existing system can handle all three. It seems that the best most researchers hope to achieve is a system that adapts very rapidly to a new speaker without any explicit teaching.

Summary

An expert system comprises two main components, a knowledge base and the inference engine. The former is information stored in a particular manner, whereas the latter is the program that drives the expert system.
The level of technology is constantly changing, although, at present, expert systems do not incorporate a natural language processor. It can be said, however, that research in this area will form the basis for future applications.

Expert systems: current general development

Before looking at the application of expert systems, we need to examine the term *expert system* in greater depth. Such a wide range of definitions exists–covering many knowledge domains, types of users and systems themselves. From these it is evident that *expert system* is a generic term, qualified before it is used in connection with any particular expert system.

The British Computer Society definition

The possible wide ranging implications of industrial expert systems are illustrated by the description of expert systems put forward by the British Computer Society Committee: [7]:

An 'Expert System' is regarded as the embodiment within a computer of a knowledge-based component from an expert skill in such a form that the machine can offer intelligent advice or take an intelligent decision about a processing function. A desirable additional characteristic, which many would regard as fundamental, is the capability of the system on demand to justify its own line of reasoning in a manner directly intelligible to the enquirer. The style adopted to attain these characteristics is rule based programming

The Committee subsequently explained that this long-winded definition of expert systems was given because it was intended to embrace several potential developments and alternatives. The implications of this definition which are relevant here: [7]

The meaning of expert skill is not closely confined (e.g., most humans are an expert in something).

These systems often initiate consultations with a human adviser (e.g., in medical diagnosis) but they can and have been applied to data processing and to on-line control systems.

This would indicate, therefore, that although a typical view of the 'expert' may be a doctor, a mathematician or a lawyer, these are not limitations on the potential area of expert systems application. Such rule-based domains as these may provide a less complex starting point from which to construct a viable system, but areas involving less certainty which may require quick and reliable decisions to be made could also be appropriate.

Types of users

Although the knowledge domains vary considerably, so too do the types of users for whom expert systems are provided. For instance: the system could be provided for a practising expert, perhaps to free him/her from some of the more routine aspects of problem solving, or alternatively to give a 'second' opinion on the problem; or the user could be less skilful than a full expert and work on more difficult decisions than he/she might otherwise manage unaided. Another possible type of user is someone who wants to learn about the knowledge domain and uses the system as an interactive teacher. Perhaps a system could be used to help clarify a complex piece of legislation [*8*].

Types of expert system

Within the last two years as commercial expert systems have appeared it has become clear that the term *expert systems* is generic and that the current (1986/87) market place definition is at the 'less expert end' of expert systems. Rather than trying to place the different types of system along a spectrum of expert systems, implying just a single dimension, it may be useful to try and place them within a two dimensional framework as shown in Fig. 3.1. One dimension could be concerned with knowledge elicitation and the other with machine learning.

Knowledge elicitation is concerned with codifying the body of knowledge so that it can be represented within an expert system. At the low end of this dimension the knowledge is already codified perhaps legislation (for example DHSS or immigration rules and regulations [*9*]), professional codes and standards (for example auditing standards) or programmed texts (for example in learning a computer programming language or learning double entry book-keeping). At the other end of this dimension the knowledge has to be explicitly brought out, perhaps involving a *knowledge engineer* as intermediary between the expert and the system. It has become clear that in many areas, codifying the implicit knowledge in a domain can be extremely difficult, and more is made of this in the following section. Perhaps fuzzy logic will be needed in the representation of the knowledge.

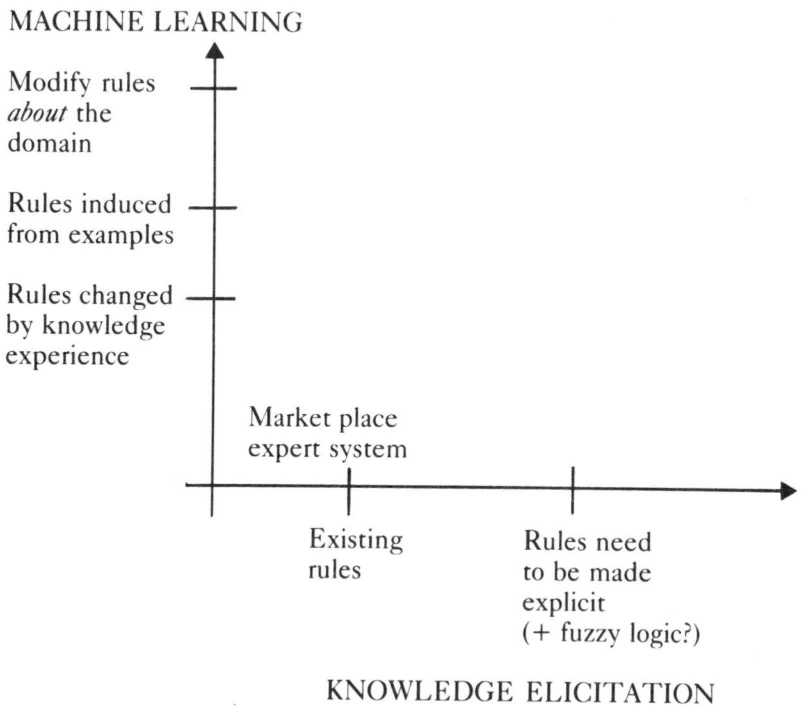

Fig. 3.1 Framework for types of expert systems

Machine learning is a large area within AI, but it is inappropriate to explore it within this chapter. This area could well be another dimension, at the lowest end, where there would be expert systems whose permanent knowledge base is not changed in any way by the system itself. At the same time human experts or knowledge engineers would be constantly updating the rules and facts as necessary. At the other end of the dimension would be systems, such as EURISKO [*10*] already referred to, which not only modify rules, but also modifies 'rules about rules'. The initial areas embraced by EURISKO were in the closed domains of mathematics and the physical sciences–although there have been recent developments in the social sciences. In between might be those systems which work from codified examples representing particular applications of knowledge and are able to induce from these examples what the underlying rules might be.

The proliferation of the 'market place' type of expert system would be placed somewhere near the origin of Fig. 3.1, such systems have been termed 'middle-level' systems and may be useful in ensuring that decisions are taken according to the same criteria over a period of time–for example the ICAS decision making on the granting of insolvency permits[8]..

A knowledge elicitation

As experience has been gained in building expert systems, it has become clear that the process of extracting knowledge from experts in the domain of concern, is much more difficult than was at first anticipated.

The fact that someone is an expert practitioner of something, does not imply that they are also expert at describing the rules they are following. (This is why a knowledge engineer is needed, and whose problem it now becomes). Perhaps the real expert's skill has long since transcended any formal procedures or rules introduced to him or her as a novice, and the expert now operates at a far more intuitive level. Figure 3.2(a) represents how the knowledge elicitation process was originally envisaged[11]. The figure also indicates the feedback to the expert once the machine expert system is being used. The weak link, at 1, is to get the expert to make explicit the knowledge being used. The numbers in the figure represent the order in which the knowledge elicitation steps may be carried out.

However, the expert may well be capable of passing on accumulated experience to an 'apprentice' by the use of illustrative examples. So a more successful approach has been to codify suitable examples; perhaps the knowledge acquisition part of the expert system can induce the rules from examples. Some expert systems have been designed to build up machine knowledge indirectly in this way. Figure 3.2(b) represents this new way of knowledge elicitation[11].

Fig. 3.2 (a) The original method of knowledge elicitation;

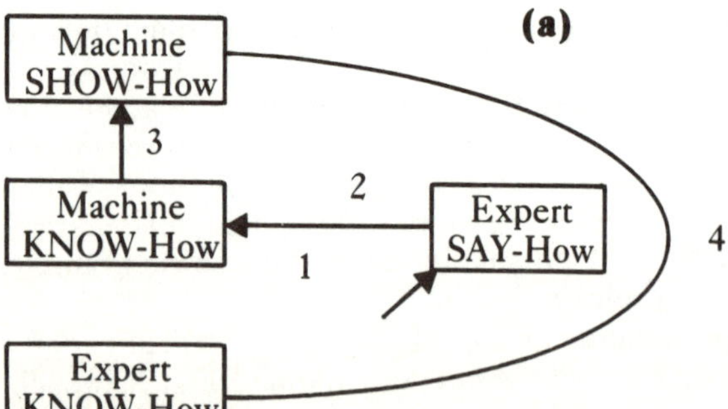

(b) more successful method of knowledge elicitation

(b)

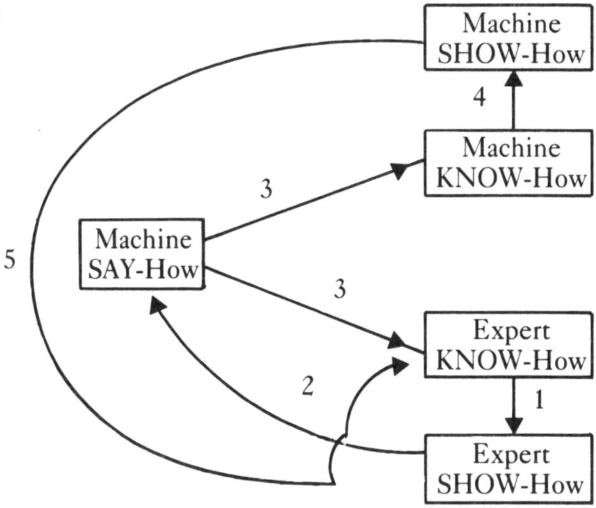

Summary

The 'market place' definition of expert systems is very much at the low end of expertise and represents knowledge that is readily captured and represented and that simulates the more routine tasks of an expert.

This trend has been accompanied by a growing awareness of the difficulty of capturing and formalising the knowledge used by human experts, before this knowledge can be encapsulated in a machine.

Expert systems: current general applications

Before assessing the application and development potential of expert systems from a business perspective, a general view looking at more widespread domains should be illustrated. A common criticism of many appraisals of successful expert systems is that the same short

list of expert system triumphs is recited, usually including DENDRAL, MYCIN and EURISKO.
Consequently, although these and similar systems are undoubtedly of prime importance and most influential within the field of knowledge based systems, the emphasis in this section will centre on more commercially viable successes and present developments. It should also be noted that, as in other areas where a developing technology or product is involved, every system that has been built will have suffered from problems and bugs. As a result, some will have been discarded as impractical or of little use, some may have become models from which future systems can be developed and there will also be those in the most favourable environments where a successful product is achieved. A favourable environment would probably be one generous in the allocation of time and funds, backed by creative thinking and perhaps incorporating an easily defined knowledge domain. Such limitations, however, are not absolute and should not detract from the achievements of a successful project team.

Expert systems in commercial and operational use

The following is a sample list of applications either in developmental stages or which have already been implemented[*12*]:

- Medical diagnosis
- Equipment failure diagnosis
- Order entry systems
- Chemical data interpretation
- Experiment planning
- Speech and image understanding
- Signal interpretation (for medicine, oil field services, military needs)
- Mineral exploration
- Military threat assessment and targeting
- Crisis management
- Advising about computer system use
- Training/teaching
- VLSI design and layout
- Air traffic control

We can consider a selection of expert systems to illustrate the diversity of applications[*13*].

PROSPECTOR

One of the more renowned systems already cited above is an aid to geologists called PROSPECTOR. Its renown is probably due to its dramatic (in terms of expert system performance) mineral find in 1982 at a site where the company previously had been dumping tailings. Its principal researchers were P. Hart and R. Duda of SRI International who were originally involved in constructing PROSPECTOR in 1979 [14]. As a geologist's aid, it helps in the evaluation of the favourability of an exploration site or region for ore deposits of particular types. The system accepts field observations from the user through an interactive dialogue and, at the termination of the diagnostic process, produces a list of possible types of deposits present and the likelihood of their presence. If the likelihood of the prescence of ore deposits is sufficiently high, then the system proceeds to determine the most favourable drilling sites.

PROSPECTOR's knowledge base

The general knowledge associated with a particular class of deposit is coded in a set of production rules, and uncertainties are then associated with these rules. Classifications of mineral types, rock types, physical forms and geological ages are also represented in the system's knowledge base.

PROSPECTOR's inference engine

An inference network or model of each deposit class shows how observations relate to intermediate hypotheses and, eventually, the ultimate hypothesis. This 'goal hypothesis' will give the user a certainty value for the presence of the relevant deposit class. The inference network is, therefore, hierarchical in nature, i.e., there is a progression from the goal assertion to subgoal assertions, which are in turn dependent upon a number of hypotheses or *antecedents*. Although it is not appropriate here to discuss PROSPECTOR's dynamics in detail, there are several facilities available to the user in PROSPECTOR that illustrate the flexibility of a well constructed expert system:

- At any point during the diagnostic process the user can interrupt the system to suggest that an alternative hypothesis is pursued, or to enter any additional observations which are considered relevant.
- Several explanatory facilities are provided, the most important being:

–*Why* a given question is asked.
–*How* a given conclusion was reached.

- The user can also ask for the geological rationale for including a question in a model.

The system, therefore, works in conjunction with the user rather than in addition to him, managing all the knowledge and processing it using the same inferences and rules an 'expert' in the field would use. To obtain an idea of the processing capabilities of PROSPECTOR, its knowledge base can be expressed in terms of the number of rules and assertions. There are 15 Models (inference networks) within the knowledge base, each consisting of more than 150 rules and 200 assertions, thereby making PROSPECTOR comprehensive in its dealing with geological details.

R1 [*15*]

Digital Equipment Corporation (DEC) of America was one of the first commercial organisations to make use of expert systems. Together with researchers from Carnegie Mellon University in Pittsburgh it developed a system called XCON–which was originally called R1–to help in the configuration of VAX computers.
The problem in specifying a computer processing unit, such as the VAX, is that it can be configured from over 400 components, each of which have up to eight properties. Consequently, inconsistencies may easily arise in a given configuration where spatial arrangements of components are also related to their shape, size and cabling considerations.
R1's knowledge base, therefore, comprising over 3000 pieces of component information together with knowledge about partial configurations and the results of various sorts of computation, should be expected to cover most aspects of VAX configuration. When combined with the various IF–AND–THEN type rules in the R1 expert system, it is potentially very successful. By 1981 R1 was achieving a success rate in excess of 90% and was being extended to cover other DEC computers.
It should be noted that there is often considerable scepticism voiced from within the engineering environment wherever the implementation of a knowledge-based system is considered. R1 proved to be no exception, but owing to its consistency in reaching realistic expectations and the continued commitment of its supporters, it flourished. According to Peter Sell, Director of

Research at SPL[*16*]
R1 has been operational since January 1980 and the company (DEC) couldn't do without it.

BL systems project[5]

A project undertaken by British Leyland Systems in the UK is on a much smaller scale than the two examples cited above. It is based on a 'why my car won't start' model and uses ISI's Micro Expert package, of which more will be said later. It is a small scale model and it should illustrate more clearly than the heavily funded R1 and PROSPECTOR models the practicality of expert systems currently used in smaller applications.

Brian Johnson, manager for advanced systems technology at BLI has been running the project, and although he has encountered many problems, he still retains enthusiasm for the idea. The system asks the user questions about the car and is directed along certain lines of questioning depending on the answers given. At an eventual level of reasoning, the system will stop asking questions and proffer advice on one or more alternative solutions to the problems. The number of questions is very important according to Johnson[*16*]:

User tolerance requires that the system asks enough questions but not too many. It also helps if a system can offer intermittent updates on what direction the situation is taking and why.

Johnson also recognises the problem of extracting knowledge from the experts, of whom he says:

[They] like to give you exceptions and then exceptions to the exceptions and have difficulty in articulating their knowledge. One minute is the best amount of time in which to extract from them the nugget with very little dross.

These problems can, however, be overcome, and the fact that people such as Brian Johnson have actually achieved viability in a system against a background of unenthusiastic users who may feel their jobs are at risk is very important. The users also accepted the advice given by the system so any problems may lie in a peripheral context such as, according to Johnson[*6*]:

The textual model is unnatural, the real world has sound, shape, colour, smell and intonation.

It could be possible, therefore, to combine viewdata with expert systems to make a package more attractive to the user; these and other problems will be discussed in more detail later.

Other examples in brief

- Elf, the French company is investigating systems for jobs such as maintenance of oil platforms.
- Britoil is interested in expert systems as a tool to help in the deciphering of complex data, for example from seismographs.
- Racal, with the MOD's Admiralty Research Establishment and the US Dept of Defense, are interested in the application of expert systems for understanding masses of code signals derived from radar.
- Unilever use expert systems for fault diagnosis in industrial plants.
- Wolverhampton Metropolitan Council were attempting to use an expert system to advise junior staff on how to allocate people to council houses.
- The Alvey Conference in 1985 in Edinburgh had 58 application projects for funding, covering a wide variety of areas, the titles of which are listed below:

001 Study for the design of a PROLOG machine

003 IKBS system architecture based on control flow

005 IDBS architecture study

006 Software house staff allocation

007 Enhancements to the POPLOG expert system development environment

008 A dictionary and morphological analyser for English language processing systems

009 A model framework for the specification of information systems

010 Natural language generation from plans

011 Experimental investigation of a computational approach to text processing

012 Applications of functional closures

013 Spatio-temporal processing and optical flow for computer vision

014 Extraction of 3D structure in low level vision by maximising invariance

017 Towards an intelligent Help file finder

018 Knowledge based systems in hydrology

019 Natural language processing

020 The knowledge engineer's assistant

021 A computational grammar of English

022 Read and write Japanese without knowing it

024 Tools for development of logic programs

025 3D surface representations and 3D model based vision from stereoscopic cues

026 Fifth generation computer architecture modelling

027 A parsing tool for the natural language theme

028 A knowledge based scheduling system for offshore work

029 An information machine incorporating an associative triple store

030 An investigation into inference with restricted quantification and a taxonomic representation

031 A flexible toolkit for building expert systems

032 IKBS applications in simulation and avionic tactical decision aids

033 Logic based front-ends for large software systems with reference to a widely-used statistical system – GLIM

034 IKBS applications in mechanical health monitoring

035 The application of expert systems to quantity surveying techniques

036 An investigation for knowledge acquisition techniques

037 A high-speed multi-user PROLOG database machine

039 An expert system for the design of spatial arrangements

040 Guided discovery learning systems in intelligent computer aided instruction

041 Learning and using PROLOG: an empirical investigation

042 An intelligent maintenance system for telecommunications networks

043 Implementation and application

044 An intelligent model-based system for diagnosis in cardiology

045 Logic for representing legislation

046 PISA–Persistent Information Space Architecture

047 Computer based techniques to assist inference under uncertainty

049 Flagship

052 Product formulation expert system

053 Temporal and cross-modality image matching for patient alignment in medical imaging

054 Real-time expert systems in process control

056 MINERVA: a prototype triple-based system incorporating

generic associative functions
058 Business applications of expert systems–an investigation

Summary

This section has illustrated the diversity, both in scale and type, of applications of expert systems. In general terms there is obviously enormous potential in this field, and hopefully the reader can now appreciate the immediacy of possible developments in areas 'closer to home'. With heavily funded systems, such as R1 and PROSPECTOR, well established in industrial use, the path has been cleared for smaller scale projects to be undertaken, such as the BL initiative. In particular business and financial applications have been shown to have great potential in the field of expert systems, a fact that is, hopefully, supported by the remaining chapters.

Practical considerations for financial and business applications

The previous section was intended to provide the reader with an insight into the extent of expert system development from a general perspective. The overall objective of this section and those that follow, is to illustrate applications relevant to those within a business environment, and particularly to members of the accounting profession; thus a closer examination of appropriate developments in this field can now be undertaken. Before entering the fray, however, with a long list of demonstrator projects, starter packs and small business packages both currently, and in the process of, being marketed, provision should be made for an explanation of exactly what the application of an expert system to business use involves. In this, considerations are not limited purely to those of financial cost. A potential user must decide upon the level of pre-packed sophistication desirable for the intended application and, consequently, the amount of time he/she is prepared to spend in developing the system to suit individual needs. Additionally, and of some importance, expert system applications, although varied, are not found in all areas.

Suitable areas for the potential expert system user

Expert systems will be more successful in some areas than others and, generally speaking, four prerequisites can be defined for the success of a knowledge-based expert system[*17*]:

(i) There must be at least one human expert acknowledged to perform the task well.

(ii) The primary source of the expert's exceptional performance must be special knowledge, judgement and experience.

(iii) It must be possible to elicit the expert's special knowledge and experience and the methods used to apply them to particular problems.

(iv) The task must have a well- bounded domain of applications

First impressions may be that these requirements are too extensive to deal adequately with complex areas of business, such as company law or financial management. However, such apparently cluttered and unstructured domains, however, can be successfully applied with the patient collaboration of subject expert and knowledge engineer (see pages 253 and 257). In some cases, illustrated below, the presence of a knowledge knowledge engineer with the expert is not necessary; after a nominal training programme, the expert can build his own system using an *advice language*.

Alternative development tools for expert system users

Within the context of a financial/business environment, it would be expected that highly trained computer programmers may not be available to spend the amount of time necessary to 'build' the appropriate reasoning software. There are alternatives, however, for

firms taking advantage of a new technology product. Larger firms, for example within the accountancy profession, that may be interested in the development of their own system from 'scratch' as an investment, would need to consider alternative programming languages and their relative cost effectiveness.
Current tools for developing expert systems are:

(i)	Algorithmic languages	(C, FORTRAN, BASIC)
(ii)	Symbolic languages	(PROLOG, LISP)
(iii)	Development environments	(POPLOG)
(iv)	Expert system shells	(SAGE, REVEAL, MICRO EXPERT, etc.)

Off-the-shelf expert systems are available but, by definition, are limited in their applications and, therefore, a potential user may have to consider that some degree of development cost will be part of the investment. The above list is in increasing order of pre-packed significance (i.e., the user is required to spend more time developing the first than the last).

Algorithmic languages

Algorithmic languages include BASIC, FORTRAN and COBOL, of which at least one will be available on most microcomputers. As shown by Duda and Gaschnig 1984[*17*], an expert system can be constructed using a language such as BASIC. The designer of such a system, however, needs to be fully aware of the internal workings of 'inference engines' in order to write a program that simulates the novel characteristics of expert systems. Given current hardware facilities, firms may regard these languages as those that lead to the most effective implementations. Reasoning software built in FORTRAN, PASCAL and BASIC will aid calls upon existing files and programs, thereby requiring the least restructuring of any existing information system. d'Agapeyeff[*18*] point out:

. . . there are snags in this practise. Conventional programming languages may be adaptable for a 'Simpler' Expert System, but it is questionable whether they are suitable for further developments.

. . . they do not facilitate an explicit representation of knowledge. This is not a problem when the knowledge base is tiny, but if [the system] is valuable it will tend to grow almost continuously and then the difficulties can become severe [*19*].

Such considerations would be very relevant to a firm interested in developing and assimilating the potential of an expert system in their environment.

Symbolic languages

For the newcomer who is prepared to learn a new language and spend some time programming, the most cost-effective entry level may lie in the use of symbolic languages such as LISP and PROLOG. LISP has been in existence for over 25 years, having been used extensively in AI research, although commercially it has not caught on. Many aspects of LISP are not standardised and take the form of additional software packages which are not available in the UK. PROLOG has been adopted by the Japanese as the core language for their Fifth Generation System (page 284-5). It is a language modelled on a form of predicate calculus (Kowalski [*20*]), and is not aimed at numerical problems but at the expression of relations. For example, a rule can be declared in the form:

x is-the-grandfather-of *y* if *x* is-the-father-of *z* and
z is-the-parent-of *y*

and then from a listing of facts such as:

Henry -7 is-the-father-of Henry 8
Henry- 8 is-the-father-of Mary

etc.

it is possible to query the listing by asking:

which (*y* Henry-7 is-the-grandfather-of *y*)

meaning[*2*]:

who are the grandchildren of Henry -7?

A knowledge base can readily be built up in PROLOG from such simple beginnings without any distinction between a fact (i.e., piece of data) and a rule (i.e., piece of program). Both are stored in the same PROLOG database and are selected by a *pattern match*. This means that there are no GOTO commands nor any other that direct the flow of program execution. Consequently, a set of PROLOG statements constitutes the specification of the program *and* the program itself.

PROLOG is, therefore, more immediately suited to the application of expert systems than conventional programming languages, though the problem may still exist that it lacks extensive file handling facilities or any ability to interact with COBOL and FORTRAN.

There are critics of PROLOG (Forsyth [*21*]), but there is also a family of PROLOG languages that have been designed to introduce people to PROLOG and some of the concepts of programming in logic. One of these, Micro PROLOG which has been developed by Logic Programming Associates, is believed to have sold well on release.

Development environments

Development environments such as POPLOG (Sloman *et al.* [22]) are an integrated combination of programming languages, in the case of POPLOG, these being POP-11, PROGOL and LISP. Sloman *et al.* see their development as capable of being used [*23*]:

for any application where program development costs are significant or where the restrictions built in to more conventional languages introduce design difficulties.

The user can work entirely within the one environment with the provision of a screen editor, program library and documentation system which can be used in the middle of a session. POPLOG, however, was not designed to be squeezed onto small machines, and Sloman *et al.* state that it should only be transferable to the new generation of microcomputers with 32-bit memory addressing capability.

More possibilities are provided with a development environment, but it requires the attention of experienced programmers capable of understanding or learning the different languages involved. In addition, the necessity of using several LISP or PERQ personal computer machines extends the costs beyond the limitations of most potential users.

Expert Systems Shells

Many *expert system shells* currently on the market provide the user with a ready made inference engine that then only requires the user to build up the relevant knowledge base. In order to do this, languages that input knowledge vary enormously in complexity, from a simple advice language for the user with no computing experience to that which requires consultation with an experienced programmer to effect a successful system. Consequently, varying degrees of simplicity in the system itself ensue and these will be detailed in the next section, where a survey of expert system shells is briefly illustrated.

Shells can be very useful to the potential user and for the new starter further development need not be limited, Forsyth [*21*]:

One relatively cheap solution is to purchase an expert system shell, use it as a prototyping tool till you know what you want, then write the production version in an efficient and portable language.

Summary

This section has been intended to introduce the potential user of an expert system to some of the alternatives involved and practical considerations to be examined. As illustrated, the choice is not a simple 'yes or no' decision, and the use of an expert system is not appropriate to every aspect of the business environment.
The latter half of this section provided a list and appraisal of alternative tools with which to develop systems apart from the purchasing of 'off the shelf' models that are available in limited applications. The next will be concerned with how businesses are interpreting such factors in their development of expert systems, and also examples of shells and other systems relevant to the field of accountancy.

Expert systems in accountancy

This section is intended to direct attention to both potential and working applications of expert systems in the field of accounting. A synopsis of expert systems shells currently available for development will precede an illustration of a number of working systems and a brief report on significant areas of research undertaken by major accountancy organisations. The appearance of many familiar areas of the accounting world in this respect should serve to illustrate the importance of technological development to the most sceptical of professions.

Developing expert systems from shells

The idea of using an expert system shell as a tool for developing an expert system for a specific application is to take the hard work out of development. It can be compared to a plastic kit taking the burden out of building a model aircraft. The shells are essentially frameworks that become complete expert systems by the addition of the expert's knowledge. This is done in various ways, the most obvious being that the expert directly inputs his knowledge into the system itself. However, problems will often arise in this respect where the expert will know much about his own subject, but very little on the use of a computer. Consequently, the alternative is for the expert to explain his know-how to a knowledge engineer who then interprets the information in a manner that enables it to be fed into the expert system.

This apparent need for an intermediary knowledge engineer is seen by some as an essential element of building an expert system given the technophobia of many experts–those within the accounting profession being no exception. Others, however, view it as an unnecessary link in the chain. ICL for instance, claim that the knowledge engineer is superfluous and that anybody can learn how to use its expert system builder if they attend a one week training course.

The cheaper systems tend to be the easiest to use, allowing the expert to interact with the computer using an *advice language*, which can be constructed in simple English grammar. Such systems, however, will by definition be simple, have less sophisticated features and be able to hold fewer rules than those further up the price range. With more flexible and sophisticated facilities, some conventional programming experience may be required, or even the presence of a knowledge engineer familiar with expert system construction. Here the discussion on knowledge elicitation is pertinent.

A summary of some expert system shells currently on the market is given below.

Expert ease

'Expert Ease' is a microcomputer system suitable for those without a programming background. It uses a spreadsheet format into which the domain expert enters examples. Rules for constructing the expert system are derived inductively by program written in PASCAL; it runs under the UCSD operating system on the IBM PC and XT, Sirius Sirius and Apricot and DEC Rainbow.

Available from Thorn EMI Software Distributors.

ICL ADVISER

This is a large scale modelling shell for ICL mainframes and demands some computer expertise. However, ICL say that non-computer people have developed systems after the standard one-week training course. Information can be entered from outside databases as well as through the keyboard, and ADVISER

incorporates an *area* construct, which positions areas of knowledge from each other so they can be developed and used independently. Applications in use include computer sizing, bonus calculation advice and fault diagnosis in telephone exchanges and manufacturing processes.
Details from ICL, Wenlock Way, Manchester.

SAGE

Offered by Systems Designers for use on VAX VMS PDF-11 RSX-11m and IBM PC under MS-DOS, SAGE is used by trained knowledge engineers to build expert systems for use by non-computer trained users. The inference engine uses Bayesian concepts, fuzzy logic and standard arithmetic with associated text for all elements of the model. Applications developed include mortgage and loan advice documentation planning, systems testing and sizing, fault finding and sensor interpretation.
Details from Systems Designers Scientific, Pembroke House, Camberley, Surrey.

ESP ADVISER

From Expert Systems International, ESP ADVISER can be implemented on microcomputers using MS-DOS or CP/M-86 by non-computer trained users. The knowledge base is written with text editing software such as Wordstar, in English then compiled into machine readable form. Uncertain reasoning is not attempted, but explanations can be provided for questions, conclusions and lines of reasoning.
Details from Expert Systems International, 9 West Way, Oxford.

MICRO EXPERT

From ISI and available on a range of microcomputers, MICRO EXPERT requires users with a conventional programming background to create the systems. 'Passive' reasoning is supported and models are constructed in an English 'advice language' before being compiled.
Details from ISI, Redhill, Surrey.

Other shells

Other shells currently available in the UK include:

ICL Reveal	ICL
Ex-Tran 7	Intelligent Terminals
Racal	Tynshare UK, Key Bridge Ho, Brentford, Middlesex
APES	Logic Programming Associates, London, SW18 3IU
Inference ART	Ferrath Computer Systems Ltd, Loch Way, Cwmbran, Gwent
Envisage	Systems Designers Scientific
TESS	Helix Expert Systems Ltd, 11 Ludgate Circus, London
Savoir	ISI
Xi	Expertech, 192 Bath Road, Slough, Berks
Personal Consultant	Texas Instruments, Manton Lane, Bedford

Applications in Accountancy

Before confronting specific issues and developments relevant to the use of expert systems in accountancy, a brief illustration should be given of potential areas where such systems may prove useful.

Accounting standards

The complexity and quantity of accounting standards that require consideration in the preparation of accounts are such that any tool which aids in their application should attract a great deal of attention. Standards could be represented with their appropriate interrelationships as rules in the knowledge base, any uncertainties being dealt with by using the fuzzy logic capabilities available in expert systems.

In addition, the possibility exists for a system to be built to aid the standard setting procedure. Such a system, though a little more abstract than the first example could be used to analyse proposed standards in relation to existing standards and law, to assess the effects on companies and to judge usefulness to readers of accounts.

Auditing

Linked to the field of accounting standards, auditing provides other areas in which the development of an expert system could be advantageous. Computer auditing in the sense of using the computer as an audit tool has already manifested itself within the offices of chartered accountants throughout the UK, and the next step of introducing expert systems would provide a further aid to the auditing process. Decisions on audit programmes, test sample sizes and the assessment of audit errors could all be covered in at least a consultative mode by an expert system. Further, the analysis of large volumes of accounting transactions, reviewing and judging of materiality are within the capabilities of a well constructed expert system. Additionally, the audit of computer systems relies heavily on the evaluation of internal control–which is initially based on a rule-based procedure.

Taxation

This area of accountancy has been the base for several attempts at developing an expert system, one of which will be discussed later. Primarily determined by complex sets of rules set down in law, tax is a highly suitable area for expert systems.
Consideration would have to be given to problems such as the frequent changes in law and the massive amount of knowledge that must be encapsulated, but even so the potential of expert systems in taxation generally is undoubted. More specifically, an expert system would prove most useful in compliance work where the best advantage is attained from a set of possible claims, and also in future income models for tax planning.

Management and control

Management and control covers a very wide domain. Expert systems can be used both in conjunction with management information systems and in the modelling results for decisions. A problem that may arise in more complex and, therefore, effective systems would be the programming to enable identification of novel problems and the acquisition of sufficient external data.
One of the Alvey Clubs (see pages 287; a *club* is a group of people from different organisations who are working on different expert systems, but in the same knowledge domain) recently formed is a 'financial' club concerned with the development of a prototype computerised financial expert. Several banks and financial institutions are expected to make use of the company 'financial health adviser' once it is completed.

Working expert systems in accountancy

Robert Michaelson and Donald Michie[*24*] have been developing their own expert system since 1982; Donald Michie having been at the forefront of British AI research with his work with the Turing Institute and at the University of Edinburgh. With Robert Michaelson, a taxation specialist and professor of accountancy at the University of Nebraska, they have developed a system called TAXADVISER[*24*] to be used in the field of legal analysis.

As long ago as the early 1970s, the first attempt was being made to apply artificial intelligence to taxation. TAXMAN was developed by L.Thorne McCarthy of Southern University of New York for evaluating the tax consequences of certain types of proposed corporate reorganisations. There was a limited degree of success due to the fact that McCarthy aimed for a deterministic model of the law and not the decision rules of an expert in corporate reorganisations. McCarthy's current research, however, given the development in systems available for modelling human thought processes, is concerned with more sophisticated models of the law.

Robert Hellawell of Columbia University made another attempt with the CORPTAX program which was designed as an aid to the professional. Written in BASIC and modelling the law only, its significance as an expert system is, however, limited.

Of more interest is the Michaelson and Michie TAXADVISER system which will be addressed in more detail later. In addition to these tax-based systems, others in the field of auditing and internal control can be cited. Andrew Bailey at the University of Minnesota, together with some former colleagues have been developing TICOM, which is a computer-assisted method of modelling and evaluating internal control systems. TICOM allows the auditor to document a review of an internal control system using a rigorous auditor description language, checking for consistency with programmed rules. Eventually, the auditor can pose questions about the internal control model using a query-processing system. Although not a pure expert system, its construction is based on AI techniques and its goals are similar to those of expert systems.

A problem of compiling the knowledge base has been overcome in the development of EDP AUDITOR in which it is recognised that the problem domain will contain hundreds of decision rules. James Hanson of Brigham Young University and William Messier of the University of Florida are developing the system to assist auditors in auditing advanced electronic data processing systems, identifying the knowledge base decision rules by protocol study. This study involved three senior computer audit specialists from a major public accounting firm and detailed reviews of edp audit questionnaires from public accounting firms.

AUDITOR[25]

Developed by Christopher Dungan at the University of Illinois, AUDITOR is an expert system that assists auditors in assessing a company's allowance for bad debts. The knowledge base was constructed by eliciting from expert auditors a number of significant factors in the allowance for bad debts. The same experts were then asked their views on the relative weight of each factor and if they recognised any interrelationships between the factors. Refinements of the system were achieved after it was assembled in rule form by interaction with the expert auditors who tested the system using real and hypothetical cases. The success of the system was confirmed in two respects. When operated against ten cases taken from audit working papers, agreement with the human expert was about 90%. With 11 real world cases in which one expert operated the system and another validated the conclusions, agreement was 91%. These led Dungan to conclude that[25]:
the validation were supportive of a belief that the systems contained the cases and weights utilised by auditors in their evaluation of trade accounts receivable.

TAXADVISOR

The TAXADVISOR system is designed to interact with a human tax consultant and its purpose is to provide estate-planning tax advice for a client. Questions are asked concerning a particular client and when the system has gained enough information to make a recommendation concerning a tax saving action, this recommendation is also displayed on the terminal screen. TAXADVISOR is capable of pursuing more than one line of reasoning, making decisions where uncertainty is involved and explaining the line of reasoning and decision. The system was verified using a 'blind' procedure whereby the recommendations of both the system and a human expert concerning a given case were judged for acceptability. No significant difference could be discerned between performance of the system and human experts.

Who's interested in expert systems in accountancy?

The Alvey Programme (see page 287) has given support to developments that are relevant to the field of accountancy. Mr David Thomas, director of the Intelligent Knowledge Based Systems (IKBS) programme has reported on the setting up of Awareness Clubs in Finance, Insurance and Econometric Modelling.

Alfex

Such a club is the Alvey Financial Community Expert System Club. Known as ALFEX, it became involved in a joint project in May, 1985, intended to last for 18 months. This club gained its full complement of members and contracted the work to Helix Software Consultants and Expert Systems International.

The objective of ALFEX is[26]:

To increase awareness of expert systems techniques and their advantages for the financial community, by developing an industry specific 'corporate health adviser'. This would provide assessment of corporate health, diagnosis of problems, and limited advice regarding solutions to these problems.

Plans for the project were on a three-phase basis:

Phase I	Selection of expert systems shell
Phase II	Development of a small business health assessor as a prototype
Phase III	Development of a corporate health advisor for a specific industry

ICAEW

The ICAEW held a seminar on expert systems on 26 October 1984 at which representatives of Arthur Young, Helix Products and Marketing Ltd, the Alvey Directorate, Imperial College and Peat, Marwick Mitchell spoke on various subjects, all involving the application of expert systems in the commercial sector.

Following this seminar the Institute made an announcement that it would, in January 1985, set up a two-year senior fellowship in Information Technology at the Department of Accounting and Management Science of the University of Southampton. The university was to develop an expert system to review the risks which surround computerised data processing in organisations. The experience which has been gained from this activity is well summarised in an article published in Accountancy[27].

Individual firms

Helix Expert Systems has already been mentioned in connection with the ALFEX club, but they have also been involved with Arthur Young, a major chartered accountancy firm, in a project half funded by the Alvey programme. The knowledge elicitation process is that an expert in a particular profession would sit down at a terminal and be interviewed by a specially developed expert system. After the interview, the machine would have an accurate idea of how the expert constructs his thought processes, and the various rules used to come to a decision.

Nick Pasricha was at the time of the venture responsible for Arthur Young's high technology group and claims that[*28*]:

if this technology can deliver only half of what it promises, then it will have a significant impact.

Using our system we could define how [experts] work and use it to train others. It could also be used as an aid to help less experienced people deal with complex problems.

Peat, Marwick Mitchell have also been actively involved in researching into expert systems opportunities. However, they have used their Amercian base on a much larger scale than their English counterparts and have allocated funds to many intelligent knowledge based systems, particularly within auditing.

Completed projects and work in progress on expert system development according to the 1985 interim report on Research Opportunities in Auditing Program of the Peat, Marwick Foundation[*29*] were undertaken at the following American Universities:

- University of Wisconsin
- Indiana University
- University of Florida
- University of Illinois
- Ohio State University
- Brigham Young University
- University of Pittsburgh
- New York University

Summary

It has been shown that the accountancy profession is not ignoring the potential of this developing technology. The reader should also recognise that, when discussing expert system shells and their developments, it must be assumed that many firms and organisations have purchased their own systems and are applying them without official public reports of their progress.

The individual members of the ALFEX club, by definition, support an interest in expert systems, and it should be noted that accountancy firms are participating fully.

Bodies of research in a world context

It may seem from the history of AI research that has been summarised here, that it has been mostly British research, with some American influences, that has provided the background of knowledge in preparation for a launch into real world development of expert systems. However, the natural scepticism inherent in the British psyche still has plenty of scope to materialise when confronted with a branch of computer science that attempts to have machines emulate intelligent behaviour. Studies in the UK have long had a bad press, presumably because an outcome would appear too exotic to be a natural candidate for investment. The USA, the 'Land of Opportunity', is conspicuous by its absence in organised national research for different reasons, which will be discussed briefly later. The very real explosion of AI interest, including expert systems, over the past half a decade was undoubtedly triggered by the Japanese. This brief precis of some of the technicalities arising from the Japanese trigger may seem unnecessary within the aim of this booklet which is, specifically, to look at the use of expert systems. However, the extent of development, in terms of performance, illustrates the vast changes that will be undergone with the advent of this implied technology. The prototype system to be described has a targeted capacity of one million LIPS (Logical Inferences per Second); one LIPS is equivalent to approximately 100–1000 machine instructions per second on a Von Neumann or conventional computer.

The Japanese initiative

In 1981, the Japanese invited the rest of the world to collaborate in a massive, futuristic project. The impact of this invitation can be likened to that of the Soviet announcement in 1956, to a stunned world, at the launching of the first artificial satellite into orbit around the earth. Now Japan has been evolving from a developing island into a nation leading the world in this new technology. After having 'bought in' expertise to form the basis of research, the Japanese now need no help in fields of technology, such as AI, where it is they who have the knowledge and potential to take advantage of the many opportunities available. In 1981 the Japanese revealed they were three years into a national research and development project in a particular field of AI. It was entitled the Fifth Generation Computer Systems (FGCS) project and combined radical hardware advances with intelligent knowledge based systems or 'expert systems' as the software. When Japan declared their plans for the Fifth Generation of Computers in October of that year, their government concluded that it planned to spend 'seed money' of about 450 dollars, with perhaps double that amount for participating industries, in the project that would eventually involve several hundred top scientists. The outlined goal was to develop intelligent computers, while by 1990 they aimed to have developed a prototype fifth generation computing system comprising a knowledge information processing system and processor. The Japanese believe this venture to be more than a technological breakthrough. In a series of lengthy reports documenting the project it was claimed that[*30*]:

these efforts will not only foster creative technology for our own computer industry, but will also provide our country (Japan) with bargaining power. We will also fulfil our duty as an economic power by investing in the development of such leading fields.

The intention is, therefore, that the Fifth Generation is not only a visionary computing project but also an acquisitive piece of economic strategy. The research body funded by the Japanese government to this end is the Institute for New Generation Computing Technology (ICOT), which is directed by Kazuhiro Fuchi. Feigenbaum points out that the Ministry of International Trade and Industry (MITI), which is supplying the funds is in, what is for Japan, an unusual position of supporting a large basic research project and seeing it through to the world market. One of the managers of the firms supplying researchers to the project agreed that nobody knows quite what will happen but pointedly remarked[*31*]:

Except; MITI never fails.

It should still be realised that neither expert systems nor even knowledge information processing in general form the limits of the research.

One of the fundamental aspects of the project is the departure from using hardware of the classic Von Neumann architecture, the traditional system, which would contain:

- A single computer incorporating processor, communications and memory
- In-line organisation of fixed sized memory cells
- A single level address space of memory cells
- A low level machine language
- A sequential, centralised control of computation
- A primitive input and output capability

According to the Fifth Generation plan, however, knowledge will be stored in a large file system known as a relational data base, where the memory is organised so as to reduce both time and the amount of information processing to be done. The database will be automatically updated by knowledge-based management software and interaction between hardware files and the software file manager will be handled by a logical language called a relational algebra. The high performance required from such a machine necessitates advanced research into Very Large Scale Integration (VLSI) processors. This should enable the accelerated development of speech and natural language processors, while all machine levels should be covered by fifth generation architecture.

An alternative of explanation of 'why FGCS?'

Another Japanese explanation of why the FGCS is necessary was also given at the time of the invitation to collaborate. It was given in conjunction with the simple diagram of Fig. 7.1 and was explained by Michie in 1986[*32*].

The left-hand circle represents the human world, the right-hand circle the machine world, and the middle circle was the Fifth Generation Project. In the human world, 'explosions' have occurred on many fronts–probably in most areas of knowledge, in most areas of human activity and in all the problems associated with the various growths. In the machine world, a similar explosion has occurred. The fourth generation computer was much discussed, even if a complete fourth generation computer system did not exist some of the features of fourth generation machines existed in isolation or in proto-type form. Very cheap primary and secondary computer memory existed; a new generation of databases (going beyond the hierarchical natural or relational structures of the 'first' generation databases) were being worked on; the use of non-procedural languages (PROLOG, LISP,

OCCAM) was becoming more widespread; new computer architecture and parallelism were being developed–in other words, there were already moves away from the Von Neumann computers mentioned in the previous section.

The important point about this picture so far described is that the two expanding worlds of human and machine were moving apart in different directions, and the concern was that the machine world would soon become too far from the human world *to be commercially useful*. The FGCS was envisaged as bridging the gap between the two worlds, and so the major emphasis was on the human-machine interface, plus multi media for capturing all forms of human information and knowledge, e.g.:

- speech recognition and synthesis
- use of everyday natural language
- handwritten input
- pictorial/graphical images
- intelligent knowledge-based systems (expert systems)

British Response to the FGCS Project

The Alvey Report

Japan invited several countries, including the UK, to discuss participation in their national project, and as a result the Alvey Committee was set up. Headed by John Alvey, a director of British Telecom, the body regarded itself as a response to the Japanese challenge. Following a study of possible areas where UK research could be established, a report was published in September, 1982. The AlveyReport[*33*]identified four key areas in which the Committee believed major technical advances were necessary:

if we are to preserve and strengthen our capability and competitiveness in information technology

These four areas, plus a fifth added later were:

- Software engineering
- Man–machine interface (MMI)
- Very large scale integration (VLSI)
- Intelligent knowledge based systems (IKBS)
- Communications

The report encouraged the undertaking of a programme to inject an impetus into the British information technology industry, which involved a high degree of collaboration between industrial and research bodies. On presentation to the Government, the project was granted a budget of £350m for a five year programme, two-thirds of which was to come directly from the Government as the direct cost. The remaining sum was to come from industry, which was also to provide the much larger sums needed to translate the results of the programme into marketable projects. The Alvey Directorate subsequently appointed was headed by Brian Oakley with four other managers appointed to govern the strategies covering the individual areas of research as stated above.

Projected Alvey research

The Alvey Committee defined the enabling technologies as follows[*33*].

(a) Software engineering
The efficient specification and generation of the instructions for the machines is crucial to success. The UK is good at software but must develop better skills if it is to stay competitive.

(b) Man–machine interface (MMI)
The interface between man and machine is also crucial. Commercial success will come to those who make their complex (or simple) products truly acceptable to their users. Visual, speech and input/output devices are the interface instruments and these need better development. This development must be supported by a better understanding of the nature of communication across the interface.

(c) Intelligent knowledge based systems (IKBS)
A prime aspect of the extension of this interface is the study of IKBS. We want more powerful information processing systems with a more effective transfer of human intelligence and knowledge to the computer. We also want computer systems that are easier to build and use, implying a better fit between humans and computers.

(d) Very large scale integration (VLSI)
The hardware to make these systems will be heavily dependent on advances in VLSI of circuits on silicon. VLSI gives the capability of efficiently interconnecting very large numbers of logic elements and these will be necessary for many applications, typical of which are new, powerful processors for IKBS or signal processing units for speech or picture recognition.

The Alvey IKBS programme

A ten year programme of research and development of IKBS was proposed in the Alvey Committee's report, the aims of which were:

(i) To promote research in all aspects of IKBS.

(ii) To ensure development from the research results.

(iii) To stimulate production of development prototypes.

Research areas were identified in the report involving academia and industry together with a list of possible demonstrator projects, although the choice and specification of these projects could not be made at the time because[33]
. . . it must depend upon the detailed research progammes and their anticipated potential, and upon discussions with prospective IKBS users and suppliers and the understanding of their needs and ambitions.
Examples such as:

- Citizens helper
- Pre-GP health adviser
- Office Manager/Personal Assistant
- Factory/Plant Manager

were offered as possible projects subject to realistic constraints.
One Alvey project that is under way is a demonstrator expert system for interpreting rules aimed at the British welfare system. The objective is to build a system that can be used by staff, claimants and policymakers at the DHSS to find their way through the maze of regulations. The DHSS, though involved in the research, is under no obligation to make use of the work, but, as with all Alvey industry based projects, it is expected to result in a profitable project. Myer Solomon, project manager of ICL who are contributing to the funding of the project, believes the DHSS system will be used as a model for a more general system that could be applied to interpret several different sets of rules.
A welcome initiative from the Alvey project has been the 'Alvey clubs'–whereby people from different organisations who are involved in one of the project activities regularly meet to try and share experience on common problems.
A time scale for developments of the IKBS Programme was also set out in the report with the final statement that[33]:
By the end of the full ten year programme even the most difficult demonstrator projects should have been implemented, if only in rather

basic form. More importantly, progress in the research programmes will have produced some IKBS demonstrators significantly more powerful than any available today.

A note of patriotism!

Alvey is an entirely British set up, to the extent that even IBM has been turned away in favour of exploiting research in Britain first. Similarly, all American firms are excluded from the Alvey Programme unless the directorate are convinced that the UK will have the first opportunity to develop the research work into applications. The success or failure of the Alvey Programme is dependent to a large extent upon the ability or partners in academia and industry to work together. If an enthusiastic commitment to the ideal can be attained, then the project should be a success not only in commercial terms, but also in improving the British information technology industry by giving it a technical lead over foreign rivals.

The European Response

As well as the all British Alvey Programme, the UK already had some involvement in the fight to keep up in the information technology race with the combined European project managed by the EEC– called ESPRIT (The European Strategic Programme for Research in Information Technology). This called together the 'bit 12' IT companies in Europe to discuss the problems. Representatives from each company formed a panel that examined the current situation in which Europe was increasingly dependent upon Japan for chip productivity and the USA for software.
Subsequently, a plan was formulated which set out six areas of research:

- Advanced microelectronics
- Software technology
- Advanced information processing
- Office automation
- Computer integrated manufacture
- Information exchange systems

Some 35 contracts were awarded in July 1983 to consortia, with both the management and funding of ESPRIT being provided by the EEC. Most projects receive 50% funding with some academic partners involved. The ideal seems to be to show ESPRIT as a very democratic program run by Europe, for Europe.

There is, however, an opinion within the industry that ESPRIT's political motivation may be sufficiently active so as to detract from its effectiveness. Three major mainframe European companies, Siemens from Germany, Bull from France, and the UK's ICL have set up an institute themselves directed at the key area of knowledge processing. Concentrating on developing software and networking techniques for future knowledge based systems, the institute believes that political influence over the direction on European industry research is forcing them into such a move. As participants in the first phase of the ESPRIT scheme, the companies are obviously looking to complement and not duplicate ESPRIT research.
The EEC council are fully supportive of such initiatives, with the then UK Parliamentary Under Secretary for Industry referring to the institute as addressing[*34*]
an area of considerable importance to the information processing industry
The future use and applications of IKBS is, therefore, being recognised by industrialists and politicians in Europe with the undertaking of these and other initiatives. The competitive nature of the three firms in the institute must make their chances of future success less than certain, so it should be hoped an EEC backed and managed group can follow this example of investment in knowledge processing research.

Russian research

The European private and public sectors are not the only bodies outside Japan involved in research into the fifth generation of computer systems. Part of a five-year plan for computing announced in Autumn 1984 at a Moscow Trade Fair by the USSR highlighted fifth generation technologies. The Moscow Academy of Sciences which will co- ordinate the Russian programme confirmed that it will cover five strategic areas:

- Design and manufacture of VLSI microprocessors
- Development of parallel and multiprocessor architectures
- Design of operating systems to support logic programming
- Creation of problem solving software
- Development of expert systems and user-responsive applications

Stressed as a civilian and not a military initiative, Academy delegates have been seeking out state-of-the- art researchers since 1982 and have also sought collaboration with Japan. The Soviet's International Committee for Computer Engineering (ICCE), an influential body based at the Academy, has co-ordinated involvement with the six East European countries of East Germany, Rumania, Bulgaria, Czechoslovakia, Hungary and Poland.

Thought of as the Russian's foremost computer scientist, Yerengyi Velikhov is believed to be the architect of this fifth generation scheme. The advanced computer division of the Academy has a team of about 150 young staff, all of whom have the ability to support state of the art research.

American research

Having discussed the British, European and Soviet response to the Japanese initiative in the fifth generation generally, and expert system applications specifically, the obvious omission would seem to be the USA. However, there is no nationally co-ordinated project involving this aspect of information technology, a fact acknowledged and disapproved of by such as Professor Edward Feigenbaum who believes[35]

The US should form a national centre for knowledge technology . . . [which would] . . . not compete with industry.

The Advance Research Projects Agency of the Department of Defence has provided the practical source of funds for work in expert systems. The agency focused highly on the application of AI techniques to military problems.

There is also a great deal of activity in independent industrial and academic bodies. MIT and Stanford University among others are engaged in expert systems development research while activity in Silicon Valley is said to be hectic. The giant IBM is refraining from making its intentions clear but its interest in Fifth Generation research and particularly expert system development is without doubt.

Summary

This section has, hopefully, provided an insight for the reader to assess the extent of interest and funded research in the subject area of this chapter. The concern is not only with UK industrial firms but international governments and corporations. It should be possible, therefore, for the reader to look at the illustrations of expert systems in the previous pages as a microcosm of the whole field of which they are part. In this context, their particular relevance and development potential can hopefully be recognised.

References

1. McLintock, D., & Fitter, R., *The Pocket Guide to Wild Flowers*, Collins, 1971.
2. Forsyth, R. (Editor), 'The Expert System Phenomenon' in *Expert Systems: Principles and Case Studies*, Chapman and Hall Computing, 1984.
3. Feigenbaum, E.A., & McCorduck, P., *The 5th Generation*, Michael Joseph Publishers, 1984.
4. Forsyth, R., 'Fuzzy Reasoning Systems' from *Expert Systems: Principles and CAse Studies*, op. cit.
5. Lenat, D., 'EURISKO: A Program that Learns New Heuristics and Domain Concepts', in *Artificial Intelligence* 21, 1982.
6. Forsyth, R. (Editor), 'The Architecture of Expert Systems' in *Expert Systems: Principles and Case Studies*, Chapman and Hall Computing, 1984.
7. BCS Committee, *Interim Report of the BCS Committee of the Specialist Group on Expert Systems*, 1982.
8. Brown, S., *Assessing Professional Expertise – DBMS v Expert System*, ICAS, 1987.
9. Sergot, M.J., Sadri, F., Kowalski, R.A., Kriwaczek, F., Harnword, D., & Cory, H.T., 'The British Nationality Act as a Logic Program', *Communications of the ACM*, May, 1986.
10. Lenat, D., 'EURISKO: A Program that Learns New Heuristics and Domain Concepts', *Artificial Intelligence*, 21, 1982.
11. Michie, D., *On Machine intelligence*, Ellis Horwood Ltd, 1986.
12. Alty, J., & Coombs, M.J., *Expert Systems: Concepts and Examples*, NCC Publications, 1984.
13. Duda, R.O., Gaschnig, J., & Hart, P.E., 'Model Design in the PROSPECTOR Consultant Program for Mineral Exploration', in D. Michie (Ed), *Expert Systems in the Microelectronic Age*, Edinburgh University Press, 1979.
14. McDermott, J., 'R1's Formative Years', *AI Magazine*, 2, 1982.
15. Bird, J., 'Airing Some Objections', *Computing*, 4 November, 1982.
16. Marsh, P., 'Opening up New Horizons', *Financial Times*, 15 April, 1985.
17. Duda, R.O., & Gaschnig, J.G., 'Knowledge Based Expert Systems come of Age', *Byte*, September, 1981.
18. D'Agapeyeff, A., *Expert Systems: 5th Generation and UK Suppliers*, NCC Publications, 1982.
19. D'Agapeyeff, A., 'Report to Alvey Directorate on a Short Survey of Expert Systems in UK Business', Supplement to *Alvey News*, 4, April, 1984.

20. Kowalski, R., 'Algorithm = Logic + Control' *Communication of ACM*, Vol. 22, No. 7, July, 1979.
21. Forsyth, R., 'The Architecture of Expert Systems', in Forsyth R. (Ed), *Expert Systems: Concepts and Examples*, NCC Publications, 1984.
22. Sloman, A., Hardy, S., & Gibson, J., 'POPLOG: A multi-language program development environment', *Information Technology: Research and Development, 2*, 1983.
23. *PROLOG, Micro Prolog Workshop*, PROLOG, August, 1984.
24. Michaelson, R., & Michie, D., 'Expert Systems in Business', *Datamation*, November, 1983.
25. Dungan, C.W., & Chandler, J.S., 'Auditor: A Microcomputer based expert system to support auditors in this field', *Expert Systems*, October, 1985.
26. Thomas, D., 1985 Chairman ALFEX.
27. Edwards, A., 'Mining for Knowledge', *Accountancy*, April, 1987.
28. Arnold, M.E., *et al.*, 'Expert Systems: As Expert as Accountants', *Management Accounting*, October, 1985.
29. (Peat, Marwick Mitchell)
30. Treleaven, P.C., & Gouveia, Lima I., 'Japan's 5th Generation Systems', *IEEE*, August, 1982.
31. Ref to come: ms p.58
32. Michie, D., *On Machine Intelligence*, Ellis Horwood Ltd., 1986.
33. Dept of Industry, 'A Programme for Advanced Information Technology: the Report of the Alvey Committee', HMSO, 1984.
34. Tate, P., *An Eye on AI*, Datamotion, January 1984.
35. Feigenbaum, E.A., & McCorduck, P., 'The 5th Generation', Michael Joseph Publications, 1984.

Further reading

1 Alty, J., & Coombs, M.J., *Expert Systems: Concepts and Examples*, NCC Publications, 1984.
2 Anon. Expert System Shells, *Expert System User*, 1985.
3 Arnold, M.E., Gambling, T. & Rush, D.G., 'Expert Systems. As Expert as Accountants', *Management Accounting*, October, 1985.
4 Brooking, A.G., 'The 5th Generation Game', in Forsyth, R. (Ed), *Expert Systems: Principles and Case Studies*, NCC Publications, 1984.
5 D'Agapeyeff, A., *Expert Systems: 5th Generation and UK Suppliers, NCC Publications, 1982.*
6 Durham, A., 'Fifth Generation Fever', *Practical Computing*, October, 1984.
7 *Financial Times*, 22 August, 1984
8 Forenski, T., 'Extracting Expert's Expertise', *Computing – The Magazine*, 25 October, 1984.
9 Forenski, T., 'UK Must Look to Alvey's Lead', *Computing – The Newspaper*, 27 September, 1984.
10 Gambling, T., 'Expert Systems: Stone Age Rules, OK?', *Accountancy*, July, 1985.
11 Gouveia, Lima I, 'Expert Systems in Business', *ICAEW Seminar on Expert Systems*, October, 1984.
12 Hayes-Roth, F., *The Knowledge-Based Expert System; A Tutorial*, IEEE, September, 1984.
13 Johnson, L., & Keravnou, E.T., *Expert Systems Technology: A Guide*, Abacus Press, 1985.
14 Kowalski, R., 'Logic as a Computing Language', in Clark & Tarnlund (Ed), *Logic Programming*, Academic Press, 1985.
15 Lamb, J., 'Alvey Is On Its Way', *Datamation*, 15 June, 1984.
16 Michaelson, R.H., Michie, D., and Boulanger, A., 'Technology of Expert Systems', *Byte*, April, 1985.
17 Michie, D., *Introductory Readings in Expert Systems*, Gordon & Breach Science, 1982.
18 Naylor, C., 'How to Build an Inference Engine', in Forsyth, C. (Ed), *Expert Systems: Concepts and Examples*, NCC Publications, 1984.
19 Stoner, G., 'Expert Systems: Jargon or Challenge?', *Accountancy*, February, 1985.
20 Walton, P., and Tate, P., 'Soviets Aim for 5th Generation', *Datamation*, July, 1984.
21 Winfield, M.J., 'Expert Systems: An Introduction to the Layman', *Computer Bulletin*, December, 1982.
22 Yazdani, M., 'Knowledge Engineering in PROLOG', in Forsyth, C. (Ed), *Expert Systems: Concepts and Examples*, NCC Publications, 1984.